AN APPEAL TO THE LADIES OF HYDERABAD
Scandal in the Raj

By Benjamin B. Cohen
Publication Date: July 2019
$28.95 | 361 pp.
15 photos
ISBN: 978-0-674-98765-4
Harvard University Press

For more information please contact:

Ellie Andrew
Deputy Manager of International Publicity
eleanor_andrew@harvard.edu
020 3463 2350

**Visit our website:
www.hup.harvard.edu**

AN APPEAL TO THE LADIES OF HYDERABAD

$\mathcal{A}$N APPEAL TO THE LADIES *of* HYDERABAD

Scandal in the $\mathcal{R}$AJ

BENJAMIN B. COHEN

Harvard University Press

CAMBRIDGE, MASSACHUSETTS ✦ LONDON, ENGLAND ✦ 2019

LIBRARY OF CONGRESS CATALOGING-IN-PUBLICATION DATA
[to come]

ISBN: 9780674987654 (cloth: alk. paper)

For Nadja

CONTENTS

NOTE ON NAMES

In almost all cases, I use the English spellings of individuals' names as they used them, except in direct quotations. Mehdi Hasan's name appears in a variety of ways—"Mahdi Hassan," "Mehdi Husain," and so on—but since he opted for "Mehdi Hasan" when he published his own work in English, I employ it here as well. Similarly, in his autobiography, the Nawab Server Jung used a particular spelling for his name—"Server" rather than "Sarvar" or "Sarwar"—so I follow suit. Other names are also spelled in various ways. Syed Jaffer Hussein, for instance, is also referred to as Husain and Hussain. I use the most common version and trust context will make alternate usage clear. I apply more modern spellings for some Indian towns and cities—thus Kanpur not Cawnpore and Ambala not Umballa—but retain earlier spellings for others—thus Calcutta not Kolkata and Bombay not Mumbai.

For readability, I refer to the couple at the center of the pamphlet scandal by their first names, Mehdi and Ellen, rather than Mr. and Mrs. Hasan. In other cases, I use the more common convention of referring to individuals by their surnames. Many of those who were hostile to Ellen referred to her by her middle name, Gertrude, but she used "Ellen" when referring to herself; honoring the couple's practice from the time, I do the same. John Seymour Keay was always referred to as simply Seymour Keay, a practice I too follow.

CAST OF CHARACTERS

Mehdi Hasan and the Donnelly Family

Mehdi Hasan Khan *Fateh Nawaz Jung*	Canning College graduate; chief justice of the Hyderabad Court; home secretary in the Nizam's government
Mrs. Mehdi Hasan, née *Ellen Gertrude Donnelly*	youngest Donnelly daughter; resident of Lucknow's back lanes; wife of Mehdi Hasan
Michael Donnelly	Donnelly patriarch; a "drunk," "man of letters," or both
Lucy Donnelly	eldest of the Donnelly daughters; married Henry Hodges; widowed
Esther Donnelly	second Donnelly daughter; married Edward Bigex; mother of Isabelle; widowed; married Egisto Amedeo Benvenuti (Chicago, Illinois); lived in Paris

Hyderabad Officials

Mahbub Ali Khan	sixth Nizam of Hyderabad, India's largest and wealthiest princely state
Osman Ali Khan	seventh Nizam of Hyderabad; son of Mahbub Ali Khan

Server Jung	private tutor to the Nizam and later private secretary; childhood classmate of Mehdi turned adult nemesis
Salar Jung I	prime minister of Hyderabad State (1853–1883); a modernizer and gifted bureaucrat
Salar Jung II	prime minister of Hyderabad State (1883–1887). Son of the first Salar Jung; known for his size and tendencies toward debauchery; friend of Mehdi and Ellen; resigned early
Asman Jah	prime minister of Hyderabad State (1887–1893).
Vicar-ul-Umra	prime minister of Hyderabad State (1893–1901).
Kishen Pershad	prime minister of Hyderabad State (1901–1912).
Mushtak Hussain	deputy prime minister under Asman Jah; ally of Mehdi; fellow north Indian; eventual co-founder of the All-India Muslim League.

The Legal Teams

O. V. Bosanquet	second assistant Resident at Hyderabad and magistrate who presided over the pamphlet scandal case

FOR THE DEFENSE:

J. B. Boyle	assistant to Norton
John Edgelow	assistant to Norton
Eardley J. Norton	chief lawyer for the defense of Mitra; an advocate of the Indian National Congress; compiler of the Norton photographic album

FOR THE PROSECUTION:

John Duncan Inverarity	chief lawyer for the prosecution
A. C. Rudra	lawyer for the prosecution; former journalist

Member of Britain's Parliament

John Seymour Keay	one-time employee of the Nizam's government; private businessman in Hyderabad; member of Parliament; indefatigable ally of Mehdi; hostile to Plowden and Server Jung

Viceroys of India

Lord Lytton	1876–1880
George Robinson, first marquess of Ripon	1880–1884
Frederick Temple Hamilton-Temple-Blackwood, first marquess of Dufferin	1884–1888
Henry Petty-Fitzmaurice, fifth marquess of Landsdowne	1888–1894
Victor Bruce, ninth earl of Elgin	1894–1899
George Curzon, first marquess Curzon of Kedleston	1899–1905

British Residents and Assistants at Hyderabad

John Cordery Resident, 1883–1888

Dennis Fitzpatrick Resident, 1889–1891

George R. Irwin first assistant Resident under Plowden

Trevor John Chicheley Plowden Resident, 1891–1898; powerful player in Hyderabad politics; discreetly hostile to Mehdi; critic of Keay; close to Server Jung.

Other Significant Figures

Steuart C. Bayley Resident at Hyderabad in 1881; secretary in the Political and Secret Department, 1890–1895; later a member of the India Council, London

Mortimer Durand foreign secretary and head of the Political Department in the Government of India

John Wodehouse, first earl of Kimberley secretary of state for India within the British government

Vasudeva Rao accused of writing the pamphlet under Syed Ali Bilgrami's dictation; an employee of the Nizam's government

Key Witnesses

Rafi-ud-din a clerk in Rai Bareilly; named in the pamphlet as a joint-stock owner; warned Mehdi of going to court; claimed to have bedded two Donnelly sisters

Yusuf-uz-Zaman *zamindar* and honorary magistrate at Banda near Lucknow; named in the pamphlet as a joint-stock owner; testified that he had sex with Ellen; double-crossed Mehdi

Syed Husain Bilgrami	testified in favor of Mehdi and had his pay cut in retribution; questioned for not exposing Ellen; accused of having been her keeper
Syed Ali Bilgrami	One-time friend of Mehdi, now hostile to him; his wife and Ellen visited with each other; contributor to the Mitra defense fund; suspected of dictating the pamphlet to Vasudeva Rao
N. Hormusji	legal advisor in the Nizam's government; worked for Mehdi to find the pamphlet's author after its release
S. M. Mitra	local Bengali journalist in Hyderabad; defendant in the legal case, charged with printing the pamphlet
Faridoonji Jamshedji	private secretary to the minister, Sir Salar Jung; aware of the secret investigation into Mehdi's marriage; later made political secretary in Hyderabad
Munshi Sajjad Husain	*zamindar*; founder, editor, and contributor to the *Oudh Punch*; hostile to Mehdi; claimed to witness Ellen in a compromising situation; collected her photograph along with that of prostitutes
Asgar Jan	Lucknow photographer; brother of well-known photographer Mushkur-ud-dowla; photographed Ellen in Indian dress
James Lauchlin	star witness for the defense; engaged to Ellen; claimed to witness an incestuous act; present at Mrs. Donnelly's grave opening
Mary Gill	schoolmate of Ellen; knew Mrs. Donnelly and Lucy; revealed accusation of incest; claimed possibility of Mrs. Donnelly being buried alive

AN APPEAL TO THE LADIES OF HYDERABAD

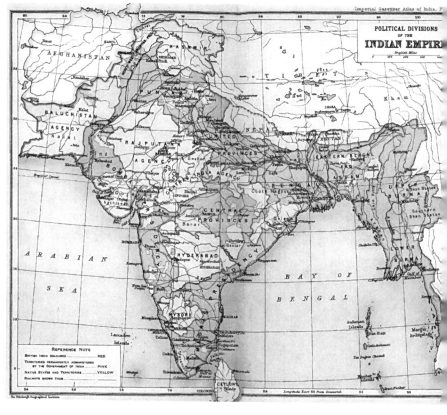

British Indian Empire, c. 1909. The darker shades show "pink" British India, the lighter shades are the "yellow" princely states.

PROLOGUE

In April 1893, Mehdi Hasan and his wife, Ellen, boarded a train from Hyderabad in southern India headed north to Lucknow. April can be a hot month, as the monsoon rains do not reach Hyderabad until early June; before that, days can turn to weeks with nothing but bright sunshine. Mehdi and Ellen directed the porters in securing their bags, ensured the compartment windows were open to catch what breeze there was, and sat down and waited for the shrill steam whistle to sound, the air brakes to release, and the train to begin its slow crawl out of Nampally Station.

The railway lines out of Hyderabad passed dirt and wood shacks that housed the city's poor, who prepared meals over open fires and looked up to catch only a glimpse of Mehdi and Ellen and a life they could never afford. In the distance, beyond the palms and fruit trees, past the jasmine and mangoes, larger palaces dotted the Hyderabad skyline. The couple had dined and been entertained by many of the nobles who inherited or built these grand structures, covered in silky *chunnam* plaster and topped with ornately carved wooden gingerbread trim. The couple might have caught a glimpse of water shimmering in the sunlight—one of Hyderabad's many lakes used for pleasure boating where one could take in the reflection of ruins from earlier empires. The train lumbered out of the city and into the countryside, blowing its whistle at wayward water buffalo and cows, ox cart drivers, bicycle riders, and a few emergent motorcars, as well as elephants, horses, camels, and other fauna. Perhaps in those moments, as Hyderabad passed beneath the carriage wheels, the couple pondered what had befallen them over the past year.

Mehdi and Ellen had come to Hyderabad a decade earlier in the winter of 1883. Mehdi had enjoyed a kind of success that made other men jealous. A young Muslim noble, he was a graduate of Canning College in Lucknow, where British educators groomed young men for service in the Government of India. There he received a competent education under the watchful eyes of British administrators. At the start of his career, he spent a few years working for the Government of India in the districts near Lucknow.

In 1872 Mehdi began courting Ellen Donnelly and married her the next year. She and her sisters and father, who was a low-ranking officer of the Indian Army, lived in Lucknow. The Donnellys rented rooms from Indian landlords in lower-middle-class neighborhoods. These were far from the posh colonial lines of tidy bungalows and the local club. Originally from Ireland, the Donnellys were members of India's population of poor whites. Ellen spoke Urdu and often dressed in local attire. She was considered quite beautiful. During her late teenage years, she befriended a group of young, handsome Indian men. Mehdi was part of this group, and after persistent efforts, Ellen converted to Islam and accepted his proposal of marriage, remaining devoted to him throughout her life.

Were it not for Mehdi's ambitions, the couple might have stayed forever in Lucknow, an example of a form of late nineteenth-century hybridity—a living bridge between Indian and European worlds—and something of an oddity at the time, as interracial marriages were less common than they had been in the eighteenth century. But Mehdi knew Sir Syed Ahmed Khan, the great north Indian reformer, and when a fellow reformer, Sir Salar Jung I, the prime minister of Hyderabad

State (also called the Nizam's Dominions), came to Lucknow on a visit, Sir Syed spoke highly of Mehdi.

Salar Jung was on tour in north India in the 1870s, recruiting educated men to come to Hyderabad and help him reform India's largest, wealthiest princely state. Salar Jung was suitably impressed by Mehdi and invited him to work in Hyderabad. Once there, Mehdi began a meteoric rise. Among his posts, he served as a judge in a local small claims court; a *taluqdar*; and puisne judge of the Hyderabad High Court. In 1887 he received the title Fateh Nawaz Jung.[1] His rise continued when he became Mir-i Majlis-i Adalat al-Aliya, or chief justice of the High Court, and soon after, home secretary—all with the blessing of the prime minister and the ruler of Hyderabad State, the Nizam, Mahbub Ali Khan.[2]

Ellen was born a Christian but converted to Islam just before she married Mehdi. Following a common practice, she maintained *purdah* after her marriage. Both Muslim and Hindu women practiced different degrees of *purdah*—from extreme social segregation to simply wearing a veil and modest attire. Ellen too observed a form of *purdah* in her early years of marriage, only to abandon the practice after being in Hyderabad for some time.

Once there, with her husband's approval, she came out more and more, dressing and behaving like a respectable British woman. She certainly socialized with other European women living in the city, but her marriage to Mehdi—at a time when relations between Indians and Britons were sometimes tense—must have made reactions to her strained. They both attended functions at the homes of Hyderabad's local elite, as well as at the Residency, home of the ranking British official at Hyderabad, the Resident. Mehdi was called to the bar in London, so the couple traveled to Britain and France in 1888.

After Mehdi's return to India, the Nizam appointed him home secretary of Hyderabad State in late 1889. In this position, Mehdi ranked just below the prime minister, himself just beneath the Nizam.

Three years passed as Mehdi and Ellen moved in ever-higher circles of Hyderabad society. Mehdi was included in social events held by the Nizam and other Indian officials because of his position. Ellen, being an Indian-born Briton and the wife of a man of rank, was invited to British social activities like tea parties or "at homes." Together, they expanded and enriched each other's social calendars and operated as a sort of late nineteenth-century power couple. Nothing, it seemed, could damage this glamorous interracial duo. Yet in April 1892, precisely one year before the couple boarded the train to Lucknow, an eight-page printed pamphlet changed everything.

I

NEW BEGINNINGS
IN HYDERABAD

MAPS OF INDIA from the late nineteenth century often have two colors, yellow and pink. Yellow was the India of its princely states, 562 in all, comprising about one-third of the subcontinent's territory.[1] Pink India was British, composed of three large administrative units known as presidencies—Madras, Bombay, and Bengal—as well as the provinces and territories that fell under the direct control of the Government of India. Mehdi and Ellen traveled between the two colors, and in some ways, that was the beginning of their problems.

The Indian subcontinent has always been a conglomeration of regions, some clearly defined by geographic features, others defined by faith, language, or dialect. Regions were cobbled together through war and conquest and took on their semi-fixed shapes over long periods of time. Hyderabad State, also known as the Nizam's Dominions, is a good example. About the same size as France, Hyderabad State, located in the heart of the south-central Deccan Plateau, was the amalgamation of earlier Deccan rulers as well as interventions from north India, including that of the Mughals. As in many other parts of the subcontinent, Hyderabad was home to several different languages and dialects. Mehdi spoke Urdu, the local language in Lucknow, which, by the late nineteenth century, was also the language of government in Hyderabad. Besides using Urdu, some educated men knew and spoke Persian, while in the countryside one could hear Telugu, Kannada, and Marathi, as well as Dakhni and other languages.[2]

The poor often remained within their natal region. India's caste system helped foster this sense of rootedness, and difficulties in long distance travel—thugs, *dacoits*, and other hazards of the road— sometimes kept inhabitants settled. Over time, a deep sense of being of the soil—a *mulki*, or local—developed.[3] Many citizens of Hyderabad city and Hyderabad State shared a feeling of localism: you were either one of us, a *mulki*, or you were not, a non-*mulki*. At the same time, opportunities arose in the nineteenth century for members of the middle and upper classes to move across the subcontinent as well as to Europe and beyond. Greater mobility was available to those Indians armed with some education in English and increasing familiarity with British norms, particularly educated Indian Muslims whose knowledge of Urdu and Persian, combined with fewer cultural restrictions on travel, made them able to operate successfully in a wide cosmopolitan network within and without India.

In 1857 the East India Company's hold on India was fundamentally shaken by an upheaval within its Indo-British army. The event, known as the Mutiny, the Uprising, or the First War of Independence, ended by 1858 when company forces prevailed and reestablished control. At that moment, the British government assumed direct control of what were once the company's possessions in India. The consolidation of British power across the subcontinent after the events of 1857, and the coming of the railroad in the decades that followed offered new possibilities. Now, inhabitants of north India like Mehdi were not just men or women of Lucknow or Delhi, of Agra or Kanpur, but also subjects of a British Empire with rights granted to them— at least in theory—by Queen Victoria herself. As subjects of the empire, and sometimes employees of the British colonial administration, they became part of a system (with roots established by the Mughal Empire before them) in which education and a shared vocabulary gave them more freedom of movement within the administrative system, and thus they were more likely to move around within the empire. Mehdi had studied in north India under British schoolmasters and worked for some years in land administration. As such, in the eyes of Prime Minister Salar Jung I, he possessed skills beneficial to the administration of Hyderabad State.

However, as a citizen of Lucknow and north India, Mehdi's foreign travels and employment in Hyderabad upset the local *mulki* community. This entrenched regionalism worked against him. While he might have considered himself a cosmopolitan man—born in one place, able to work in another, and weighing in on the imperial world around him—such an outlook was less common among Hyderabad's local elites, if not downright threatening. Thus, the story of Mehdi and Ellen is, in part, one of insiders and outsiders. The latter never have an easy time of it.

The couple's experiences in the two cities of Lucknow and Hyderabad were radically different: Lucknow was home, with family close by and deep connections across a variety of social networks, but it offered only basic opportunities for Mehdi. Hyderabad was full of potential, but foreign territory. The dialect of Urdu spoken there was different from that of Lucknow, and Mehdi and Ellen knew almost no one in the city. Yet Hyderabad officials (and Salar Jung in particular) sought out men like Mehdi to bring their experience to Hyderabad. For someone who worked hard and had the essential social graces—aided by a wife of European descent—opportunities were plentiful.

If Mehdi was an outsider in Hyderabad, Ellen faced an entirely different challenge. She represented a different group in late nineteenth-century India. Part of her story arguably began on New Year's Eve, 1600, when Queen Elizabeth granted an exclusive charter to the newly minted East India Company.[4] For the next two hundred and fifty years the company, slowly at first and then with greater speed, expanded its footprint in India. Early contacts between company officials and then Mughal rulers were not successful at first. But by the mid-seventeenth century, the British had small footholds at Madras, Calcutta, and Bombay. From these towns, which became the presidency capitals, the company became increasingly involved in local Indian politics and warfare. Company officials, taking a page from their French competitors in India, trained Indian *sepoys* for their army and then either lent them to local Indian rulers or used them under direct command to annex principalities that bolstered their position as a commercial force.

Across India, rulers of princely states were seen as important players in the affairs of the East India Company. Officials of the company and Crown sent British employees to these princely capitals as representatives, with the title of Political Resident. Being posted to a large and wealthy princely state elevated the Resident's own prestige within company ranks. Among the most important and largest courts in India was that in Hyderabad. By the eighteenth century, at Hyderabad and across India, Britons began taking a new interest in things Indian. For instance, James Achilles Kirkpatrick (1764–1805), then the Resident at Hyderabad, adopted Indian dress, language, and food. He also took an Indian wife.[5] Kirkpatrick's love interests were formed within the company and Hyderabad's elite, whereas the story of Mehdi and Ellen—he from humble origins and she from a poor white family—was one of love within a different stratum of Indo-British society.

According to her baptismal record, Ellen Gertrude Donnelly was born on 3 June 1854 to Michael Ross Donnelly and Eliza Mitchell. Mitchell was the daughter of a military captain who had served in

Meerut.[6] Her parents had several stepchildren, who formed the greater Mitchell clan.[7] Although the Mitchells appear to have spent some time in Meerut, when Eliza married Michael Donnelly in April 1841, the wedding took place at Fort William in Calcutta. Michael and Eliza's marriage produced three daughters. Ellen was the youngest. The two elder sisters were both role models and playmates for Ellen, and she remained in contact with them throughout her life.

Michael Donnelly was of Irish descent and lived his adult life in India, leaving only once to travel to Ireland, where perhaps he still had family.[8] He had a position in the Commissariat Department of the Indian Army, which procured supplies. He never seemed to have climbed in rank, and those who knew him contrarily testified that he was either a drunk, a learned man, or possibly both at the same time. When Michael Donnelly died in the north Indian town of Ambala in or around 1892, only his eldest daughter Lucy was at his bedside and funeral.

Lucy was born on 4 October in 1845 or 1846. At the age of thirteen, she married Henry Melville Hodges, son of Robert Hodges, who worked in the Indian princely state of Kapurthala, southeast of Amritsar. The Hodges family resembled the Donnellys—both low-ranking British families living and working in India. Henry and Lucy had at least one child, Edward.[9] Henry may also have had a sister who married into the Kapurthala royal family.[10] Lucy and Henry's wedding took place at Jalandhar on 20 May 1859. Ellen would later testify that Lucy "always dressed then in Punjabi (native) dress" and that this was because she used to "live among a lot of natives."[11] Less than fourteen years later, by the time of Mehdi and Ellen's marriage in 1873, Lucy was a widow.[12] She died around 1892 at Ajmer.[13] Ellen and Lucy, the youngest and oldest sisters, were apparently close, since in her will, Ellen asked to be buried next to her eldest sister. However, tragedy would prevent this from happening.

The second daughter, Esther Caroline Donnelly, was born on 19 July 1850 in Wazirabad, not far from Amritsar. At the age of sixteen, she married Edward Bigex (also spelled Begex) in Amritsar. Edward Bigex, the son of Victor Bigex, was also a member of a less affluent class of Europeans living and working in India. While in India, Edward and Esther had one child, Lucy Isabelle Bigex, called "Isabelle" by her family.[14] The young couple and daughter would later move to Europe, where Esther and Isabelle would reunite with Mehdi and Ellen when the latter two were on tour. The young Isabelle spent several days traveling with Mehdi in Geneva and acting as interpreter for him.

Lucy, Esther, and Ellen were baptized, the older two within a year of their births and Ellen when she was seven. The locations of their baptisms reflect the peripatetic life of Michael and Eliza Donnelly throughout the Bengal Presidency: Lucy's baptism occurred at Kanpur, Esther's at Agra, and Ellen's at Sanawar (a small hill-station town north of Delhi). Ellen would later testify that she thought she might also have had a brother who died, but no evidence exists to suggest a fourth Donnelly child.[15]

While there are no known photographs of the greater Donnelly family, there is one definitive photograph of Ellen. The photograph was hand printed and glued into the frontispiece of the published transcript of the trial that Mehdi initiated. Likely taken in her late teens when she lived in Lucknow, the photograph shows Ellen's hair as black and parted down the middle, combed, and pulled tightly back behind her ears, dropping out of sight behind her sari. She has thick eyebrows that set off narrow eyes peering past the camera. Her lips are thin, reaching out to full cheeks and a rounded chin. The sepia photograph belies any hint of her skin tone, but given the contrast between her face and hair, she appears more fair than not.

In the photograph, Ellen is dressed in a sari, standing next to a draped table with a dressing mirror. The mirror suggests a degree of intimacy, as if the viewer has been invited into her dressing room. Her right arm rests on the mirror; her left hand is extended across her body and clutches the end of her sari. The *dupatta* covers the back of her head and drapes down and across her chest. The space where the *dupatta* is draped above her chest exposes a bejeweled *choli* and the swell of her breast.

In 1874, around the same time this photograph was likely taken, a book appeared that presented the "beauties of Lucknow" in twenty-four photographs. The images of these "beauties" and the one of Ellen bear striking resemblances. The images are of Indian women: actresses, dancers, and other celebrities in the city of Lucknow, once capital of the north Indian princely state of Oudh. The author wrote, "I have been particularly requested . . . to prepare a series of photographs of the dancing girls, singers, and actresses who may be termed the celebrities of Lucknow on account of their beauty or talent."[16] The studio scenes for Ellen and the other women are similar. In all of them, an ornate carpet grounds the scene, with a curtain appearing behind. Each has one main prop: for Ellen, it is a table and mirror; for the others, it is a tufted chair or mirror. Like Ellen, the other women have bejeweled ears, neck, and wrists. Ellen and her Lucknow counterparts wear their hair in the same style: parted in the middle and pulled tight behind the ears. Some of the women have their saris arranged to reveal the outline of one or both breasts. Like Ellen, many of the women of Lucknow wore pleated skirts or saris of strong geometric-patterned fabric that wrapped just below the chest. At the very least, the photographer of these pictures used the same type of setting for Ellen's photograph and those of the Lucknow collection. The similarities raise interesting possibilities: perhaps the same photographer took all of the images; perhaps the sartorial choice was the fashion of the day used by women across a social spectrum; perhaps Ellen consciously

Ellen Gertrude Donnelly

imitated the look; perhaps she unknowingly imitated a style that had meanings she did not understand; or perhaps she was manipulated by the photographer to meet his needs rather than hers.

Although Ellen is dressed in Indian fashion in the photograph, her name and parentage are of Irish extraction. Yet at times she was called "Eurasian," a term that suggested she had Indian blood in her veins. The great contemporary tome on Indo-English language, *Hobson Jobson* (1886), explains that the term was a "modern name" for persons of mixed Indian and European heritage.[17] Later, "Anglo-Indian" also came into use, a term that was not particularly precise: at different times, it could mean either a person of British birth who lived or had lived in India, or a "Eurasian," thus opening the possibility that "Anglo-Indian" could refer to someone of mixed birth.[18] Thus, depending on the time and point of view, Ellen was certainly Irish, but also very much British, and quite possibly Eurasian and Anglo-Indian as well.[19] Ellen's ambiguous identity would come into play later in her life.

While photographs of Ellen are exceedingly rare, Mehdi appears in many photographs of the time. Indeed, he seemed to be fond of public attention—especially from women—and was not shy about having his photograph taken.[20] In his decade of service in Hyderabad, dozens, if not hundreds, of photographs show the mustached Mehdi alongside the full range of Hyderabad and British nobility. Mehdi was not particularly tall and displayed a barrel chest that filled out his *sherwani*. His portly shape likely did not help the gout that affected his feet and kept him bedridden at times. He sported a long, drooping mustache, but, unlike some of his counterparts, he kept his chin clean-shaven, which showed off a cleft that gave him an attractive look. He wore the popular bushy sideburns of the day, and, in some portraits, he appears slightly cross-eyed.

Mehdi Hasan

Mehdi was likely born in 1852. We can approximate his age because when he was about fifteen, he entered Canning College to begin his formal education. The family home was Fatehpur, a village not far from Lucknow. Mehdi's father, Shaykh Lutf-i Husayn, worked as a revenue collector in Oudh.[21] His mother died in Fatehpur in the fall of 1892.

In some accounts, Mehdi had a brother, Hyder Hussain, but this might be the same person identified as his cousin, Sirdar Hussain.[22] During the trial, Ellen would admit to knowing this relative of Mehdi's (she calls him his cousin).[23] Also, a man named Fakhrudeen was sometimes identified as Mehdi's brother, sometimes as his cousin, and also appears briefly in the trial. At the height of their popularity, when Mehdi and Ellen were leaving India for London, Fakhrudeen traveled with Ellen to meet Mehdi in Bombay for their departure.[24] Mehdi called both Sirdar and Fakhrudeen cousins, but the term could mean a variety of possible relationships. In at least one account, when the two men arrived in London, Fakhrudeen was referred to as Mehdi's brother, not cousin.[25] Mehdi made no mention of Fakhrudeen in his account of his time in London, but Fakhrudeen reappears momentarily after both Mehdi and Ellen's deaths.

Mehdi was first educated at home, and then attended a middle school in Kaiser Bagh in Lucknow.[26] From his time at middle school, a fellow north Indian named Server Jung described the young Mehdi and his relation, Hyder:

> He and his brother Hyder Hussain read with us in the school at Kaiser Bagh for a short time, but he did not do very well, though he became well-known in buffoonery. Later on he was posted as Munsiff in Oudh, and kept an Anglo-Indian woman whose character was well-known. However he made her observe "Purdah," and was able to acquire some English from her,

so as to be able to read and write it. But he was intelligent, and had read some Arabic in his boyhood.[27]

Mehdi spent the early part of his career working for the Government of India in and around Lucknow. After graduating, he served as a *tahsildar* of Pratapgarh, beginning in 1873, and then as a *munsif* at Ragiri. He continued in different positions for a time, all the while contributing toward his pension. A decade later, when Sir Syed Ahmed Khan recommended Mehdi to Hyderabad's prime minister, Salar Jung, Mehdi applied for and received permission from the Government of India to work in Hyderabad.

Thus, in the spring of 1883, Mehdi began his new position in Hyderabad. He must have felt a considerable degree of pride as he took up his new duties as an employee of the Nizam's government: he held a degree from a well-known college; he was married to a woman of European descent; his training and work in law and land revenue would serve him well in Hyderabad; and he had already contributed to his pension with the Government of India, thus believing that he was sowing the seeds of financial security for his future.

Mehdi and Ellen began and ended their lives in the north Indian city of Lucknow. The city is located in the middle of the wide alluvial plain dominated by the Ganges River, about 325 miles from Delhi and 800 miles north of Hyderabad. As in Hyderabad, a river bisects Lucknow. The Gomati River flows from west to east through the city, moving in a southeasterly direction until bending in an easterly direction about halfway through the heart of the city. Cool breezes could then be had along the river's edge, mixed with the scent of flowers like India's *raat ki rani*, or queen of the night (jasmine). Throughout Lucknow, five times a day, the call to prayer sounded through the warm north Indian air as members of the city's predominantly Muslim population made their way to one of the city's mosques.

South of the Gomati was the railway line, with the heart of the city sitting on the west side of the tracks, and the British residential neighborhoods on the east. The latter, known as the "civil lines," were home to the city's *sahibs* and *memsahibs,* that is, members of the British community who retreated from Lucknow's narrow lanes and crowded bazaars to this area's widely spaced roads and tidy gardens. Here those belonging to the middle- and upper-class British community could find God in their local churches, the dead in the adjoining cemeteries (more than one), and drinks in the club. From the civil lines, across Bruce's Bridge, where the Gomati begins flowing to the east, was Canning College, where Mehdi received his education.

The city of Lucknow rose to prominence when it served as the capital of the princely state of Oudh. Although elements of the city possibly date from the reign of Rama, king of Ayodhya during an ancient past, the chronology of the city's growth becomes clearer with the first nawab of Oudh, Saddat Khan (1680–1739). His descendants, and in particular the fourth nawab, Asaf-ud-Daula (1748–1797), fashioned the city into an opulent princely capital, rich with architectural assets. Palaces, bridges, mosques, and other infrastructure arose—perhaps the most spectacular being the Bara Imambara building and complex. For Shia Muslims, an *imambara* is a place to perform ceremonies, especially those related to Muharram. Built by Asaf-ud-Daula in the late eighteenth century, this cream-colored structure has rich, scalloped doorways, cupolas along its walls, and a dizzying set of smaller stone arches that ring the top of the building.

As Mughal power in north India waned during the first decades of the eighteenth century, Lucknow, Hyderabad, and their respective rulers prospered. Once vassals to the Mughal Empire, these successors threw off their allegiance and established themselves as independent princely states. Yet, by the early decades of the nineteenth century, growing British power challenged these regional elites. In Lucknow, the last of the great Lucknow rulers was Wajid Ali (r. 1847–1856). The end of his career saw his state annexed by the East India Company. This provocation heightened tensions across north India, which erupted in the 1857 uprising. However, before Wajid Ali was finally dethroned, he constructed the largest of the Lucknow palaces, the Kaisar Bagh, a large, multistoried building with columned porticos on the lower levels and a grand dome above. It cost the immense sum of eighty *lakhs*.

The Donnelly family home was in the shadow of the Kaisar Bagh. This was a largely Indian neighborhood. Their social circles were a mix of both Indian and British friends, the latter also drawn from a lower socioeconomic stratum of the British society in Lucknow at the time. This community was somewhat different than those Britons living in Lucknow's civil lines. In other terms, the Donnellys were not "clubbable," or respectable enough to be voted into a club, whereas the inhabitants of the civil lines likely were. For Ellen, her move to Hyderabad would mark the beginning of her rise from a relatively poor social position to that of a respectable Englishwoman.

Hyderabad city lies in the middle of south-central India, which is marked by its high, flat plateau. This semi-arid region is geographically distinct from the north or the deep south. The Hyderabad that Mehdi and Ellen saw when they arrived had three major areas. The first was the older center of Hyderabad, located on the south bank of the Musi River, which flows from west to east. The second area held the newer settlements along the north bank, including the British Residency and its bazaars. At the head of this northern half of the city was a large lake or "tank," Hussain Sagar. Wrapping around the shimmering water body on the east side was the newest and third section of greater Hyderabad: the British military, civil, and commercial areas.

These British areas together comprised the city of Secunderabad. Still further north of Hyderabad and Secunderabad by about nine miles was the outpost of Bolarum, a military cantonment of the Hyderabad Contingent. In this more salubrious locale, a home, office, and garden served as a second lodging of the British Resident.

Hyderabad city in the late nineteenth century was a colorful feast for newly arrived eyes. In the streets, camels, horses, and elephants jostled together with water buffalos, cows, and other beasts of burden. Local elites wore either English suits or Indian *sherwani* and tight *kurta* pajama pants. Hyderabad officialdom had its own headwear, a yellow beehive-shaped turban. These could be seen in the markets and bazaars alongside Britons donning "solar topees" (pith helmets) and women in bonnets tied tightly around the chin to keep sun and dust out of their hair. Parasols, umbrellas, caparisoned elephants, and horses added splashes of crimson, navy, gold, and purple to the street life. Lower classes moved about on foot, steering clear of animal traffic as well as buggies and phaetons. Bicycles were now an old technology, and, by the end of the century, the motorcar would start to ply Hyderabad's streets. Away from the old city and into Secunderabad, or in the enclave of the Residency, the architecture shifted from a mix of Indo-Islamic forms with pillars, arches, minars, and *jaalis* to tidy groves of trees, potted plants by the thousands, neat white fences, and the crosses and bells of St. George and St. John churches. Most of Hyderabad's architecture sported semicircular clay tile roofs that helped abate the heat of the summer and protect inhabitants from torrential monsoon rains. Intricate latticework shaded deep verandahs for men and women stationed in Secunderabad's civil lines. Near the Residency, decorative street lamps marked the newer business district; an area anchored by the large building housing A. Abid and Company, "Drapers, Tailors and Outfitters."[28] To this day, this part of town bears the name "Abid's" in memory of that shop.

Below Hussain Sagar were neighborhoods that contained the Public Gardens as well as Nampally Railway Station. The gardens sported fountains, manicured lawns, and faux castle gates. The British Residency compound sat on the north side of the Musi River, anchored by the Residency structure itself, completed in 1805.[29] Guests would arrive at the foot of a wide staircase from which six massive columns reached upward to support the neoclassical rooflines. Two lion statues flanked the steps, and, high above, the crest of the East India Company graced the portico. Inside, symmetrical curved staircases led to the second floor. Music and the tinkling of crystal must have often wafted down the steps and into the night. On the other side of the building, a graceful semicircular façade broke up the boxiness of the building. Off to each side were screened rooms to catch some of the breezes that blew in from the Musi. The compound also had gardens, fountains, other administrative structures, and a graveyard where many of Hyderabad's British officialdom and sometimes their families, as well as some prominent Muslim members of the city, were laid to rest.

The Residency Bazaars were immediately adjacent to the Residency compound. This area was under the jurisdiction of the Resident, and it was in the court of the Residency Bazaars that Mehdi would later file his case. The area had about 2,800 homes and 12,400 occupants. The second assistant Resident held the position of superintendent of the Residency Bazaars and exercised duties that resembled those of a cantonment magistrate or judge, hearing legal cases that fell within the area's jurisdiction.[30]

Crossing one of several bridges that spanned the Musi, the older part of Hyderabad unfolded. The Nizams resided in the Chowmahalla palace complex. Completed in 1769 by Nizam Ali Khan, the complex contained several buildings as well as gurgling cisterns and enclosed courtyards. These low buildings, covered in cream-colored plasterwork, had arched doorways and matching cupolas. Inside, large rooms with checkerboard floors, ornate glass chandeliers, and yellow and cream stucco decorated every space.[31]

At the crossroads of the old city lay the Char Minar—the city's defining icon—a four-minaret structure built by the Qutb Shahi ruler Muhammad Quli Qutb Shah in 1591. American Bishop John Fletcher Hurst, on tour in Hyderabad in 1888, called the Char Minar the "'scandal point' of the idle loiterers of Hyderabad."[32] South of the Char Minar was the immense Mecca Masjid. To the east and west of the city were the great pleasure tanks built by Mir Alam and Mir Jumla, each providing a cool and watery respite from the hot southern sun. On the city's outskirts were the remains of the fort of Golconda, from which Muhammad Quli Qutb Shah shifted his capital to create the new city of Hyderabad.

When Mehdi and Ellen stepped down from the train onto the Nampally Station platform on 9 February 1883, he was thirty-one years old, and she was twenty-nine. Not visible to the naked eye but surrounding them was Hyderabad's complex political networks in which they would play an increasing role for the next decade.[33]

At the center of the political order was the Nizam, ruler of Hyderabad State. In 1724, as the Mughal Empire was breaking apart, the first Nizam, Asaf Jah I, established his independence from the Mughals, and Hyderabad as an autonomous princely domain began its 224-year existence. By the late nineteenth century, Hyderabad State was just over 83,000 square miles in size. At the time of Mehdi's arrival, the sixth Nizam, Mahbub Ali Khan, was readying himself to be installed with his full ruling rights, having been, up to this time, a minor under the care of guardians. In photographs and paintings of Mahbub Ali Khan as a young man during the time of the pamphlet case, he appears fair-skinned, sporting a thin mustache that curled down to meet bushy sideburns. He has almond-shaped eyes and delicate eyebrows, with a high forehead. In some images, the Nizam sports the simpler style of turban with one fold across the front— similar to what Mehdi wore—whereas for more formal portraits and pictures, he wears the beehive yellow high turban with a jewel-encrusted ornamental top-piece.

Second to the Nizam in Hyderabad's political system was the position of prime minister. This individual was in many ways the de facto ruler, handling the day-to-day administration of the state, while the Nizams participated in governance to varying degrees, largely according to their own interests. The prime minister who looms largest in Hyderabad history is Salar Jung I.[34] Images of Salar Jung usually show him wearing a round disc-like turban, a sash over his shoulder, and the large Order of the Star of India pinned on the left chest of his *sherwani*. He sports a long mustache but a clean-shaven square jaw. In many photographs, his lips appear almost pursed, as if he wished the moment would end so that he might return to his desk piled high with the paperwork of a burgeoning bureaucracy.

When Salar Jung went to north India to recruit British-trained Indian civil servants, including Mehdi, to work in Hyderabad State, his efforts were not entirely popular with locals. Joseph Rock, who served as an agent for the Nizam through his position in Rogers Rock, Merchants and East India Agents, wrote in 1897: "Their services were, no doubt, in the first place necessary; but, as these aliens monopolised the eligible posts, prevented the Hyderabadis acquiring any experience or knowledge, and with the instinct of nepotism recruited their own ranks from their kinsmen and relations, the presence of this foreign element soon became a scandal and an abuse."[35] A similar account of outsiders in Hyderabad came from Morton Frewen, soon to be the assistant of Salar Jung's son, Salar Jung II. He wrote, "Hyderabad politics are being run at this moment to fill the pockets of a gang of foreign swindlers and, to do this better, they are leaving and have left no stone unturned to make the Nizam quarrel with the

The Nizam, Mahbub Ali Khan

native Nawabs, and to make the Nawabs fight among themselves."[36] Mehdi thus joined other north Indians in Hyderabad who bore sobriquets of "alien" and "foreign swindler."

Among those north Indians, deep in the labyrinth of the Nizam's palace complex, was the Nawab Server Jung. He would play a central role in the scandal. Also known by his full name of Nawab Agha Mirza Beg Khan, Server Jung, Server-ud-Dowlah, Server-ul-Mulk Bahadur, he was born in Delhi and a few years older than Mehdi.[37] His father died when he was a young child, and his uncle, Mirza Abbas Beg Khan, raised him and his brothers.[38] Server Jung was living in Delhi when a ragtag group of *sepoys* from Meerut arrived in the city in 1857. They badgered the elderly Mughal ruler, Bahadur Shah II, to join them in a rebellion against the British—Delhi was quickly engulfed in violence.[39] Server Jung and his family fled to Alwar, southwest of Delhi, where his uncle provided refuge. At Alwar, Server Jung's father received a post of *hakim* in a local district. However, the family did not remain long at Alwar and returned briefly to the outskirts of Delhi before finally being summoned by Server Jung's benevolent uncle, Abbas Beg. Server Jung and his immediate family settled in Sitapur. Here he began his education in earnest. In his own words, he was not a promising student: "I was far behind them [his cousins at school]; and because, in addition, I was fond of play and sport, and had no desire for learning. When I joined school I knew hardly anything."[40] A few years later, Server Jung moved to Lucknow where he, like Mehdi, attended Canning College.

Given Abbas Beg's prominent service to the East India Company and his high position in Lucknow society, Server Jung received special attention from General Lousada Barrow, the chief commissioner of Oudh. When Salar Jung I came from Hyderabad on a recruiting visit, Barrow likely recommended Server Jung. Arriving as a young man in Hyderabad in early 1873, Server Jung spent some time simply trying to get the prime minister's attention. Layers of bureaucrats guarded the prime minister, controlling admission to his *durbar*. They used endless stall-and-delay tactics or demanded large bribes, the payment of which were not guaranteed to secure a meeting. Frustrated, Server Jung was on the verge of leaving Hyderabad altogether. "I was young and inexperienced, and proud of my family traditions, and had been educated and brought up in a lordly style; and having on two occasions waited in vain for an audience, I was dismally disappointed."[41] He consulted a friend who, after prayer, encouraged him to go to the prime minister without bothering to heed the bureaucratic intermediaries. Still not motivated to go, Server Jung had a more mystical encounter that finally gave him the courage to seek out the prime minister again. As he recounted it, he would see a man dressed only in a loincloth and carrying a walking stick pass by his home each day and return later. One day this man walked directly up to Server Jung, took a long drag from his pipe, looked him in the eyes, and said, "They are calling you, and you won't go."[42] When this happened a second time, a stunned Server Jung finally made his way—unimpeded—to the prime minister's *durbar*.

The young Server Jung found an initial position in the Public Works Department in mid-December 1873. He was not there long; two or three months later, a docket arrived requesting him to come to the palace. Server Jung's family background and education secured him a position as tutor to Salar Jung's two sons, Salar Jung II and Nawab Munir-ul-Mulk. At the time, the boys were just twelve and eleven years old. His work teaching these noble youths did not go unnoticed.

In 1875, the Nizam, Mahbub Ali Khan, was nine years old. His father had died in 1869, and Salar Jung I and the Amir-i-Kabir formed a regency to oversee his education. Salar Jung I had carefully overseen the tutoring of his own sons by Server Jung and, when the moment arrived, put forward his name to become one of the Nizam's tutors. Server Jung would instruct the Nizam in Urdu.[43] From this moment until his departure from Hyderabad twenty-four years later, Server Jung was at the Nizam's side. Eventually he was named peshi secretary, a kind of personal assistant, and through this role he was able to shape the politics of the city and state, bestowing boons on those who met his favor and ruining those who, like Mehdi, did not.

In this milieu Mehdi and Ellen thus began a new chapter of their lives. Hyderabad was a princely state capital that offered Mehdi promising job prospects. Although they left behind their family connections in north India, they had a few friends and acquaintances from Lucknow who already lived in Hyderabad and would play important roles in their lives. This support was particularly urgent because Salar Jung, who had recruited Mehdi, died shortly before Mehdi began his appointment. Mehdi would need connections to help him get started and navigate the now uncertain political waters in which he and Ellen found themselves.

2

A GRAND TOUR

TO THE HEART

OF EMPIRE

WHEN THEY ARRIVED in Hyderabad, Mehdi and Ellen found the city in mourning. On 8 February 1883, Salar Jung I had died. When news of the prime minister's death reached the young Nizam, he wept bitterly. The streets of Hyderabad were silent as the city became a site of collective mourning. "Those who visited the city that night describe it as wearing the appearance of a city of the dead. There was no life, no noise, no bustle in the streets. But few people were about, and those that were, looked like men stricken with some sudden and most terrible calamity."[1] The next morning, the funeral procession began, and "immense crowds of sobbing and wailing people proved how deep had been the affection of all for the deceased prime minister. At the casements above the streets, women beat their bosoms and uttered shrill cries of sorrow; below, in the procession, rugged featured Arabs, Rohillas, Pathans, and others who had known his bounty, wept bitterly for their dead benefactor; and around and about was a sobbing crowd."[2] Through a city deep in a state of shock and mourning, Mehdi and Ellen made their way. For Mehdi, Salar Jung I's death must have brought a sense of unease. In his personal papers, he carried with him a letter of introduction addressed to Salar

Jung I from Sir Syed Ahmed Khan.[3] With the prime minister gone, the surety of his appointment in Hyderabad now faced unforeseen challenges.

Mehdi and Ellen arrived in Hyderabad in February and by April—with the help of fellow north Indian friends—he had secured his first post as a judge in a "small causes court." His starting salary was a modest 800 rupees per month. He secured that first job in part from his letter of introduction, but also with the help of his former classmate, Server Jung. At least in the beginning, Mehdi and Server Jung were on good terms, but this would not last. The next year Mehdi was promoted to *taluqdar*, and the year after that, promoted again to puisne judge of the Hyderabad High Court. His power grew again in 1885 when he was appointed as acting chief justice of the Hyderabad High Court, and then made permanent chief justice in 1887, commanding a handsome salary of 2,000 rupees per month.[4]

Within a short time after the death of Salar Jung I, Nizam Mahbub Ali Khan was invested with full ruling power. Among his many acts was the appointment of Salar Jung I's son, Salar Jung II, as the new prime minister of Hyderabad State. Salar Jung II did not have a long career, serving only four years. He was, according to Joseph Rock, "the tool of designing persons who were not natives of Hyderabad."[5] The mention of non-natives of Hyderabad was a direct reference to the "aliens" and "foreigners" from north India. Pundits in part attributed Salar Jung II's failure to his closeness in age to the Nizam. He was more a friend than an advisor to the ruler. His physical appearance was certainly far different from the young Nizam's: Salar Jung II was six feet four inches tall and weighed over two hundred pounds.[6]

From the British perspective, the blame for the trouble between Salar Jung II and the Nizam fell squarely on Server Jung. Joseph Rock described the end of Salar Jung II's term in office: "Owing to Survar Jung's machinations, the trivial differences between the Nizam and Salar Jung II were magnified into an irreparable breach, their intercourse necessary for the transaction of business ceased, and in 1886 [sic] Sir Salar Yung [sic], feeling how utterly impossible it was to continue in his office without the sympathy of his sovereign, resigned."[7] Server Jung had his own ideas why Salar Jung II resigned. He placed the blame squarely at the feet of Mehdi and Ellen: "But in the short regime of Nawab Laik Ali Khan, he [Mehdi] and his mistress [Ellen] secured such influence that, when the Nawab was relieved of his office, he, with the aid of Moulvi Mushtak Hussain, became a companion and adviser to Nawab Sir Asman Jah."[8] In Server Jung's opinion, Mehdi and his friend Mushtak Hussain played a complex political game by helping usher Salar Jung II from office while securing his successor, Asman Jah, a man they felt they could more easily influence and control.

Once Salar Jung II was out of office, he left Hyderabad and began a tour of the Middle East. Helping him navigate the politics of British imperialism in that part of the world was Morton Frewen. Frewen was a close friend to Lord Randolph Churchill (father of Winston Churchill), who had recommended Frewen for the job.[9] Frewen would be mentioned in the trial, and his wife, Clare (also known as Lady Frewen), played an important role during Ellen's visit to London.

Salar Jung II's replacement as prime minister of Hyderabad State, Asman Jah, had been the minister for justice. Asman Jah was descended from a group of royal nobles, the Paigahs of Hyderabad. His father was Bashir ul-Mulk, and his mother was the sixth daughter of Nizam ul-Mulk. He would serve as prime minister until 1893, in office when the pamphlet scandal broke. In fact, he would appear as a witness at Ellen and Mehdi's trial.

Mehdi's friend Mushtak Hussain served as deputy prime minister under Asman Jah. Mushtak Hussain, Server Jung, and Mehdi shared a similar background. Mushtak Hussain was born in Meerut into a

A party at Saroornagar. Asman Jah is seated second from right, bottom row. Fitzpatrick is seated to next to him, third from right. Mehdi is standing fourth from right, top row. The seated figure in a white hat behind Fitzpatrick could be Ellen.

family who, like Server Jung's family, had served the Mughal emperors. He was a boy during the uprising of 1857. All three men rose through the ranks upon their arrival in Hyderabad. Mushtak Hussain began as law secretary, worked in the Revenue Department, was governor of Warangal, then revenue secretary, and finally became deputy prime minister under Asman Jah.[10] In 1892, Hussain left Hyderabad and returned to north India, where he took up a position at Aligarh. He was a supporter of Sir Syed Ahmed Khan and was one of the four men who, in December 1906, launched the All-India Muslim League, of which he became the general secretary.

Mushtak Hussain amassed a good deal of power in Hyderabad and chose Mehdi as his junior colleague. This relationship of Asman Jah to Hussain and Mehdi was widely known. Newspapers freely commented on the prime minister's weakness at the latters' hands.

> It is an open secret that Sir Asmanjah could not—at any rate, does not—dispose of any single 'paper,' although hundreds of such papers are submitted to him daily. In the first instance each paper goes to Mushtak Husain who reads it and pins to it a scrap of paper containing an endorsement or opinion for the Minister to copy out thereon . . . Mehdi Hassan as being next in rank to Mushtak Husain is accorded the privilege of submitting papers from his office direct to the Minister. And even *he* can get no orders passed without the knowledge of the Minister *de facto*. Whenever Mehdi Hussan is announced at the Minister's place, the Minister inquires if Mushtak Husain is there; and if the wise Mushtak is *non est* Mehdi Hussan, however important and urgent in character his papers may be, is made to await his arrival. And then both are ushered into the Minister's presence.[11]

Reflecting on his own time in Hyderabad, Server Jung commented on the three-way relationship between Asman Jah, Hussain, and Mehdi: "In important and urgent matters alone, representations were made by Moulvi Mushtak Hussain in the name of the Minister, who had only to sign his name, while Mushtak Hussain was 'de facto' Minister, and had for his partner Fatteh Nawaz Jung Bahadur [Mehdi Hasan]."[12] To a degree, the actual power of Asman Jah as prime minister was less than the title he bore. Mushtak Hussain, with the support of Mehdi, clearly held sway over Asman Jah, but Mehdi was apparently unable to exert the same kind of control on his own. Mehdi was deeply loyal to Hussain. When the latter traveled to London in 1888, he wrote in his diary that Mushtak Hussain "is one of the most thorough gentlemen in Hyderabad, but the black intrigues of the place have always prevented his virtue being done justice to."[13]

The relationship between Mushtak Hussain and Mehdi seems to have started with Mehdi's arrival in Hyderabad. Like Server Jung himself, Mehdi found it difficult to obtain a meeting in order to present his letter of introduction. Mushtak Hussain helped him. The two men approached Server Jung and "pressed a long-standing claim" on him. Server Jung knew Mehdi from their Lucknow days and helped him find his first position within the government. Although Server Jung pleaded that he had no "locus standi" in the administration, he said he would nonetheless try to help. Server Jung described what happened next: "However, I began to think how I could interfere re the man's appointment. The Maharaja was already ill-disposed towards Upper Indian men [north Indians], and was about to lay hold of Moulvi Mushtak Hussain himself, but the fact that Mehdi Hussain had been my school-fellow, influenced me in his favour."[14] Server Jung took credit for helping Mehdi navigate Hyderabad's political waters. "He [Mehdi Hasan] brought a letter of recommendation from Sir Syed Ahmed Khan to the late Minister, but as the latter had died, Moulvi Mushtak Hussain brought him over to me during the Prime Ministership of the Maharaja, and I had recommended and got him employed in the Judicial Department."[15] The Maharaja was Narender Bahadur, who, along with Salar Jung II, served as co-administrator of the council in the year after Salar Jung I's death and before Salar Jung II assumed full power. Server Jung carried out a plan whereby he would vouch for Mehdi's abilities and help him land his first position in the Hyderabad government administration.

When Mehdi and Ellen arrived in the city, life in Hyderabad in the 1880s was a combination of princely Indian and high Victorian

Mehdi Hasan (*right*) and friend in "fancy dress"

cultures. For instance, the calendar was punctuated by important events from multiple communities: the Langar Procession, widely observed as part of Muharram in the old city; festivals of Hindu deities; Eid and Ramadan; Christmas and Easter; the birthdays and anniversaries of the Nizam and Queen Victoria; and inaugurations and jubilees. These and other events were moments for the elite of Hyderabad and the expatriate British community to separately close ranks and celebrate. At the same time, such occasions were often moments for each community to extend invitations to the other and practice, in the term of the day, "social intercourse," whereby Indians and Britons socialized together.

The Nizam's palace—Chowmahalla—and the Residency were the two largest centers of power, and, when the occasion warranted, their doors opened to the Hyderabad elite, Indian and British. Inside, immense crystal chandeliers hung down and illuminated walls covered with paintings that depicted former Nizams or Residents, stuffed animal heads, and other bric-a-brac of late nineteenth-century India. Rich Persian and Indian carpets covered the floors, and the scent of roses wafted through the halls. At mealtimes, bearers laid immense tables prepared for over one hundred guests with dishes such as biryanis of rice and meat, dozens of curries, and sickly sweet desserts like sherbet or fruits with cream, all prepared by an army of chefs.

Centers of power beyond Chowmahalla and the Residency included the two major social clubs: the Secunderabad Club and the Nizam Club. The former was largely for the British community of Secunderabad, while the latter was for the Indian elite of Hyderabad, which included Britons who wished to become members. Mehdi served as the first secretary of the Nizam Club from 1884 to 1892, taking the position just a year after his arrival in Hyderabad. He had experience in India's clubs that predated his time in Hyderabad. For instance, an account from the *Pioneer* in 1877 notes that Mehdi delivered a lecture on the principles of civilization at the Roy Bareilly

Mehdi Hasan, Asman Jah, and friends at a breakfast party. Asman Jah is seated, center, in white. Mehdi is standing, second row, third from left.

Reform Club (now Raebareli), where he served as club secretary.[16] At that time he was a *tahsildar* near Lucknow, while Ellen was keeping *purdah*. The secretary of an Indian social club was far more powerful than its president. The president's position was honorary and usually lasted just one year. The secretary could hold power for years on end, dictating the direction and agenda for the club.[17] For his part, from his position as secretary of the Nizam Club, Mehdi organized lavish dinners for himself and his friends.

By 1887, Mehdi had been promoted to chief justice of the High Court, where he seems to have found his voice and shared his opinion on different topics. That year brought with it three significant events related to Mehdi and Ellen. The first was the celebration of the Golden Jubilee of Queen Victoria, observed on 19 February. In his position as secretary of the Nizam Club, Mehdi organized and hosted a dinner at the club on 21 February. This event was a reflection of his power at the club and his ability to summon Hyderabad's most elite members to his own event. He distributed 150 invitations, including ones to the Nizam, the prime minister, military officials, the Residency staff, and those in service to the Nizam.

Later that year, a second event transpired to which Mehdi lent his voice. Between August and September 1887, a proposal circulated for the reshaping of Hyderabad's administration. Known as the Cabinet Scheme, it proposed a system with two secretaries at the top of the political echelon, with the current secretaries in the administration becoming their assistants. The proposed system would have disrupted Hyderabad's political hierarchy and carried with it a whiff of criticism of the current system.

Mehdi made his opinions about Hyderabad affairs known through the newspapers. On 20 September 1887, he wrote to the *Pioneer* in his role as chief justice.[18] He summarized the feelings of Hyderabad officialdom in their opposition to the Cabinet Scheme: "I never witnessed such unanimity in condemning an unfortunate scheme as that which has been shown in Hyderabad on this occasion." He pointed out that A. J. Dunlop had previously "mooted" the idea of a dual secretary system. Dunlop served as the respected revenue secretary in the Nizam's government and held the rank of Companion of the Order of the Indian Empire. The proposal implicitly questioned the loyalty and motivations of the current batch of Hyderabad officials. Mehdi drew a distinction between "native British subjects" like himself and the local Hyderabadis. He responded, "There is no better or more loyal class of native British subjects in India than those serving in Hyderabad. It is they who more plainly see the real difference between the British and native systems of administration, and it is certainly they who are better able to appreciate the former." Mehdi continued by invoking the late Salar Jung I, who, he claimed, "regarded such matters with great caution."[19]

In this tense atmosphere, a rumor emerged that Mehdi and the British Resident, John Graham Cordery, were at odds. As rumor and accusation circulated between the Residency, the Nizam's palace, and the offices of the different ministers concerning the Cabinet Scheme, Mehdi explained his own relationship with Cordery as well as with Colonel C. H. T. Marshall of the Nizam's forces. Marshall served as a private secretary and advisor to the Nizam from March 1887 to November 1888, helping oversee the state's business in the time between Salar Jung II's death and the appointment of Asman Jah. Mehdi leapt to the defense of Cordery against rumors that he had been behind the Cabinet Scheme: "It is simply absurd to suppose that Mr. Cordery had anything to do with the scheme." Furthermore, accusations of ill will between Mehdi and Colonel Marshall were also quickly dispatched. Mehdi had hosted Marshall at the Nizam Club at some earlier point and reiterated his feelings for the military man: "I say plainly that I never met a better Englishman than Colonel Marshall, the most generous, the most noble-hearted, the most liberal-minded of men. He has so loyally identified himself with the best interests of the State that we already look on him as one of us."[20]

A third event of 1887 took place in more intimate settings, far from the political spotlight that shone increasingly on Mehdi. In that year, in blue ink on cream paper, Ellen composed her last will and testament. It would appear in the trial as evidence. There is no reason to believe she felt death was near, but Mehdi and Ellen were about to begin a dramatic new chapter of their lives, and so, perhaps in advance of this next, uncertain phase, she prepared the document. In the will, Ellen identified herself as "Ellen Gertrude Mehdi Hasan, the wife of Mehdi Hasan Khan, Fatteh Nawaz Jung." She appointed her husband as sole executor of her will and left anything she might have to him. The will was executed on 27 October 1887 and had two witnesses: James B. Buchanan, an executive engineer in the Nizam's service, and Dora White, also in the Nizam's service, who was identified as a *zenana* doctor—one who provided medical care to women in their homes.[21]

It had been an important year for the couple. The jubilee celebration marked Mehdi's emergence as a prominent member of Hyderabad's elite circles who was able to muster them at the Nizam Club, and the Cabinet Scheme marked his entry into public debates over the nature of Hyderabad's government. Ellen's will demonstrated a degree of planning and forethought concerning the couple's future. It was also one of many instances in which she identified herself as the lawfully wedded wife of Mehdi Hasan—information that would later prove critical to her fate.

By early 1888, the couple temporarily traded their Hyderabad address for lodgings in London when they took an extended trip to the heart of the empire. Feeling secure in his position in Hyderabad, and perhaps intent on expanding his power, Mehdi left India for Britain with Ellen in February. He had business to conduct on behalf of the Nizam's government, and she would visit her sister Esther and niece Isabelle.[22] Mehdi wrote about his travels in a diary that he privately published in 1890. It was not an uncommon practice for nobles to keep and sometimes publish a diary; for instance, Amar Singh of Rajasthan kept a diary for forty-four years between 1898 and 1944, missing only one day of writing.[23] Thus, for a period of time, we are privy to Mehdi's opinions and activities in some depth. The diary begins on 2 February 1888 as he prepared to leave Hyderabad. Members of the city's elite gave a farewell dinner at the Nizam Club and also saw him off at Nampally Station en route to Bombay. There, he and Ellen met his relation Fakhrudeen. The couple then boarded the steamer *Sutlej* along with their dog, "Petty." The *Sutlej* made its way across the Arabian Sea, docking in Aden to take on coal. It proceeded to the Bay of Suez, where Mehdi disembarked alone. Ellen traveled on to London.

Mehdi's itinerary was something of a Grand Tour. On these tours, popular in the nineteenth century with Britons, other Europeans, and even Americans, individuals or groups would visit sites associated with Europe's antiquity and renaissance. Mehdi's similar itinerary suggests something of a desire to be "polished" by the experience as a cosmopolitan man of the British Empire.[24] Yet, by the time he reached Egypt and disembarked for the first part of the tour, his mood had already soured. After only a few weeks of travel, he was already reflecting on the earlier portion of the trip onboard the *Sutlej*.

> I do not know why, but I am very much depressed to-day. It is too gloomy to sit in the cabin, and too cold to sit on deck. I keep on thinking of the "Sutlej," and wishing I were back on her. I regret having broken my journey in Egypt. Not having heard from my wife, nor received a line from my friends in Hyderabad during the past twenty days, causes me torture. Even the Indian papers cannot be obtained, and I have passed a tedious, miserable day. The journey from Bombay to Suez was the happiest one of my life.[25]

From Egypt Mehdi traveled to Italy, where he visited Bologna, Venice, and Milan. Throughout his journey, he noted with particular attention the women he saw or met. While in Milan, he commented, "The women seem to me more attractive than in Venice, their beauty is of that saucy kind that has a peculiar relish in it."[26] Such comments, peppered throughout the diary, give credence to the depiction of Mehdi in his youth as a flirt and somewhat of a buffoon. By his thirties, his buffoonery—as Server Jung had called it—had turned into pride and arrogance, and his flirtatiousness had become more private, revealing itself through his wandering eyes and the attention he paid to women who, more often than not, were not his wife. In Milan, Mehdi attended the opera. This performance of Richard Wagner's

Lohengrin was participatory: audience members were expected to come in costume. Mehdi wore a turban, *sherwani,* and pajama pants— what he called "native costume." He noted with evident pride that his attire had additional effects: "I had purposely gone in native costume, and am proud to say that I was the lodestar for all the ladies' eyes in the house."[27]

The culmination of his tour through the Middle East and Europe was his arrival in London. Over a century before, Indians came to London as servants, accompanying returning members of the East India Company. Sailors sometimes jumped ship and stayed in London.[28] But by the eighteenth and nineteenth centuries, Indians came to London on official visits, for pleasure or school, or as political participants. As the community grew, so too did the amenities to support it: Indian restaurants, including London's first, the Hindoostanee Coffee House, which opened in 1810; temples and mosques, and community associations and organizations. While in London, Mehdi met a variety of individuals from this British-Indian community as well as British politicians connected directly to the Raj.

For Mehdi, a staunch supporter of the British Empire, his arrival in London was a pivotal moment. He felt himself to be an Indian-born citizen of the Raj visiting its capital city. Mehdi reached London on March 14, noting he "felt as if I were realising the dream of my life."[29] He made no mention of his reunion with Ellen, and, in fact, made little mention of her at all throughout the diary. Mehdi checked into the Alexandra Hotel, near Hyde Park. This four-story Victorian hotel, located at 159–161 Sussex Garden, is still in business. One can imagine Mehdi looking up at the tan-brown brick structure with its cement lintels, pushing through the front door past the columned front portico toward a room warmed by a fire in the hearth. From the Alexandra, he began a fairly active routine of work on behalf of the Nizam's government, meeting friends and officials, and visiting sites in and around London. While living his "dream" in London, news from

Hyderabad periodically disturbed him. Mehdi's comments reveal his opinions of Hyderabad in less than flattering terms. When the Indian mail arrived at his hotel on 19 March, he wrote of his friends' letters: "They tell me of the intrigues of Hyderabad. I am sorry that they mention these, for so long as I am in England I want to forget the dirty intrigues of Hyderabad, to enjoy the pure atmosphere of London, and to meet honest, straightforward, intelligent people, which is a great treat to me. I dislike having my enjoyment interrupted by this kind of news."[30] The insinuation that Hyderabadis were neither honest nor straightforward or intelligent undoubtedly angered many when his published diary circulated in the city. Making his opinions on the city's intrigues so clearly known could not have helped his reputation.

While Mehdi was in London, the Indian National Congress was in its third year of existence and beginning to attract national and international attention. Established in 1885 by like-minded Indians and Britons, the early Congress—heavily influenced by its Bengali cohort—sought ways to enable British power in India to better meet the needs of the Indian people. Over time, and with Mahatma Gandhi's return to India in 1915, the Congress became the major party of India's independence movement. Yet from the start, not everyone, including Mehdi, was enthusiastic about this new organization or its agenda.

As spring unfolded in London, Mehdi's position as chief justice of the Hyderabad Court made him something of a minor celebrity in London, and he was interviewed for his opinions on Congress affairs. The interview recounts, "A representative of a News Agency had an interview on Wednesday with his Honour the Mussalman Chief Justice of Hyderabad, the Nawab Fettah Nawaz Jung Mehdi Hassan, who has just reached this country on a pleasure tour, accompanied by his wife." Nothing further was said about Ellen. The journalist commented on Mehdi's personal side: "He is well known to Indian jurists and scholars, and speaks English with rare purity of accent and diction." The substance of the interview began with news from Calcutta. A group of well-wishers had gathered to make valedictory addresses for Lord Dufferin while another group gathered to organize a counterdemonstration. In his interview, Mehdi offered soothing words to a British audience: "The entire native community is at one in its loyalty to the British Government. There is no real difference on this point between the different races of India." He argued that, under British rule, the educated classes had enjoyed unprecedented peace and prosperity while the uneducated classes had enjoyed the "more practical and tangible advantages which spring from that rule." As for the counterdemonstrators, apparently led by Bengalis, Mehdi said, "Our educated Bengali fellow subjects, for whom I have otherwise a high esteem, are getting too Radical." He continued by praising the viceroy, and his handling of affairs in Central Asia (by avoiding a war), as well as the British annexation of Burma. Mehdi extended his support for Britain and the British government by speaking not just for himself, but, he claimed, for all Muslims. "From the Mohammedan point of view (we are not very Radical in our politics) this [the counter demonstration] involved an insult to every one of us. Politically we are one nation with the English, and an affront offered to the Government of the Queen is felt by all of us." Mehdi concluded the interview with remarks on the loyalty of the princely states.[31]

Also in March, Mehdi wrote a letter to the editor of the *Times,* concerning the Indian National Congress. The letter was nearly four full page-length columns under the title, "Mr. Hume's 'Loose Dynamite' In India." "Mr. Hume" was Allen Octavian Hume, the founder of the Congress and an outspoken critic of many policies pursued by the Government of India. Hume argued that India's poor were akin to a pile of loose dynamite that could explode at any moment. Mehdi took exception to this characterization, refuting Hume's premise point by point for his British audience. Part of Mehdi's argument was that the princely states were far from backward, in large part owing to the employment of British-educated men (like himself) who now staffed their ranks. If he had not already offended those in Hyderabad who followed the English language press, he surely did now.

> If the administration of many of the native States of the present day is remarkable for ability, justice, and wisdom, this is because able men who have established some character for experience in administration in British India often find in the capitals of native States a wider field for their genius and activity, the result being that the administration of native States is now generally worked on a system devised by perhaps the ablest bureaucratic service the world has seen, modified, of course, by careful regard to local circumstances.[32]

Mehdi's outspoken criticism of Hume, the Congress, the population of the princely states (benefiting from the "able men" of British India), and the large Bengali cohort that dominated the Congress would not be forgotten.[33]

Beyond politics, London offered Mehdi a view, literally, of women that was different than what was possible in India. One evening at the end of March, he took himself to the Alhambra Theatre, where he witnessed nearly one hundred young women in fishnet stockings and airborne skirts dancing in unison, "which was the grandest sight I ever saw."[34] His theater outing included an additional activity—some flirting with young, attractive women who worked at small bars set up on each floor of the theater building. The bars were kept by "very pretty girls," he said, adding that "Those who do not really care to have any refreshment sometimes order some with the object of having a little chat." For a Muslim, unlikely to drink alcohol, the beer or spirits held little attraction at such venues. But for Mehdi, the opportunity to speak flirtatiously with different "pretty girls" was perhaps both novel and entertaining. A few weeks later, on a Bank Holiday Monday, he went to visit a friend (unnamed, but of Indian origin) who lived with a British family outside of London. In the home were the proprietor's "four pretty and highly educated daughters," one of whom Mehdi came to learn was engaged to his friend. Mehdi was overjoyed not only for his friend's happiness but for the broader prospect of such "international marriages," in which he himself had partaken. "Nothing can be more advantageous for our social and intellectual progress, nothing more conducive to the harmony of the political relationships of the two countries, than these international marriages," he wrote, noting how in India such marriages often met with "hatred," but that this would not affect the couple "in the long run."[35]

Such marriages were not entirely uncommon. Love across race and religious lines arguably peaked in the eighteenth century, the days of "White Mughals." But the practice continued into the nineteenth century, although it was perhaps less well accepted as racial identities hardened during the high noon of the British Raj. Some Indian princes took up with British women, or "wicked" British women sought wealthy Indian husbands.[36] Less common, or at least less commonly explored, were examples like that of Mehdi and Ellen, involving couples who came from more humble backgrounds. Indeed, were it not for the pamphlet case, their relationship might have been lost to history.[37]

If Mehdi's trip to Europe earned him the credential of having completed the Grand Tour, allowed him to weigh in on political matters involving Indian nationalism and the Congress, and provided the opportunity to enjoy encounters with women at the opera and elsewhere, his being called to the bar bestowed upon him a significant

legal credential. Within English legal practice, those desiring to practice law before the High Court (a barrister) became members of one
of four Inns of Court: Gray's Inn, Middle Temple, Lincoln's Inn, or
Inner Temple. When they qualified to practice, they were said to have
been "called to the bar." The Inner Temple, to which Mehdi sought
and was invited for membership, boasted such past members as Geo-
ffrey Chaucer; James Boswell, Dr. Johnson's friend and biographer,
and nearly a decade later, another young Indian, Mohandas K. Gandhi.

When Mehdi's call to the bar was first announced in Hyderabad,
it raised a flurry of criticism in India, even though the event was a few
months away. In an editorial, the *Indian Daily News,* a newspaper hostile to him, questioned both his qualifications—invoking his wife as
an accomplice in his ineptitude in the English language—and the
value of being called to the bar, if the bar was so low as to admit him.
The attack began, "As far as we have been able to ascertain, this lucky
gentleman has not the rudimentary linguistic qualifications to begin
with. He is not even an indifferent English scholar, having had no education whatever in an English school. He has only a smattering of
English, which he has picked up probably from his English partner
in life, and has acquired a facility in speaking from his visit to England.
We are told he is unable to write two lines in decent English."[38] This
critique offered a challenge to Mehdi as a type of Indian-born
Englishman, flattered in other newspaper accounts for his command
of the English language. "We have gone to this length in describing the
Moulvie's [a Muslim legal scholar] qualifications, simply to inquire of
the eminent lawyers of India and England, whether, in their opinion,
the authorities of the Temple were justified in calling an individual
with such qualifications to the Bar."[39] Being from Lucknow (part of
British India), Mehdi's entrance to the Inner Temple required the permission of the Government of India. In communications with the
treasurer of the Inner Temple, the under-secretary of state for India,
J. A. Godley, stated that "there is no objection on the part of this

office" to Mehdi's admission to the Inner Temple. With government approval, the process went forward unhindered.[40]

As April dawned, Mehdi and Ellen continued to circulate in London society. He met Dadabhai Naroji, a leader in India and among Indians in Britain. Dadabhai was the first Indian to be a British member of Parliament, and an intellectual known fondly as the "Grand Old Man of India."[41] Mehdi also went to several London clubs and enjoyed the city's nightlife, taking in a performance of *David Garrick* at the Criterion Theater. On April 11, he recorded in his diary, "In the evening my wife and I went to the 'At Home' of the Right Hon. W. H. Smith, the First Lord of the Treasury."[42] Here is the first mention of Ellen in the diary since they boarded the *Sutlej* months earlier.[43] In other parts of the diary, it is unclear whether Mehdi's use of the first person plural when attending events meant that Ellen was by his side. If not, where was she? Although Ellen and Mehdi arrived and departed London at different times, we know that, on at least a few occasions, they attended events together. Later in the month, Mehdi's London adventures were once again interrupted by news from Hyderabad. Abdul Huq, also known as Sirdar Diler-ul-Mulk, had been suspended from his office. This, according to Mehdi, created quite the "sensation" in London's India circles.

Like Mehdi and Server Jung, Abdul Huq was not from Hyderabad; he had come to the city from India's western Konkan coast. He was fluent in English and good with finances. Twice he was dispatched to London to help with a nascent Hyderabad railway effort and was amply rewarded for his success in turning around that venture, as well as for securing investments in Hyderabad's coalfields. Yet his acceptance of large rewards for his service appeared distasteful, and eventually he fell out of favor in Hyderabad. While in office, Huq had great influence in the India Office, some claimed, and men like Asman Jah (prime minister at the time) were said to be obsequious in dealing with him. Perhaps sympathetic to a fellow non-*mulki*, Mehdi wrote in his diary, "I sympathise with the poor Sirdar, and hope he will be able to defend his honour."[44]

On the last day of April, Mehdi attended Queen Victoria's levée, without Ellen. The Prince of Wales hosted the event at St. James Palace. Mehdi opted to wear "native dress": a *sherwani* and pajama pants. This was clearly strategic: "As I had a foreign name, and was in my Indian Court dress, I attracted particular notice, and his Royal Highness, who is always very gracious to the Indian subjects of her Majesty, condescended to pay me especial attention, which was immensely gratifying to me."[45] Mehdi was overcome at the sight of the prince. "I forgot all the Anglicised feelings which have been forced upon me by circumstances during the past fifteen years of my life, and felt inclined, as if by the force of some spell, to revert to the Oriental custom, to throw myself at the feet of that noble Prince, and to kiss his hand."[46] Mehdi revealed that, despite his schooling and professed loyalty to the British Empire, in an emotional moment, he drew from his Indian roots. This was the first time that Mehdi had an audience with members of the royal family, but it would not be his last.

On May 9, Mehdi and Ellen attended a drawing room event in Buckingham Palace. Their presentation to the queen was made possible through connections to Morton Frewen and, more importantly, his wife, Lady Clare Frewen. She seems to have befriended Ellen, or at least used her own social standing and connections to arrange the visit to Buckingham Palace. These drawing room events were predominantly for women, men being only their companions. Furthermore, an individual could only be presented once in a year to the queen or member of the royal family. Mehdi requested and received special permission from the Lord Chamberlain to accompany Ellen. Mehdi describes a scene of several hundred women, dressed in their lavish best, slowly making their way through several saloons until reaching the room where Queen Victoria herself was seated. The sound of rustling silk and hushed admiration for the palace must have filled the galleries. "I felt as if I were in the heaven of a dream," he wrote.[47] The excited and ethereal mood continued as he was about to see Victoria herself:

> My heart beat high at the thought of seeing that lady under whose rule I was born, and whose name (in our language Malika Victoria) was poured into my ears when I was in the cradle, a lady whom I was taught to love, and about whose virtues, good nature, and splendid appearance (which we call Ikbal) I had heard so many stories in my childhood. My heart was filled with the enthusiasm of love and loyalty. Whoever would have thought that I should come across the sea many thousand miles and have the good fortune to see my beloved sovereign?[48]

When Mehdi's name was read, he made a low bow. When he looked up, "I saw her nodding to me with such a gracious smile that tears of joy and love came to my eyes, so that I could see neither her nor the princesses, and passed on."[49] Mehdi made no mention of Ellen, but some Indian newspapers reported on his presentation. The *Madras Mail* noted that Ellen was introduced by Mrs. Morton Frewen, and then cited the *Deccan Times:* "We congratulate . . . our Chief Justice on the position he has acquired in English society, and the good-will of the leaders of London society in thus honouring representative men from the Hyderabad State is justly appreciated."[50] Their presence before the queen—especially Ellen's—became a point of contention.

At this very moment, rumors began to circulate in London that Mehdi and Ellen were not actually married. It was even whispered behind their backs that Ellen had come from a dishonorable past. Such rumors percolated up the rungs of power until a response became necessary. Taking up the issue was Mortimer Durand, the foreign secretary and head of the Political Department of the Government of India. Durand would be immortalized in South Asian history for the line bearing his name (c. 1893) that separated spheres of influence between Afghanistan and British-controlled India. Durand wrote to Asman Jah seeking some sort of assurances regarding Mehdi and Ellen's marriage.

> Very unpleasant rumours are afloated in England, with regard to this matter. It is said that the lady who is known as Mrs. Mehdi Hasan was not Mehdi Hasan's wife when she was presented to her Majesty, but was merely living with him as his mistress. From your experience of England you must be aware that presentations to Her Majesty, are, as a rule, subjected to the most jealous scrutiny; and if there is any truth in these rumours, it will be a most unpleasant business. For obvious reason I do not like to impose upon Mr. Howell the duty of enquiring into this matter after recent occurrences, and I therefore write to you direct in the hope that you will be able to give me satisfactory assurances as to the lady's position. If so, I shall be greatly relieved. If not, I shall be unable to avoid further action.[51]

Asman Jah replied that, to the best of his knowledge, Ellen was Mehdi's lawfully wedded wife, and the inquiry went no further. These unattributed rumors were the very earliest signs of impending trouble and would return to haunt Mehdi and Ellen.

Perhaps infused with a greater sense of self-importance after having visited Buckingham Palace, from London Mehdi took it upon himself to comment on Hyderabad affairs. He did this not through the Nizam or his own office, but rather by writing directly to Donald Mackenzie Wallace, private secretary to the viceroy. His letter concerned some "unperceived mistakes" by Cordery, the Resident at Hyderabad. Mehdi believed that Cordery had been taken advantage of by unscrupulous and sometimes feuding members of the Nizam's government. As a loyal subject, Mehdi took it upon himself to report such dealings to Wallace. His tone and motivation for writing were those of someone trying to ingratiate himself with a higher power—a character trait frequently attributed to Mehdi. He wrote, "I think it the duty of a loyal subject and servant of the Government of India like myself to take the first possible opportunity, at whatever risk, of expressing his views on the subject. Believing as I do that the Government of India mean to do good to the country and so wish to be well informed, I think the time has come for me to lay before you a few facts."[52] He continued, gilding the lily, "I have, and can have, no other motive in doing this than pure loyalty to the English Government and sincere regard for His Excellency personally."[53]

In what way was Cordery taken advantage of? Mehdi lay before Wallace three instances when the Resident, knowingly or not, had faltered in the performance of his duties. First, Cordery lent his support to the appointment of Sirajul Hassan (Abdul Huq's brother) to a position within the Nizam's government. Initially, Asman Jah had disapproved of Sirajul Hassan, but Cordery appealed directly to the Nizam, circumventing him, thereby placing the Nizam in an awkward position while at the same time embarrassing his prime minister. The second instance occurred after Asman Jah sought to place Mushtak Hussain in the position of revenue secretary. Abdul Huq opposed this and was able to get a letter from Cordery, with the help of Colonel Marshall, asking the Nizam not to make the appointment. Again, according to Mehdi, Cordery was taken advantage of by men like Abdul Huq. Finally, Mehdi angrily denounced Cordery's support of Major Neville, who had in some way insulted Salar Jung. "I honestly tell you that his continuance in Hyderabad is a standing insult to the whole native community, and that he is a thorn in the side of His Highness the Nizam and his Minister."[54]

In conclusion, Mehdi again brought his own loyalty to the fore, while at the same time directly and indirectly attacking the Indian National Congress and its predominantly Bengali composition. He wrote, "I have come before you as a loyal subject, feeling as sincere loyalty as any Englishman can feel, and not in the fashion of a Bengal critic of the British Government."[55] Mehdi then bluntly criticized what he considered the "dangerous" work of the Congress. Along with its members who were "Bengal critics," Congress served as the foil for Mehdi's own loyalty to the Government of India. "I consider the spread of Radicalism in India most dangerous to all of us, and so have stated my reasons for disagreeing with the National Congress resolutions. I am enjoying my visit to London immensely. The weather has at last become warm and pleasant. I saw the Queen for the first time in my life, and was very much impressed by her graciousness."[56]

Mehdi and Ellen were soon joined in London by the Nawab Mohsin-ul-Mulk Mehdi Ali. Mehdi Ali was a noble originally from the north Indian town of Etawah, located about halfway between Agra and Lucknow. Having passed the civil service exam, Ali went to work in Uttar Pradesh as a district deputy collector. Ali began his tenure in Hyderabad in the Settlement Department, moved on to be revenue secretary, and was then appointed to the Political and Finance Department. In Hyderabad for nearly two decades, Ali had worked to conduct the settlement of the Marathwada part of the state, as well as working hard to avert the disaster of the famine of 1876–1877. Ali weighed in on larger matters, too, writing a letter of support when Russia made advances in India's direction, and defending the loyalty of the princely states, especially Hyderabad. Ali had done well in Hyderabad: he was reported to have amassed a fortune of thirty *lakhs*. His time in north India both before and after his Hyderabad sojourn is well known because of his connection to Aligarh and the All-India Muslim League. His work in Hyderabad and his friend-ship with Mehdi are less well known, but they played an important role in the pamphlet scandal. Ali knew Sir Syed Ahmed Khan, and after working in Hyderabad from 1874 to 1893, he (like Mushtak Hussain) returned to Khan's side in the north Indian city of Aligarh. He was active in the growing Muslim political organization of the late nineteenth century and lived long enough to be a co-writer of a draft of the All-India Muslim League's constitution.

By the early twentieth century, many Indian Muslims felt that the Indian National Congress did not have their best interests at heart. To better represent these, the All-India Muslim League was formed in 1906. Sir Syed Ahmed Khan was at the core of this organization, which sprang from a literary movement in Aligarh. The league would grow to lead the movement for a separate homeland for South Asia's Muslim community, eventually materializing as Pakistan.

An edict from the Nizam of 2 May 1888 had conferred upon Ali powers of negotiation in business related to mining in Hyderabad State. His arrival in London, in conjunction with the Deccan Mining Company, and his relationship to Mehdi did not escape the notice of the viceroy, Lord Dufferin. The politics and potential profits involved had long since attracted the interests of John Seymour Keay—a one-time businessman in Hyderabad, a member of Parliament, and a staunch ally of Mehdi. Dufferin was at pains to keep Ali out of Keay's grasp and instructed the acting Resident at Hyderabad, Arthur Howell, to be sure that Ali checked in with the India Office in London upon arrival. "You had better take care that the delegate of the Nizam's Government pursues this line of conduct [checking in]. It is not de-sirable that he should become a tool in the hand of Seymour Keay & Co."[57] The next day, Howell telegrammed back to Dufferin his assur-

ances that he had given Ali both a stern warning and proper intro-
ductions for the latter's mission. "I will represent the matter strongly
to Minister. I have already twice warned and dissuaded him from official relations with Keay & Company, and do not now anticipate
any. I gave Mehdi Ali's letter of introduction to Bradford, with request
to introduce him to the Council and give him official support, without
which mission could not fully succeed."[58]

As spring bloomed, Mehdi again used letters to the London
newspapers as a means to express his views—this time on a personal
subject, that of "social intercourse" between Indians and Britons.
This subject was an obvious one for him to address. He had married
a woman of European descent, supported his Indian friend's engagement to a British woman, and generally believed that more interaction between ruler and ruled—even marriage—would benefit both
communities, especially as he perceived a growing distance between
them. His opinions were not always popular, but his views of the
increasing estrangement between Indians and Britons elicited a
double-edged response from the *Times* at Lahore. The editors were
deeply critical of Mehdi's opinions on political matters: "We never
thought that we should ever find it possible to agree with the views
of a man who entertains such phenomenally stupid, retrograde, and
selfish views on political subjects." Having lambasted Mehdi regarding politics, the paper took an entirely different view of his opinions on Indo-British social relations. "But we must confess that we
have found it possible to agree with many of his opinions on the
subjects of the estrangement between the rulers and the ruled in
India."[59] His opinions brought yet another opinion from the *Indian
Spectator*: "After reading this letter, we very much wish that a friend
of the Nawab would advise him to attend to business which he was
more fitted to discharge, than that of giving to the world his original
views on old subjects."[60]

The month of May had been eventful for Mehdi and Ellen. They had seen the queen, welcomed Ali to London, and attended several functions together. Mehdi was about to be called to the bar, and several of his letters on British-Indian affairs had been published in the British newspapers. Now, on 30 May 1888, it was Derby Day. Thousands of Londoners made their way to Epsom, about eighteen miles from the city. As fashionable British men of the day did, Mehdi hired a private coach to make the journey. Separately, Ellen, her sister Esther, Esther's daughter Isabelle, and Ali traveled by a special royal train reserved for the Prince of Wales and select guests. By accessing his growing network of connections in London, Mehdi had managed to secure an invitation on the train for his wife and the others. Once at Epsom, the group enjoyed the festive nature of the Derby, comparing it favorably with festivals in Lucknow.

About two weeks after Derby Day, Mehdi experienced a "memorable day in my life"—the call to the bar. Along with seven others, he received this honor on June 13. At the event, he made a brief speech in which he recognized the gratitude he felt in receiving the call and acknowledged the honor that was being extended to the Nizam and prime minister through his recognition. He received praise for his appearance at the Inner Temple in the *Deccan Times*, a paper sympathetic to him. Its story stated that Mehdi had been called to the bar "without terms and without examination, a tribute to the position which he occupies in the State which is both flattering to the Government which he serves and highly honourable to the recipient himself."[61] He received warm praise from both the prime minister and the Nizam. A telegram, the contents of which were published in the *Deccan Times*, conveyed the expressions of support for him. "His Excellency the Minister has sent a telegram warmly congratulating Nawab Fatheh Nawaz Jung (Chief Justice of Hyderabad) on his success and call to the Bar. The telegram also states that the Nawab will be gratified to learn that His Highness has likewise been very much pleased to hear of his success, and that His Excellency, by express command, also congratulates the Chief Justice on behalf of His Highness the Nizam."[62]

As Mehdi's fortunes continued to rise, his friend Mehdi Ali found his own position in decline. Ali's work in London was being undermined by his diminishing power in Hyderabad's political structure and by those who wished to see him fail. As outlined in a secret memorandum by British officials, an edict from the Nizam granting Ali powers of negotiation should have given him a degree of comfort and power in London, but his every effort was checked, and his ability to receive clear and timely replies from Hyderabad undermined. As outlined in the memo, these difficulties foreshadowed the change of power from Ali to Mehdi about to occur.

> It may seem strange that the Nawab [Mehdi Ali], who derives the most ample powers by virtue of the edict issued in India, should be under the necessity of referring all important questions which arise during the progress of the negotiations for order to Hyderabad, but the tenure of office in most Native States, and especially in Hyderabad, is precarious, and no official, however influential he may be, can afford to dispense with the recognized safeguards which applications for approval of proceedings supply. This is the more necessary in Nawab Mehdi Ali's case, as his influence at Hyderabad has, temporarily at least, diminished during his absence, a state of things which is instanced by the unsatisfactory replies to telegrams which he has received, as well as by a direct snub, in an order that Nawab Mehdi Hassan was to be freely consulted on all matters as a junior member, and to be free to telegraph his opinion independently for the Minister's consideration.[63]

Ali's effectiveness had shifted from bad to worse. His weaknesses in British eyes triggered a character assessment and raised the prospect of Mehdi replacing him.

British officials in London, Hyderabad, and Simla (summer home of the viceroy) were increasingly concerned about what appeared to be an impending transfer of power from Ali to Mehdi, a change they did not look favorably upon. The first to offer his opinion was a military major named Robertson.[64] His critique of Mehdi insinuated that there were deeper problems with his character than just those that might affect his role of negotiator.

> I have no hesitation in stating that he is eminently unfitted to undertake any work in which reticence, straightforwardness, and stability of character are essential qualifications. Though not intentionally dishonest, he has, mainly with the idea of pushing himself forward as a person of consequence, been intriguing with the opposite side, doubtless to the prejudice of a more favourable settlement, and so much is he distrusted that, up to the time of the Nawab Mehdi Ali's leaving England, he (Mehdi Hassan) had not been told, so far as I am aware, that a compromise was in course of preparation. He earnestly pressed upon me that I should agree to remain in England with him were he appointed Hyderabad Representative, but, knowing that to entrust the negotiations to him was seriously to prejudice the chances of a successful termination, I unhesitatingly declined. Sir Edward Bradford is aware of the Nawab Mehdi Ali's opinion of Mehdi Hassan.[65]

Although writing at some distance from the time of the events, Server Jung, in his autobiography, added his own assessment of Mehdi, one not far afield from Robertson's: "He was quite as pushing a man as the Moulvi and in the capacity of a minister of Hyderabad, he presented his wife at the levee of the Queen Empress, and himself became a barrister in name,—The pride of these Ministers knew no bounds!"[66]

This desire to be a "person of consequence" revealed Mehdi's desire to advance himself in multiple ways in late nineteenth-century Indian and British society. As such, the choice of a British wife might be seen, in part, as a strategic move to link his fortunes with a woman who gave him access to circles that might have otherwise remained closed. His choices regarding his private life could have public advantages in his professional career. With a British wife, they would *both* be invited to functions at the Residency, the Nizam's palace, or at Government of India functions. Had Mehdi married an Indian Muslim woman, it is unlikely that she would have been invited to dinners and dances, or, if invited, attended. Social restrictions specific to Indian Muslim women did not apply to Ellen, who was slowly rekindling her Christian roots and no longer living as a Muslim woman.

At the end of September, Mehdi and Ellen, now joined by Ali, left London for Paris, where they stayed at the Grand Hotel and toured the sights. Mehdi noted that the Eiffel Tower was well underway, but remarked, "I do not see anything remarkable in it, except of course its great height."[67] A few weeks later, he left Paris for Geneva, with his niece, Isabelle Bigex, as his guide. Isabelle's mother, Esther, was the second daughter in the Donnelly family. Mehdi and Isabelle had something of an adventure in traveling from Paris to Geneva by train. The two misunderstood whether they needed to switch trains and, in a moment of doubt, followed the crowd and stepped off their train. This resulted in their late arrival into Geneva at 2 A.M., drenched by pouring rains. Mehdi wrote, "I was never so disgusted before."[68] Mehdi and Isabelle managed to find lodging and spend a few days in Switzerland. In sum, Mehdi wrote of their adventure, "I consider it very fortunate that I had a person with me who spoke French, otherwise I cannot imagine what would have been the result."[69]

Two weeks into October 1888, a new edict came from Hyderabad making official what many had speculated: Mehdi was to replace Ali as Hyderabad State's negotiator in London. The edict granted Mehdi "full authority to act on behalf of His Highness's Government and to represent the same in and negotiate on their behalf."[70] For the time being, Ali licked his wounds and retreated from the public spotlight.

By the end of October, Mehdi's diary ends. The last entry is from 24 October in Naples. The conclusion of his Grand Tour and his journey back to India are unrecorded. However, we know that Ellen stayed on in Britain, visiting with her sister Esther and niece Isabelle, and did not return to Hyderabad for some time. Mehdi reached Hyderabad first, arriving in January 1889. While we lose Mehdi's voice from his diary during these last two months of 1888, members of the Government of India were not so reticent in expressing their thoughts.

Opinions of Mehdi, none very complimentary, continued to circulate within confidential British circles. Durand wrote from Simla, "In my opinion Fateh Nawaz Jang is incompetent and untrustworthy, and will require close watching. If allowed to act on his own account he will land us in another scandal."[71] The foreign secretary's words were surely prophetic. Mehdi would indeed land in the middle of a scandal, not one involving his politics and the Government of India, as feared, but a more personal and unsavory one that would, by its salaciousness, reflect badly across the Raj. Further judgment of Mehdi's character came from the viceroy himself. Parroting Durand, Dufferin wrote, "I am of opinion that it will be necessary to watch and control with much care the proceedings of the new representative, who is believed to be inferior to his predecessor in ability and discretion."[72] The viceroy's opinion laid bare the imperial desire to survey and control its subjects, especially those whose character was in question.

Undoubtedly, Mehdi had supporters. He had been recruited by Salar Jung I and enjoyed the support (for a limited time) of his successor as well as of the Nizam. Such support was public knowledge, affirmed in the local press. At the time of his return from London to Hyderabad on 9 January 1889, Mehdi met the prime minister, Asman Jah, while out for a carriage ride. The *Deccan Times* recounted the relationship between the two men, as well as between Mehdi and the Nizam. "The Nawab [Hasan] was always a favourite with His Highness, and was especially a good deal in attendance on him some time before he left for England. As being *persona grata*, therefore, His Excellency the Minister had very little trouble in obtaining His Highness' sanction to the transfer of the Nawab from the High Court to the Home Secretariat as a recognition of his services in England. It must have been gratifying to the Nawab to find that he had still a place in His Highness' favour."[73] Shortly after this meeting, the Nizam received Mehdi at his *durbar*. "Among the presents brought by the Nawab for His Highness, none seemed to please him better than a magnificent album of the Royal Family . . . After listening to some accounts of the Nawab's travels and experiences, he congratulated him cordially on his success, and the tact and intelligence with which he had conducted the very difficult negotiations with which he was entrusted."[74] The exchange lent further proof to Mehdi's positive relationship with the Nizam, making the former's ultimate fate all the more painful.

In March 1889, the deal that Mehdi had conducted in London concerning the Deccan mining affair came to a satisfactory conclusion. Asman Jah, the Nizam, and the viceroy examined the final document and approved it.[75] It was then forwarded to the secretary of state and Lord Cross, who both gave their assent. Finally the shareholders of the company approved the deal. The terms stipulated that the concessionaries would provide £150,000 additional working capital; the prospecting period was extended; full recognition of the company's title was granted; and those who sold the concession and other rights recognized the sale.[76] It seemed Mehdi's talent knew no bounds.

Mehdi and Ellen's visit to Europe had been by all accounts a success. He came to London as the chief justice of the High Court of India's largest and wealthiest princely state, having risen rapidly through the ranks of Hyderabad officialdom. Along the way, he had become secretary to the new Nizam Club and used that social space as one to host and entertain both Indian and British elites alike. Ellen had emerged from *purdah* and began circulating more and more among members of both the Nizam's government and the British government in India. The couple's Indo-British composition made them likely to be invited to events hosted by the British Resident and those of local Indian officials. In London they moved in ever-higher social circles and were received by Queen Victoria herself. Yet behind their backs, whispers and rumors suggested shocking claims about the couple that would haunt them for the rest of their lives.

3

THE PINNACLE
OF POWER

Nearly a year after the Deccan mining agreement was reached, Mehdi found himself mired in Hyderabad politics. Since his time together with Mehdi Ali in London, and Ali's subsequent removal from his position as negotiator on behalf of the Nizam's government, Mehdi's relationship with Ali had been increasingly tense. On the surface, they appeared cordial, even close, but that only papered over deeper divisions between the two men. Tension between them was deleterious to the administration of the state, and although they undoubtedly realized this, little seemed to change.

Once again, the Nizam Club provided an outlet for these two and others to publicly declare their friendship and goodwill toward each other, knowing that the local newspapers would report their speeches in full while at the same time allowing them their private machinations behind closed doors. So it was in December 1889 that Mehdi hosted a dinner for Ali at the club. In the dining saloon, candlelit tables were filled with the chef's finest biryanis and curries, and as dinner concluded, Mehdi offered toasts to Queen Victoria and to the Nizam, and also to Mehdi Ali.[1]

Delivered in English, Mehdi's toast heaped praise on his colleague. He began, "The last toast which I have the pleasure and honour of proposing to-night is the health of my esteemed friend the Nawab

Mohsin-ul-Mulk Mehdi Ali." Mehdi continued, publicly declaring his loyalty and friendship to Ali. "There is no need, nor does it become the humble position I have the honour to occupy in His Highness' Service, for me to make public speeches, and indeed had it not been for my unavoidable absence from the banquet which my friend Mehdi Ali gave some months ago, at which he paid me a compliment and which I could not before publicly acknowledge. I should not now, conscious as I am of my want of sufficient words, attempt even briefly to express my feelings."[2] Mehdi described the "unbounded pleasure" he had had in working with Ali, mentioning how the two had "nursed each other in sickness" during their joint time in London and how they had shared social occasions, such as attending the opera while in Paris. Mehdi was aware that a rift between the two men had been reported in the newspapers. Even though the rift was unsubstantiated, he chose to address this directly:

> The newspapers may cast doubts upon our friendship and people may invent fictions, but for my part I believe that, even if in this world there is no such thing as unselfishness, yet our long acquaintance, the various relations which bind us together, and last, though not least, the community of our object loyalty to H. H. the Nizam as our Sovereign and to H. E. the Minister as our chief—all these form an inseparable union between us.[3]

Mehdi offered a few further remarks and took his chair.

Then the "Grand old man of Hyderabad," as Ali was called, rose and addressed the guests. After apologizing to his "English friends" for the lack of wine and his choice of speaking in Urdu, Ali also publicly addressed concerns of a rift between the two men. "Our friend and host Mehdi Hassan has spoken of me in very high terms indeed, higher than I deserve; but a friend does not thank another friend for his friendliness, rather will I thank God that my friend's doubts and suspicions have been removed from his mind: that the estrangement that he had towards me has been removed and that our old cordial relations have been fully restored." He continued, almost chiding Mehdi: "I knew all along that the time would come when the light of truth would show to him that his doubts and suspicions were wrong: and this is what has happened. (Applause.) He is now convinced that he was wrong in his opinion of my conduct; the light of truth has shone into his mind, and the doubts and suspicions have flown away, like flying-foxes, to obscurity, never I hope to come forth again." After offering a few further kind words and giving thanks to God, Ali asked that guests "drink to the health of our good friend and host, and as the rules of the Club we are in prohibit us from drinking it in anything stronger, we will do so in soda-water."[4] Thus, for the moment, the two men seemed to have mended their disputes.

On New Year's Eve, two weeks after the Nizam Club dinner for Ali, John Seymour Keay, member of Britain's Parliament, addressed a lengthy letter to John Charles Ardagh, the private secretary to Viceroys Lansdowne and Elgin. Keay was visiting Hyderabad for December and part of January before returning to London for the opening session of Parliament. Keay, a staunch ally of Mehdi, described the positive effects in Hyderabad resulting from the departure of Arthur Howell as acting Resident and the arrival of Sir Dennis Fitzpatrick, the new Resident.[5] Keay writes of Fitzpatrick, "He has already made himself the master of much valuable information, and I may add that I have the fullest confidence that he will be found quite equal to cope with all questions, however intricate, which may from time to time arise."

From behind the scenes, Keay wanted to control the degree of interference the Government of India might deploy in a princely state.

With the niceties complete, Keay launched into a scathing attack of Ali. His critique suggests some of the tensions that Mehdi and Ali sought to gloss over at the Nizam Club. Perhaps Keay was making explicit what Mehdi—like Ali, a fellow member of the Nizam's government—could not. He began, "He is a man of great ability and much plausibility and charm of manner, but unfortunately he is the victim of a restless and boundless personal ambition, which he continually seeks to gratify by planning and executing intrigues of the most subtle character." What Keay sought was the withdrawal of government support for Ali. He hoped that, by describing some of Ali's past follies, the viceroy might support the Nizam in accepting Ali's resignation.

> I will now, though most reluctantly, give a few of the many facts which might be adduced with regard to the Nawab Mehdi Ali's past position and career here, from which His Excellency the Viceroy will be enabled to judge whether the Government of India would be justified in extending to him their support, and thereby securing him in office here with extended powers, or whether, on the other hand, they should support the Native Government in accepting his resignation.[6]

Keay proceeded to lay out three examples of Ali's foibles. The first accusation related to the time of Salar Jung II's ministry. Salar Jung II and the Nizam did not always have an easy relationship, and Keay charged that Ali was responsible. It was Ali, he claimed, "whose plan was first to get the Nizam's mind worked into a state of exasperation against his young Minister, and then to ingratiate himself with the Nizam by proving to him that he was indebted to him [Ali] for getting rid of him."[7] Keay outlined the exact transaction that led to the resignation of Salar Jung II. Lord Dufferin sent a message to the minister by way of John Graham Cordery, who was Resident at the time, which noted, "That if the young Minister should not conduct the administration properly, and should thereby fail to act up to the pledges which he had given to the Viceroy, then in that case the Government of India would not be able to support him any longer."[8] According to Keay, Cordery, not understanding the politics of Hyderabad, entrusted Ali to deliver the message. Ali used this opportunity to twist the message to his own advantage and, again according to Keay, told Salar Jung II, "that the Government of India would not support him any longer, and that he had better tender his resignation voluntarily in order to save the indignity of being dismissed."[9] Furthermore, Ali had taken the liberty of drawing up a letter of resignation, which he presented to Salar Jung II, who panicked and signed the letter, thus ending his term of office.

The second supposed offense that Keay claimed Ali had committed was related to Mehdi. It unfolded during the previous year, when all three had been in London negotiating the Deccan mining deal. Keay found Mehdi of indisputable character, being "an officer who has all along possessed that confidence and influence with His Highness from which the Nawab Mehdi Ali's own tortuous conduct has necessarily debarred him." According to Keay, Ali suggested that Mehdi was not conducting the mining negotiations in the best interests of the Nizam's government. To advance this prejudice, Ali withheld two telegrams from Mehdi in London regarding the mining discussions. This had the effect of making Mehdi look as if he were working for the concessionaries in the mining case rather than on behalf of the Nizam's government. Howell, the acting Resident, believed that Mehdi was at the center of the duplicity, his trust in Mehdi having already been weakened by insinuations from Ali. By the time the "missing" telegrams were found, Howell admitted to having been on the "wrong tack" while the Nizam switched from Ali to Mehdi as chief negotiator in London.

The final charge Keay leveled against Ali concerned the latter's support from the viceroy and Resident. Seeking to enlarge his power through the Nizam, according to Keay, Ali wrote to the Government of India inquiring about a possible decoration for himself based on service in Hyderabad and beyond. The Government of India's reply was noncommittal, but, to raise his value in the Nizam's eyes, Ali shared the letter or a summary of its contents with the Nizam. Believing he had the Nizam's support, Ali then went about openly discussing his possible resignation, hoping to prompt the Nizam into supporting his plans for greater boons from the Government of India.

Keay's letters to the Government of India often required responses from the current Resident, providing us with an alternative perspective. Early in 1890, Fitzpatrick wrote to Ardagh about Keay's letter. Fitzpatrick described the situation when he arrived at the Residency: Mushtak Hussain, allied with Mehdi, wielded great influence over Asman Jah. Ali, who once enjoyed a close relationship with the prime minister, now found himself marginalized. As Fitzpatrick characterized it, "there was war to the death between Mehdi Ali and Mehdi Hassan, the latter being supported by Moostak Hossain."[10] Fitzpatrick wrote to the prime minister regarding the secretaries in the Nizam's government, saying, "the result was that all promised to be friends—a promise which, so far as outward appearances go, has been kept up to this point, the parties having silenced their respective newspapers and always meeting on a footing of even exaggerated friendship."[11]

The matter became more complex when Mehdi was nominated for home secretary.[12] Fitzpatrick was not in favor of Mehdi's appointment and went so far as to express his opinion to the prime minister and Nizam: "[I] put the fat in the fire again, and told the Minister and the Nizam I thought the arrangement a bad one, I, as I have said, stood (after referring to the Foreign Secretary) out of the way of it."[13]

Fitzpatrick felt that Mehdi's promotion would only further consolidate his alliance with Mushtak Hussain and increase his powers. Fitzpatrick condemned their attempts at intrigue. "I have added that it would be extreme folly on their part to make any such attempts, as their doing so would not only stamp them as intriguers, but would further discredit the policy of comparative non-interference recently adopted under the orders of the Government of India which admitted of Mehdi Hassan's appointment being given effect to."[14]

Fitzpatrick claimed that these men (Mehdi, Mushtak Hussain, and Keay) had all but taken control of much of the Nizam's government; what lay at the core of their machinations was not a real threat to their power but, rather, a perceived one. "Their anxiety is not, I think, so much the result of any desire for greater power, for they really have things almost entirely in their own hands, as of that constant dread of intrigue, which is the source of at least half of the intrigue here, and which it is impossible to persuade them is exaggerated."[15] Ali served as a bulwark against what Fitzpatrick called the "dominant party." While Fitzpatrick did not view Ali with naïve eyes (he described him as "an unscrupulous man"), he recognized that Ali was, in a sense, a check on the others. Rather than speak ill of Ali to the prime minister or Nizam, Fitzpatrick was more reserved, suggesting that Ali could retain his position. "I have no desire to see the administration weak, indeed the want of strength here as in other Native Administration, is the source of most of the mischiefs, but some internal check is necessary, and I don't see where it is to be got if Mehdi Ali goes."[16]

Fitzpatrick saw Keay as a pawn of Mehdi, whom he disliked, and Mushtak Hussain. He believed Keay was "altogether in the hands of Mehdi Hassan, Mehdi Ali's enemy, who I, like all my predecessors, much distrust." Mehdi and Mushtak Hussain both believed that Ali was intriguing against them and trying to co-opt the prime minister and Nizam. Mushtak Hussain—according to Fitzpatrick—"seems to regard Mehdi Ali as a sort of demon, endowed with superhuman intelligence."[17]

Fitzpatrick's correspondence circulated only through the private networks of the Political Department within the Government of India. By the 1890s, however, the newspapers in and around Hyderabad increasingly participated in conversations about and condemnations of local and nonlocal officials. Eventually, Mehdi would be a subject of such reportage. In his capacity as home secretary, he would work to curtail it. Perhaps the beginning of his problems came with the *Hindu's* coverage of the upcoming visit of his friend and ally, Keay. The paper quipped, "Mr. Seymore Keay's visit is looked forward to anxiously by many in Hyderabad . . . But this may be said, that Mr. Keay, such as he has proved himself to be, now that he can be meddlesome with impunity is not likely to keep his hands clean of Hyderabad affairs."[18]

Further criticism of members of the Nizam's government continued to fill the pages of the *Hindu*. Published from Madras (a bastion of British power in south India), the newspaper seems to have delighted in reporting scandals and intrigues of neighboring Hyderabad State. The newspaper correspondent wrote:

> Men in high places are never idle here. They have the pluck to fight their adversaries, if not in open daylight at least in the gloaming. And when they have not work in the enemy's camp they find work in their own. And thus we are destined ever to be "tickled" by the effects of "powder and shot"—covert and overt. In a case—to come—which promises to be not a bit less sensational than the sensational "cases" all the world has heard of, Sir Kurshedjah and Sir Asmanjah figure as complainant and

defendant respectively. With advancing age the craving for notoriety, or the desire to do things which one would not do in youth or manhood seems to grow more and more morbid.[19]

By late 1890, Mehdi found himself and Mushtak Hussain under constant attack by the press. The two men were by now close allies. On one occasion, Mehdi had honored Hussain at Jeedikal village (in modern Warangal District), where a great *mela* was held to honor the Sri Ramaswami Temple. Such occasions were an opportunity for Hyderabad officials to leave their urban confines for the countryside, participating in the state's plural society while offering felicities to each other. Mehdi spoke at the event, recognizing Hussain in his capacity as revenue secretary and describing him as "one whose name was inseparably connected with the advance, the prosperity and well-being of the Eastern Division."[20]

This type of public flattery raised the hackles of the *Hindu* correspondents, who used it as an opportunity to dredge up the past. The newspaper recounted that Hussain publicly congratulated Mehdi when he was called to the bar in London. Hussain, in his capacity as revenue secretary, sent a circular soliciting money from lesser nobles who supported Mehdi. The *Hindu* correspondent wrote, "He issued a circular that every one of those that wished to congratulate the Nawab on his success by wire might send him money enough to cover the cost of a telegram to England. And lots of money poured in from the revenue officials in the Districts."[21] The *Hindu* correspondent wondered how a similar circular might have fared if it had not come from the revenue secretary. The cost of the telegram was not prohibitive, so by asking multiple participants to contribute, the extra money would have been understood by the donors as a form of *nazr* given from lesser officials to the revenue secretary. Such public accusations and questioning from the media seem to have pushed Mehdi to act.

In his role as home secretary, Mehdi issued a circular in June 1891 to all of the local newspapers. He required that the press not publish anything that would "threaten an injury to a Government servant" or "tend to prejudice the mind of the people against His Highness the Nizam's Government or any of its officers."[22] Such a gag order drew immediate condemnation and ridicule from the newspapers. The *Hindu*, published from Madras and thus not subject to Mehdi's circular, viewed it as an example of the "despotism" that ran rife throughout the state, calling the order "hectoring or terrorising." The reporter concluded his critique by suggesting that Mehdi might have better worked for the tsar of Russia, then added sarcastically, "But then I forget that in Russia people do not rise by flattery and wield power without intelligence."[23] The *Hindu* correspondent, in a subsequent installment, continued to attack:

> I hitherto gave the Nawab Mehdi Hussan credit for keen-sightedness, but I see now that I was mistaken. He seems to be quite at a loss to understand the circumstances amidst which he is placed, to read the signs of the times in which he finds himself possessed of enormous power. Does he know that Hyderabad has not been at a stand-still for a quarter of a century, that days when any wickedness and injustice could be perpetrated safe from the eyes of the people or authority belong to ancient history, now that public opinion—it does not matter by whom guided—is gaining in volume and strength day by day, that agitation for justice which was an unknown factor formerly has given his Government endless trouble? If he does, it is impossible to comprehend how he could commit the blunder of issuing a circular with a view to gag the Moglai Press, and aggravate it by suppressing the paper the Editor of which had the honesty and moral courage to protest against it.[24]

Thus, beginning around 1890, Mehdi and his allies Mushtak Hussain and Seymour Keay, among other Hyderabad elites, faced criticism for what was viewed by some newspapers as "despotic" behavior. They were accused of raising "sensational cases" against one another, engaging in gratuitous flattery and fundraising, and, finally, issuing and enforcing a "blundering" gag order on the local press.

Hyderabad had a new political intrigue to digest a few months after Mehdi's roundly criticized order to the press: the resignation of Mehdi Ali. In October 1891, Ali wrote to Mortimer Durand asking for the Government of India's support in accepting his resignation from Hyderabad and transfer to some other post. He asked for help in "relieving me from a position which has become well-nigh intolerable to me. I dare say you are not ignorant of the course of events which has brought me to my present condition of a mere nonentity in the State, and reduced my office to a perfect *sinecure*. You will admit that such a condition of affairs is neither advantageous to the State, nor quite agreeable to my feelings."[25] With Ali now off Hyderabad's political stage, power continued to consolidate in the hands of Mehdi and Mushtak Hussain, with Seymour Keay serving as a valuable ally and whip when matters required it.

In November, a glimpse—albeit not a clear one—can be seen of Ellen. A minor incident occurred that momentarily brings her back into the archival record. In Hyderabad, a woman named Mrs. Giaccino appealed to the Nizam's government to hold a lottery. Told that she did not require the government's permission, she commenced to advertise the lottery, print tickets, and incur a sizable debt (4,000 rupees). She had sold about 1,500 tickets before Mehdi, acting as home secretary, gave an order without explanation for her to stop the lottery from continuing. A report noted that Ellen was among the first to buy one of the lottery tickets. Giaccino, unnerved at the seeming arbitrariness of the decision, hired a lawyer to sue the Nizam's government to recover her losses. No further news emerged of the ill-fated lottery or of Ellen and her participation in the event. But the connection between Mehdi's order to stop the lottery and Ellen's participation in it hints at foul play: Did Ellen oversubscribe? Did Mehdi end the lottery before the couple suffered financial and social humiliation?[26] What was Ellen's relationship with Giaccino?

Another change in Hyderabad's political scene also unfolded in 1891 when Sir Dennis Fitzpatrick announced his departure from Hyderabad. The newspapers immediately weighed in with some judgments of his performance. The *Hindu* wrote: "There cannot be two opinions about Sir Dennis's character as an official. He is upright, conscientious, even-handed in his dealings with the meanest as well as the highest, and in short he is as good a specimen of a British Indian official as it is possible to have."[27] Nonetheless, the paper did not believe he had done any good for Hyderabad in his tenure. It noted that his predecessors, Cordery and Howell, both succumbed to the deep factions running through Hyderabad's political and social circles. "Verily Hyderabad proved, in their cases a grave of political reputations."[28] The paper recognized that Fitzpatrick, aware of his predecessors' mistakes, charted a path of noninterference in a variety of social and political circles, something the newspaper believed was a mistake. The second problem under Fitzpatrick was the consolidation of power by men from north India. Fitzpatrick was blamed for allowing various cases—ones involving treasury fraud, a city murder, and a scandal in the Anagundi *samasthan*—to unfold at the hands of nonlocals. This was capped by Mehdi's own unchecked attempt to gag the local press.[29]

Replacing Fitzpatrick as Resident at Hyderabad was Trevor John Chicheley Plowden. Plowden, who assumed his duties on 12

November 1891, would soon find himself mired in the pamphlet scandal trial. After the viceroy issued a *kharita* for Plowden's appointment to Hyderabad, the Nizam wrote to the viceroy:

> According to your Excellency's intimation the said gentleman attended my darbar and personally delivered your Excellency's friendly letter. Mr. J. C. Plowden is a high minded gentleman and an undoubted well wisher and possesses excellent qualities and approved manners. Therefore I am confident that this gentleman will perform the duties entrusted to him in such an excellent manner as will strengthen and consolidate the foundation of friendship and cordiality and union which has existed for such a length of time between the two sublime governments, and being desirous of raising the standard of affection and intimacy, he will render services in such an approved manner as will afford me pleasure and satisfaction, and become the means of obtaining your Excellency's thanks.[30]

Plowden was a member of a distinguished family. For decades, Plowdens served in India, from Kashmir to Meerut and from Bengal to Hyderabad. When Walter Chicheley Plowden compiled the family's history in 1914, no fewer than thirteen family members had served in the Bengal Civil Service—fourteen in the Indian army, five in the Indian police, two in Parliament, and two as "Directors of John Company."[31] Being servants of the British Raj was decidedly a family business.

Plowden began his own career in India by joining the Bengal Civil Service and then transferring to the Political Department, where he became Resident, first in Kashmir and then in Hyderabad. He married twice, having two daughters in each marriage. He retired from his position at Hyderabad in 1898 and was awarded the Knight Commander of the Order of the Star of India before his death, in

Trevor John Chicheley Plowden, Lord Wenlock (governor of the Madras Presidency), and Asman Jah. Standing between and behind Wenlock and Asman Jah is Dossabhoy Nusserwanji Chenoy

England, in 1905. Walter Chicheley Plowden remembered him as "a brilliant scholar at Winchester, and showed great capacity for rule during his long service."[32]

Mehdi and Ellen had now reached the pinnacle of their power and acceptance in Hyderabad. They had met and married in Lucknow, where, through the benefits of the British Empire, Mehdi had received an education and attracted the notice of Hyderabad's prime minister, Salar Jung. The couple transgressed the division within India between directly controlled, colonial India and the indirectly controlled India of the princely states. They found old acquaintances in Hyderabad from their Lucknow days, none more important than Server Jung, who served at the side of the Nizam and wielded great power with the prime minister.

The couple had found fertile ground in Hyderabad for his professional success and her social mobility. Leaving behind the *purdah* she had maintained in Lucknow, Ellen moved about in Hyderabad society wearing European dress and acting more like a British Christian wife of a rising Muslim nobleman in an important city and court. Whereas her enemies in Lucknow had referred to her as "Gertrude," she now went by "Ellen" as she remade herself in Hyderabad. The couple was entertained at the Nizam's palace, at the British Residency, and in the homes of Britons and Indians alike; moreover, Mehdi participated in the establishment of the influential Nizam Club. Mehdi and Ellen had successfully toured Europe and visited the heart of the empire. Being called to the bar, being made chiefly responsible for the Deccan mining affair, and having an audience with Queen Victoria were realizations of Mehdi's dream. Ellen left India for the first time in her life, was received within London's Indo-British circles as a respectable Victorian woman, shared in the honor of meeting the queen, and was reunited with her sister and niece. After returning to Hyderabad, the couple settled back into their daily routines. In the spring of 1892, they visited Kashmir. Mehdi returned early to go on a shooting trip while Ellen stayed on. While she was still away, and Mehdi prepared to leave the city for several days of hunting, a pamphlet was printed and mailed to Hyderabad's nobility. Its appearance marked the end of Mehdi and Ellen's social ascent.

4

THE SCANDAL

UNLEASHED

THE PAMPHLET AT the epicenter of the scandal was eight pages long and four by six inches in size, a little over 2,100 words. On the last page, the name Mirza Bakir Hussain appeared, together with Aminabad, the name of a neighborhood in Lucknow. The pamphlet was in English, titled "An appeal to the ladies of Hyderabad," and its allegations shocked Hyderabad society to its core. It charged that Ellen and her sister Lucy had been prostitutes when they lived in Lucknow in the late 1860s and early 1870s. It claimed that Ellen had been "kept"—for sexual pleasure—by the writer of the pamphlet and that Rafi-ud-din, Yusuf-uz-Zaman, Mahomed Akbar, and the author had formed a joint-stock company to call on her services whenever they desired. It labeled Ellen as Mehdi's mistress, who passed as his wife but had never in fact married him. Moreover, it charged that Mehdi had "pimped" his wife to the young prime minster of Hyderabad, Salar Jung II, to hoist himself up the career ladder. The pamphlet accused Mehdi of knowingly passing off Ellen as his wife before Queen Victoria. Finally, it alleged that many men in the Nizam's government knew of Ellen's past and had availed themselves of her sexual services, but that they did nothing about it when she arrived in Hyderabad.

The tone of the pamphlet was one of an excited confidant through which the author related his own experiences with Mehdi and Ellen. This intimacy not only made for more compelling reading (replete with exclamation marks, bold, italicized, and capitalized text) but also lent credibility to the author's story. He remembered both Mehdi and Ellen; he partook in her pleasures (as did others); and now, having visited Hyderabad, he was shocked and tormented with the seeming fraud the couple perpetrated on Hyderabad society.

The pamphlet was printed at the Hyderabad Residency Press in late March and early April 1892. At the time the pamphlet was being proofed, typeset, and printed, Mehdi and Ellen were on holiday in Kashmir. Ellen remained away from Hyderabad while Mehdi returned in March. On April 6, copies were mailed to three hundred prominent individuals in and around Hyderabad. Mehdi received a copy mailed to the Nizam Club. The timing is significant, as Hyderabad elites knew that Mehdi was going on a shooting expedition with Asman Jah on the morning of April 7.

The choice of language in the pamphlet suggests much about the intended audience, as it clearly targeted the elite, English-speaking community of Hyderabad. Hyderabad State of the late nineteenth century was a linguistic conglomerate that included Urdu and English speakers, who dominated the capital city; beyond that, the country-side rang with Telugu, Tamil, Marathi, and Kannada speakers as well. As English was the language of the Government of India and of its local representative in Hyderabad (the Resident), the pamphlet was designed to be read and clearly understood by members of British officialdom. Its "appeal to the ladies of Hyderabad" suggests that the audience was not merely British elites, but British women in particular. The author appealed to their sense of propriety, hoping their revulsion would be directed at Ellen. By appealing to such "ladies" in a pamphlet largely about Ellen, the author locates her outside that community of British women. This was a community she had begun to socialize with, but it was now being called upon to judge her. The pamphlet was also readily accessible to the English-speaking Indian elite of the city. Thus, the pamphlet aimed to shock the very society Mehdi and Ellen moved in.

The pamphlet began with these words: "Facts are stranger than fiction," leading the reader to expect a cool and rational recitation of "facts," not speculation.[1] What he was about to unveil, he wrote, "beats the record even of a sensational novel." Yet fictions abound in the pamphlet. No individual with the name "Mirza Bakir Hussain" was ever found; it was widely believed that this was a *nom de guerre* used by someone in Hyderabad. (Server Jung was the prime suspect, with others also implicated.)[2] And, the neighborhood of Aminabad listed on the pamphlet suggested a specific place in Lucknow where it had been printed, when in fact it was printed in Hyderabad.

A close reading of the pamphlet reveals issues that placed much of Hyderabad society squarely within the larger fabric of late nineteenth-century colonial India, from marriage across lines of race and religion to norms and taboos of sexual practice, and from participation and support of an imperial world to clashing views of newly emergent Indian nationalism.

The pamphlet was primarily a political weapon aimed at bringing about Mehdi's downfall, yet the bulk of the pamphlet's accusations concerned Ellen. It sought to reveal facts about the couple that would irrevocably harm them. Such attacks, either in printed form (libel) or in speech (slander), were common at this time in Hyderabad and throughout India. Both Indians and Britons participated in attacks on each other's character. Often, such libel or slander took place both *within* and *between* these communities.

Four decades after the 1857 uprising, relations between Indians and Britons had reached an even greater degree of racial separation and antagonism. Inexpensive print media—cheap books, newspapers, pamphlets, and so on—fueled the rise of associational life, allowing individuals and groups to attack one another. Hyderabad city enjoyed several English and Urdu newspapers and presses (the first papers in English and Urdu being the *Deccan Times* and *Khursheed-e-Deccan*, respectively).[3] Each provided its own outlets for individuals to vent while anonymous editors hurled charges at each other. Furthermore, with the installation of India's telegraph system and the growth of transportation networks, especially the railway, such attacks could travel much faster and farther than they once might have.

With mudslinging made easy, resort to the court of law skyrocketed. By the late nineteenth century, the British judicial machinery established in India had often become the venue of choice for settling such disputes. In the princely states, some Indians felt British justice—if they could afford it—was somehow more impartial than their local courts. The trajectory of the pamphlet scandal in Hyderabad was no different.[4] The pamphlet's author repeatedly requested the reader to assemble a commission of European (i.e., British) gentlemen to investigate the couple's affairs. Britons, especially men, were thus portrayed as the prime source of judicial fairness.

In these courts, under the eyes of Indian and British justices, cases from petty land disputes to monumental claims of wealth could be settled. Yet, the path to justice was not always smooth. Eight years before the pamphlet case was filed, much of British India was awash in controversy regarding the Illbert Bill. This bill allowed Indian magistrates to hear cases involving British (European) subjects. Britons in India cried foul, claiming that the ruled should not pass judgment on the rulers, while Indians felt belittled by the final bill's form, which weakened their position. The controversy that the Illbert Bill created helped spur the formation of the Indian National Congress the next year, in 1885, and did little to improve relations between Indians and Britons across the subcontinent. Yet, in light of the Illbert Bill controversy, Mehdi's choice to file his case under a British magistrate suggests that his own affinities were sympathetic to the British rather than the Indian judicial processes. Mehdi chose to file the case in the Residency Bazaar Court not only because the pamphlet was printed at a shop within the Residency Bazaar and was thus under this particular court's jurisdiction, but also because he recognized his own conflict of interest, having once been the chief justice of Hyderabad's court. Mehdi harbored loyalty to the British Raj, and his choice to file a case under such jurisdiction stemmed from a belief in British justice.

To add grist for such a move to the courts, the author's narrative throughout the pamphlet invokes the language of an "investigation" and the collection of "facts," no matter how "strange" they seemed. The pamphlet juxtaposes this narrative with the rhetoric and conventions of fiction and drama, casting Ellen as the protagonist. Not only does the author thereby achieve an engaging rhetorical style but also positions himself as the guardian of facts—facts that could be investigated by a commission or court of law and found to be completely accurate as claimed.

The pamphlet also sheds light on the highly gendered space that was late nineteenth-century India and, by extension, Britain and its empire. It appealed to the ladies of Hyderabad; it called upon their "self-respect" and morality to bring them to action; it invoked their children, who needed protection from such immorality; and it contrasted Ellen's transgressions with that bastion of morality at the time, Queen Victoria. Women were to be shocked and outraged, men were to gather and search for the truth, and children were to be protected from the likes of Ellen. For the author and others, prostitutes were sex objects to be used by those who could afford them, but they were not to circulate in good society and certainly not to be presented to the queen. To make the crimes outlined in the pamphlet more disturbing, the author positioned Ellen as a prostitute at one end of a social spectrum and upstanding British women at the other. The latter were modeled after the highest example of morality, the queen herself, while Ellen was portrayed as the basest of human beings.

Men, on the other hand, were in some way victims who had become unwilling participants in this brewing scandal. Included in that group were middlemen, like the author and the others he named, who served as loyal and morally upright citizens of the empire. Although they may have committed transgressions in their youth, they had matured and were now calling for an investigation of the couple. At the pinnacle of morality and goodness, "European gentlemen" could form a commission and investigate the scandal in its entirety.

The pamphlet's author offers sensational details. "Inured in the pleasures of a Lucknow *zenana*, I did not much care for what was going on outside the walls of my earthly paradise."[5] A man able to retreat from the world into his own "earthly paradise" was a man of financial means. Furthermore, this was someone who participated in *zenana* life, a renaissance man who was not bothered with social practices like marriage. Yet marriage—or the claim of marriage—was at the center of the scandal. On a trip to Hyderabad, the author continues, friends introduced him to a Hyderabad official's wife, whom he immediately recognized. "I was staggered at the brass which the woman displayed." The author does not reveal if this woman recognized him; if she did, presumably she would have disguised any such recognition to protect her reputation. She exuded such "brass" because she was now married to a powerful noble of the state government and because (apparently) her reputation was not known to those who fêted her and her husband. In short, the author had come face to face with his former lover.

Nineteenth-century Indian society offered a variety of types of women who could provide sexual services and sometimes more. At one end of the social spectrum were courtesans. These women were artists, poets, musicians, and dancers who were highly regarded within society.[6] Powerful men, including India's princes and members of their courts, competed for their attention and paid large sums to share their bed.[7] Beneath courtesans socially were concubines. These women were in some way "kept" by a man, or a group of men, for their exclusive pleasure. The women would receive a regular stipend and be expected to share their affections only with the man or men with whom they had such an arrangement. Less cultured than the courtesans, these women occupied an intermediate position: beneath a courtesan but above a prostitute.[8]

At the far end of the spectrum from the courtesan was the prostitute. These women offered their services on a transactional, short-term basis. No terms of exclusivity were expected, and trysts were short and perfunctory. Perhaps the occasional prostitute found herself to be so desirable that her services would be reserved, and thus she might become a kept woman or concubine. Also, a courtesan who no longer held the attention of the most elite men might find herself engaged in relationships that resembled those of a concubine or, if matters deteriorated significantly, those of a prostitute. That the pamphlet's author refers to Ellen as a concubine alludes to his relationship with her, one in which he and friends paid her for their exclusive use. However, labeling her as a concubine allowed the possibility of her having been a prostitute who gained some notoriety and thus was now being kept as a concubine.

Having spent a restless night visited by memories of his past, the pamphlet author declares, "I would not rest until I cleared the seeming mystery." He then began his investigation into the "facts." He defers to the reader, whom he claims he does not want to trouble, saying, "it is neither desirable nor pleasant . . . to follow the thread of the story and to take the reader with me in all the difficulties and troubles that I got entangled to trace this woman." His quest was difficult and personal, but what really mattered was exposing the identity of his former concubine, now socializing with Hyderabad's elite.

The author wastes little time in revealing her identity. "I therefore proceed to give a connected story of the person who in Hyderabad is known as MRS. MEHDI HASSAN." Ellen's identity in Hyderabad circles as the wife of a nobleman is consistently undermined throughout the pamphlet. She "is known as" Mrs. Mehdi Hasan: the implication is that her real identity might be something else. Immediately following this revelation, the author makes an appeal to European (British) women of Hyderabad to call upon male society to do something, referencing Roman characters to add weight to the plea.

> Reader! I do not want that you should take the truth of my statements on my credit alone. *Ladies! If you have any self-respect, if you have a thought for your innocent daughters and sisters, if you care for happiness in this world and the next, I pray you do not let the grass grow under your feet until you have got a Commission of honorable European gentlemen appointed to sift this matter to the bottom. Caesar's* wife must be above suspicion. And one who is invited to the State banquets in Hyderabad and moves in the highest circles ought to be like Caesar's wife.[9]

The author notes his statements should not be taken at face value but corroborated through an investigation. The plea for action is to the "Ladies," women of rank and those who held respectable positions within society. They were not mere citizens or commoners, but a specific group that embodied the morality of the day. These women were filled with "self-respect" and would naturally care a great deal for their daughters and sisters. The language of the pamphlet specifically targets areas of concern for the community of European women in

Hyderabad. These women were to relay their indignation and concern to European gentlemen; for the author, a woman's duty was to be sensitized to moral outrage but to take no further action than to turn over the matter to a man. Adding to the Eurocentric target of the pamphlet's message was the invocation of Caesar and his wife (Pompeia). Had the pamphlet targeted the Indian community, perhaps kings of the Persian *Shahnameh* or Rama and Sita of the *Ramayana* might have been cited instead. But since the pamphlet was meant for European consumption and subsequent outrage and action, it invokes a classical Roman reference.

The author shifts back to the time when he first met Ellen. He states that he had lived in Lucknow eighteen years earlier, near the *koti* of Mirza Abbas Beg. This would put events as having occurred around 1873 or 1874. In that year, Ellen would have been between seventeen and nineteen years old. Uncertain of her exact birth year, she claimed she was born in the year of the uprising, either 1856 or 1857, although her baptismal record indicates 1854. The author writes that Ellen had an elder sister, Lucy, known at the time of the pamphlet as Mrs. Hodges (the pamphlet mistakenly calls her Mrs. Hodgson). In the 1870s, the author claims, the two girls were "prostitutes by profession and Eurasians by extraction." As the pamphlet recounts, Ellen became a kept woman of the author. Thus, her position changed from prostitute to something more like a concubine.

By describing Ellen and her sister as "Eurasian by extraction," the author casts some doubt on their racial background. Some prostitutes in India were of mixed birth, uncomfortable reminders to the British of liaisons between the ruler and the ruled.[10] While Ellen's father was a known figure in the lower ranks of the Indian Army, the same could not be said for her mother. Thus, it was possible that the girls had Indian blood in their veins. Likewise, others described Ellen as "Anglo-Indian"—another term that could mean one of mixed birth. In his autobiography, Server Jung—suspected author of the pamphlet—

refers to Ellen as an "Anglo-Indian lady."[11] By suggesting that Ellen had a mixed racial background, the pamphlet author aligns this facet of her identity with a trait of some prostitutes.

The author writes that he was a student at Canning College in 1874 in Lucknow. He brags of his affluence, sexual prowess, and ability to keep a woman for his pleasure. "In college days, boys, or rather young men, sow their wild oats, and I was no exception to this rule." The author reveals further details of his own background. "My father, being a rich man, allowed me a superabundance of pocket-money for which he never took any account." According to the pamphlet, Ellen was well known in Lucknow at the time, especially among young men. "The bewitching charms of GERTRUDE that had well nigh turned the heads of every Mussulman rake of fashion in Lucknow entranced my weak heart, and my choice of a mistress fell on her." Gertrude was Ellen's middle name. She referred to herself as Ellen, but her middle name is used in the pamphlet and among her enemies in the pamphlet case. The author continues: although he was not short of spending money, he entered into an agreement with friends to share Ellen. "In the year 1873 a Joint Stock Company was formed consisting of myself as the paying partner and three others—Rufiuddin, Yusuf-uz-Zaman, and Mahomed Akbar." The pamphlet author omits naming any one person as the founder of the joint-stock company but does not hesitate to name his partners. These men were far from fictions.

These four young men pooled their resources and thus were able to keep Ellen for themselves. Of their experience, the author coyly states, "We kept this sweet *Gertrude*, for *sweet* she was in those days." Additionally, she was a "Venus" who cost her holders dearly. This situation was short-lived; the author and some of his fellow stockholders were recruited from college into jobs, and "Soon we tired of this siren, or rather she of us, and she began to bestow her favours elsewhere, and thus our connection had to cease." The suggestion that

Ellen made the choice to end her relationship with the men alludes to her power in this dynamic. If true, she would be thought of not as a victim but rather as empowered, freely able to choose with whom she spent her time.

Mir Shujat Ali, the pamphlet author notes, also "kept" Ellen after their joint-stock arrangement concluded. Both Ali and the members of the joint-stock company, excluding the pamphlet author, would later testify about their relationship with Ellen. The author then states that Ellen lived with others whose reputations "I do not want to injure by mentioning their names." Thus, only some individuals' reputations were available for injury. At this point, the pamphlet's author unleashes an even more serious charge, one that would both undermine Mehdi and disgrace Ellen. He writes (italics in original), "*Mehdi was never married to Gertrude in any shape or form.*" If this were true, then the couple had misrepresented their relationship in Hyderabad circles, and Mehdi had brought a woman who was not his wife (and of questionable background) into not only the highest social circles of Hyderabad State but the innermost moral circle of all the British Empire, Queen Victoria's levée. In the author's opinion, given Ellen's background, "marriage was out of the question."

Although Mehdi's relationship with Ellen in Lucknow had been discreet, the author claims, this changed with his employment in Hyderabad. With a fresh start, the couple could "come out" with their hybrid relationship—one they presented as that of a married couple—and mingle with Hyderabad's elites. He names Mr. and Mrs. Sabapathy and Dr. and Mrs. Aghornath Chattopadhyaya. The latter were the highly respected parents of Indian nationalist and poetess Sarojini Naidu. Yet, the author sneers, Ellen initially mingled with "no better company than" these individuals.

Unsatisfied with ruining only Mehdi and Ellen, the pamphlet author levels the accusation that Mehdi had offered his wife to Salar Jung II in exchange for his own promotion. As the pamphlet describes it, the "debauched" young Salar Jung II became ill, or feigned illness, and went to stay in the Bolarum Palace. Mehdi offered Ellen, "whose charms had by no means faded" to act as a nurse to the smitten prime minister. "Sir Salar Jung gladly consented, and the acquaintance which Sir Salar Jung formed with *Gertrude* as his nurse soon ripened into an intimacy, and the two—Salar and Gertrude—were seen together at all hours of the day and night."[12] The author would have the reader believe not only that Ellen was an unwed prostitute, but that she—at Mehdi's urging—formed a relationship with Hyderabad's highest official.

The pamphlet suggests that Mehdi and Ellen enjoyed a meteoric rise within Hyderabad circles as a result of their unsavory connection with Salar Jung II. A tinge of jealousy is now apparent in the pamphlet author's writing. An account of Mehdi and Ellen's social life is described thus: "Through the influence of this great man, Gertrude was suddenly hoisted into Hyderabad society and was admitted into the *elite* of circles. She was invited to all the State entertainments . . . Another outcome of the intimacy is that Mehdi's position in the Nizam's service was secured for ever. He is the *youngest* Secretary and draws the *highest* salary."[13] Years later, Server Jung would also suggest that Mehdi benefited from his wife's role. Mehdi, he said, "came into prominence and notoriety more through the diplomatic moves of the Anglo-Indian lady referred to. As the poet says: 'Not the curtain, but we, did fall, when she showed her beauty, by lifting the veil.'"[14] Such rhetoric might come from one who resented the success of the couple, as the pamphlet author seems to do. Ellen was not only beautiful, but used her charms to benefit herself and Mehdi.

The pamphlet addresses the trip to London by Mehdi and Ellen in 1888. Although countless Indians formed a "counter flow to colonialism," what so deeply troubled the pamphlet's author was how and to whom Ellen presented herself. "As a Nawab he was accompanied by Gertrude, who gave herself out as—LADY GERTRUDE MEHDI HASSAN." Here, the scandal had two facets: first, that Ellen presented herself as "Lady." This term was the feminine equivalent of the male title Lord, and, more generally, a polite appellation for a woman of some position. To the author of the pamphlet, Ellen was neither. Equally objectionable was their continued presentation as married.

Yet the offenses committed by the couple were about to reach a higher level of scandal: Mehdi and Ellen were presented to Queen Victoria. The pamphlet reaches new heights of vitriol with this revelation. "Not only did Mehdi during his stay in England palm off *this common harlot* of Lucknow as his wedded wife in all the best of English circles, but he had the audacious shamefacedness to connive at the presentation of this *stinking wench* to the noblest, the purest, the most virtuous and the chastest sovereigns the world has ever seen, in the person of Her Most Gracious Majesty Victoria, Queen-Empress of India."[15] On a practical level, during her marriage, Victoria was often held up as something of a model wife, thus Ellen's character is portrayed as the polar opposite of the monarch's.[16] On a rhetorical level, the abuses heaped upon Ellen—"common harlot" and "stinking wench"—were, then and now, extraordinary.

In explaining his own feelings about such a meeting, the author again juxtaposes truth and fiction, stressing how the reality or truth of events can be so much more upsetting than fiction. "But the *reality*—words cannot express my unbound indignities when I learnt this in the course of my inquiries." Further, he once more brings his role as detective or investigator to the fore. The author had informants who shared information with him during his investigation, revealing facts or realities beyond what he could have imagined. Being presented to the queen was not, according to the author, something Mehdi or Ellen had plotted; the idea seemed to have come to them during their time in London, where their access to certain individuals (the Frewens) made the meeting possible. Whether this speculation has any merit would be difficult to establish one way or another, but the brashness of the plan and its spontaneity gave the pamphleteer another opportunity to deplore what had happened.

The meeting with the queen was a high point for Mehdi and Ellen, but it also marked a turning point in Mehdi's fortunes in Hyderabad, according to the pamphlet author. The presentation to the queen "excited the jealousy of his [Mehdi Hasan's] enemies," and rumors swirled around the couple. London officials heard such rumors concerning Ellen's background. However, when Prime Minister Asman Jah wrote that he knew nothing untoward about Ellen's past, the matter seemed to end. At this point, according to the pamphlet's author, Mehdi's success began to reap tangible reactions among jealous onlookers. "A feeble attempt was made to investigate the scandal, *but interest and influence that reign paramount in Hyderabad were instrumental in hushing up the matter.*" Those favorable to Mehdi in Hyderabad—especially his friend Mushtak Hussain—are accused of having conspired to cover up anything untoward in the couple's past. Leaving no stone unturned, the pamphlet author stood poised to topple Mehdi and his entourage. Those who once knew about Ellen and had forgotten, or who chose to keep silent, were on the cusp of exposure. "The thought that no one at this distance of time could remember or trace the history of her antecedents only strengthened their fancied security." This security was about to be shattered.

The pamphlet reveals the names of several individuals who knew Ellen's past. The author lists several of Hyderabad's most prominent individuals, questioning their silence in the matter. Among them are Syed Husain Bilgrami, Syed Ali Bilgrami, and Server Jung. That Server Jung is named in the pamphlet suggests that either he was guilty of participating in the silence regarding Ellen's past, or he used a clever ruse, if he wrote the pamphlet himself, that allowed him to speak as if reluctantly divulging what he knew. The pamphlet author sets the text in italics and suggests the bystanders' moral responsibility: "*either* [they] *know the antecedents of this infamous woman or had enjoyed her personal favours . . . Nay, they have been guilty of conniving.*" To stress his shock at the cover-up, which all but validated the royal meeting, the author held the named men guilty as well. Their silence made them complicit in the meeting between Ellen and the queen. This was "an unpardonable insult that was gratuitously offered to the chastest and most maternal sovereign that rules over the destinies of an empire and over which the sun never sets! *Oh tempore! oh mores!*"[17] The author's use of a classical reference to Cicero suggests something of the intended audience—well-educated, upper class, and European.

Near the end, the pamphlet reflects its earlier tone. The author suggests, "the scene of the inquiry should be laid in Lucknow, the home of Gertrude's youth, where she captivated and ruined many a promising youth." By focusing on Lucknow, the author calls upon investigators to examine Ellen's possible early life as a prostitute rather than her later life in Hyderabad as a married, respectable woman. Yet, many of the individuals with whom she was supposedly intimate now resided in Hyderabad itself. An investigation at Lucknow would likely have turned up others who would be more forthcoming than those in Hyderabad about Ellen's past. The author reaffirms that the individuals mentioned in the pamphlet could "testify to the truth of the statements contained herein." These were reputable individuals, and if their word were not sufficient, the author lists several other individuals by name who would suffice: Nissar Hussain, Yusuf-uz-Zaman, and Mahomed Akbar. Hussain worked in the judicial commissioner's office in Lucknow; Zaman was a landlord in Banda; and Akbar worked for the Nizam's police department.

In its penultimate paragraph, the author claims the pamphlet is a "history." The author has recounted a series of facts, none of which could be easily discarded by a commission. Even if a commission found evidence that contradicted the pamphlet, surely the investigation itself would ruin both Mehdi and Ellen. This was the goal of the pamphlet from the start.

The author concludes with a final appeal to the public of Hyderabad. His audience expands from the ladies mentioned in the earlier pages to include men—Indians and Britons alike. One final time the author appeals to their sense of morality: "LADIES AND GENTLEMEN! FATHERS AND MOTHERS! EUROPEAN AND NATIVE! IF YOU HAVE AN ATOM OF SELF-RESPECT FOR YOU, IF YOU CARE FOR YOUR REPUTATIONS, IF YOU HAVE A THOUGHT FOR THE FUTURE HAPPINESS OF YOUR UNOFFENDING AND INNOCENT CHILDREN BUDDING UP INTO YOUTH, RISE AND DEMAND AN INQUIRY FROM THE BRITISH COURTS."[18] Goading the reader further, the author rhetorically asks if not one "lady of rank" could be found to press for an investigation of Ellen and her "scandalous character." Returning to the first person voice, the pamphlet's author concluded with a cool quip, "I hope sincerely that this is not the last the public hears of this unprecedented social scandal in high life." Indeed, it would not be.

The first Mehdi knew of the pamphlet was when he received a copy mailed to the Nizam Club, where he was secretary. He immediately began investigating who had written and printed the pamphlet, but time was short. He was about to leave town for a hunting trip with the prime minister. At the railway station, he had conversations with E. S. Ludlow, Hyderabad's inspector general of police, and Ludlow's men to ascertain what they knew and whether they could help. He called for a commission to investigate the pamphlet. While on his hunting trip, he exchanged a series of letters with old acquaintances, Yusuf-uz-Zaman and Rafi-ud-din, to see what they knew. Mehdi soon discovered that a local man, S. M. Mitra, had printed the pamphlet but was unlikely, Mehdi thought, to be the author. Despite this conclusion, by the beginning of May, a month after the pamphlet was released, Mehdi had all but decided he would take Mitra to court. He asked permission from the prime minister to sue Server Jung as well. The relationship between the onetime friends had now badly deteriorated: Server Jung was angered by Mehdi's prideful attitude and Ellen's entry into Hyderabad high society, and Mehdi at one point tried to sue Server Jung for libel. While waiting for an answer, he announced an obscenely large reward of 5,000 rupees for information regarding the pamphlet's author, an offer he later withdrew.

From the jungles of Hyderabad State where he was hunting, only a week after the pamphlet went into the mail, Mehdi, Yusuf-uz-Zaman, and Rafi-ud-din exchanged a series of letters. All three names had appeared in the pamphlet. These letters are useful for what they reflect about Mehdi's reaction to the pamphlet and his attempts to align allies early in the scandal.

At the time, Yusuf-uz-Zaman was the honorary magistrate of Banda, a small town southwest of Lucknow. He wrote to Mehdi after the district magistrate called him for an interview. The magistrate may very well have been responding to a request from Ludlow, now involved in the case at Mehdi's behest. The magistrate, according to Zaman, held a lengthy telegram in his hand and, with no introduction, asked him if he knew a woman named Ellen Gertrude Donnelly, who had once lived near Abbas Beg's *koti* in Lucknow. Zaman wrote, "I was not at all prepared to answer this abrupt interrogation. I cannot possibly guess the case of this enquiry after 20 years. You might be connected with the matter also, as I am sure your name was also mentioned in the telegram."[19] Zaman's letter waited unanswered for a few days while Mehdi was shooting in the jungle. In his reply, Mehdi told Zaman what he should and should not say about Ellen. First, he spoonfed Zaman the idea that he (Zaman) did not remember the lady in question—something Zaman had not said in his letter. In fact, he remembered Ellen in vivid detail. Second, Mehdi planted the event of his marriage and date as 1873. Undoubtedly concerned, Mehdi asked his old friend for the latter's "detailed reply" to the magistrate's questions.[20]

Zaman responded on May 10. Throughout the correspondence, Mehdi chose his words carefully, never stating that his wife was Ellen Donnelly, only that he was married, and his wife was known as Mrs. Mehdi Hasan. Zaman, on the other hand, wrote back to Mehdi about the Ellen he had known but did not link Mehdi and Ellen as husband and wife. Zaman raised the issue of Ellen's abandonment of the custom of observing *purdah*. He blamed Mehdi for this, noting how, as Mehdi achieved greater success, he had allowed Ellen to come out of *purdah*.

> All your acquaintances condemn you on your taking her out of *purdah*. The scandal has spread far and wide. She must be a bold woman if she still persists in moving in the high circle. Who the fool [*sic*] advised you to press for a commission to investigate the scandal without any preparation of any kind. Her previous conduct in Nanpara and Lucknow was no secret from you or her. Many persons are still living who knew her intimately, and as you raised your head above the common level, she acquired greater notoriety.[21]

Mehdi wrote back, "You are perfectly right in saying that you do not know my wife." To which Zaman finally responded, "In reply I can positively assert I know nothing against the private character of your wife, whom you said you married in 1873."[22] At this point, Zaman seems to have taken Mehdi's hint that, technically speaking, he (Zaman) did not know Mehdi's wife because the link between Ellen as Mehdi's wife was never acknowledged in their correspondence.

While Mehdi was trying to shape his friend's recollection of the past, Server Jung was using a different version of the past to accomplish the same goal. Server Jung wrote to Zaman and described to him the pamphlet and impending court case. Perhaps sensing the gravity of the situation, Zaman backed away from any further involvement. In his response, Zaman stated that he could not aid in the defense of S. M. Mitra, the Bengali printer charged by Mehdi in court.[23]

Zaman wrote, "I have more than once told you that I cannot identify Mrs. Mehdi Hasan or any woman of such position, and can say nothing against her [in] private, much less in court." He continued, warning Server Jung against pursuing his presence in court, "You should never try to produce me in court, otherwise you might be sorry for this rashness." He concluded by remarking that he was "ignorant" of "these intrigues and conspiracies rife in Hyderabad."[24]

Server Jung also wrote to the Raja Shaban Ali Khan. The raja's father, Raja Nawab Ali Khan Saheb, had been a friend of Server Jung's famous uncle, Mirza Abbas Beg. Now, playing on the friendship between men of a different generation, Server Jung asked the young raja if he had any information about "a moon-faced, venus-like European lady" who lived in Aminabad twenty years earlier. In particular, Server Jung was after a photograph of Ellen in Indian dress. He added that Ellen had lived with Mehdi, and, at the moment (May 1892), "she has now fled to Kashmere, taking a considerable sum with her leaving him (Mehdi Hasan) poor."[25] The record does not indicate whether the raja responded to Server Jung's request, but in the only known photograph of Ellen, she wears Indian attire.

Server Jung also wrote to his friend and Lucknow photographer Asgar Jan in search of photographs of Ellen. In the course of asking for these photos, he explained the situation in Hyderabad, revealing his view of the couple. About Mehdi, he said, "he is a pushing man [and] he made much progress very soon but he made a mistake that he brought forward [this *memsahib*] into society here and did away with the purda and when he went on leave to England he also presented her to Her Majesty the Queen Empress." For Server Jung, part of Mehdi's problem was his pushiness and part was bringing Ellen into open society, but perhaps the underlying problem was Mehdi's prideful attitude. "However this man afterwards gradually began to conduct himself with pride towards his old companions." Server Jung explained how Mehdi had once charged him with libel and had attempted to sue him, although that had failed.[26] Asgar Jan's response seemed to indicate that he recognized his impossible position. Both sides in the trial were trying to obtain the photographs they knew he had. In his letter to Server Jung in August 1892, he said, "I am afraid of the world and sought a shelter in a corner. Therefore I cannot comply with your order."[27]

Rafi-ud-din, also mentioned in the pamphlet, wrote to Mehdi in April and May 1892. In his first letter, he explained that a telegram had arrived from the inspector general of police at Hyderabad, asking him a series of questions about the pamphlet. Rafi-ud-din wondered if his old friend Mehdi had somehow turned against him, hoping this was not the case. "Whatever the cause may be, I hope, that you do not consider me mean enough to write against an old friend, especially when in the same breath I have been asking him to lend me a helping hand. Howsoever your worldly success may have removed you far above me, let me assure you that I still consider you the same friend of my younger days that you once were, but of course with proper and due regard to our changed mutual circumstances." He concluded, "With my best compliments to Mrs. Mehdi Hasan if she remembers me and be in town."[28]

His next letter to Mehdi was less ornate. Having heard that Mehdi intended to take the pamphlet case to court, Rafi-ud-din prophetically writes, "I fear you are ill-advised. I for one would never advise you to do so. You cannot expect to gain anything by such a step, and may possibly lose much." Regarding the large reward of 5,000 rupees for information regarding the pamphlet's author, Rafi-ud-din chided his old friend, "But really I think you are joking about this reward, the sum being so very large for a small matter."[29] Mehdi initially ignored his friend's warnings. At the same time, Rafi-ud-din wrote to Server Jung. He seemed to be currying favor with both sides, possibly preparing his own protection should he be called to testify. Of Mehdi he said, "You know he is awfully cunning," and of his own writing, "I said nothing which can tell in his favour or against me."[30]

While Mehdi's enemies began to align, so did his allies. In April, he received a letter from Syed Husain Bilgrami. Bilgrami wasted no superlatives in condemning the pamphlet. He began, "The vile libel fulminated against Mrs. Mehdi Hasan and yourself is so absolutely false and so villainously filthy and ill-natured, that it could only have been conceived and published by some one completely lost to all sense of shame and self-respect." He continued by referencing the two sisters who had a notorious reputation in Lucknow twenty years earlier, but rejecting any possibility that one of them could be the current Mrs. Mehdi Hasan. He railed, "the attempt to identify one of them with Mrs. Mehdi Hasan is a feat of audacity in satanic invention of which the great 'Artificer of Fraud' may himself be proud. It is a work of superrogation [sic] to add that within my memory and knowledge never has a breath of scandal been breathed over the name of your good wife either here or at Lucknow."[31]

During the summer of 1892, Mehdi also sent several letters to Asman Jah. What remains are copies of the letters sent, but not the prime minister's replies. From Mehdi's letters, however, we can gather that Asman Jah hesitated if not obstructed the matter. In his first letter, Mehdi tried to preemptively frame the narrative concerning the pamphlet. He told the prime minister that he could not describe the "pain and anguish" he felt concerning the "scandalous" pamphlet. The objective of the pamphlet, said Mehdi, was political. He assured Asman Jah that he was taking all the necessary steps to find, and bring justice to, the author and printer.[32]

As the month of May progressed, Mehdi and N. Hormusji, legal advisor within the Nizam's government, had discovered Mitra's involvement in the pamphlet. Mitra had little voice in the case itself, since it was widely accepted that Mehdi's case was aimed at other enemies. Those enemies came to Mitra's defense, supplying the funds necessary to pay for substantial legal costs. Mitra himself was not wealthy, but he served as the target in the center of a larger group that Mehdi chose to attack. Mehdi understood and speculated that it was not really Mitra at all who was responsible for the pamphlet. He wrote to Asman Jah,

> The question, however, which has lately engrossed my most anxious and serious attention is whether this man Mitra is really the author of this scandalous pamphlet and whether by prosecuting him and having him punished I shall have discharged that duty which lies on me of punishing the principal offender, *viz.*, the originator or inspirer of the pamphlet, which I do not believe for one moment that this man Mitra is.[33]

The main purpose of this letter, besides updating Asman Jah on his progress, was to ask the prime minister's advice and help. Mehdi asked "whether I should go through the most obnoxious and disgusting ordeal of becoming a prosecutor against a mere hireling and such an insignificant man as Mitra." Mehdi, his pride and indignation rising, continued, "and even though I may succeed, of which there is not much doubt in my own mind, in having this hireling convicted and punished it would be a very poor satisfaction to us and to the public." He concluded his letter by asking Asman Jah if he, as prime minister, could deal with Mitra as he would any other "intriguer and mischief-maker."[34]

Mehdi understood that his real target should be Server Jung. In a follow-up letter to Asman Jah, he accused Server Jung of leaking information to the press and claiming that the contents of the pamphlet were true, all but giving them the Nizam's government stamp of approval. Mehdi asked that the prime minister turn over any communication he had had with Server Jung on this matter and then requested permission to prosecute Server Jung for defamation.[35] No reply came from Asman Jah.

In April and May 1892, the *Indian Daily News*, among other newspapers, paid considerable attention to the unfolding scandal in Hyderabad. Sympathetic to Mehdi after the pamphlet's release, the paper claimed that the "Penal Code does not provide a punishment adequate to the offence of its publication." Not only did such pamphlets reflect poorly on their authors and subjects, but they reflected poorly on the administration of the state. The paper prophesized that a court case "could make perhaps very undesirable revelations."[36] By early May, the pamphlet scandal had continued to grow in scope. The same paper reported, "The 'scandal' pamphlet which has been widely scattered over the land, and it is said even in England, has caused naturally much sensation in Hyderabad, where the parties chiefly concerned, occupy conspicuous positions."[37] The paper called the search for information in Lucknow a "ruse" designed to throw people "off the scent." The newspaper noted that the large reward offered for finding the author during the early inquiries had caused a rush of would-be detectives to emerge. The reward was subsequently withdrawn, and the inquiry into the assertions of the pamphlet transitioned into a general belief that the contents of the pamphlet were true.[38] The *Evening Mail* printed a story entitled "The Lucknow Pamphlet," all but verifying that it was Server Jung who had vouched for the truth of the pamphlet to Asman Jah, and thus brought the initial frenetic period of inquiry to an end. The paper argued that it was Mehdi's "duty" to sue Server Jung for having vouched for the truth of the pamphlet, libeling Mehdi and

Ellen in the process.[39] In some circles, the early handling of the case was blamed on the Nizam; the *Indian Daily News* suggested he stop going on hunting trips out of the city and instead seek the counsel of the viceroy on how to assert more control over his government.[40] However, as we shall see, the Nizam remained silent regarding the case. In the meantime, Mehdi went forward with his plans.

By early June, against the advice of several friends, Mehdi finalized plans to pursue legal action against Mitra. In writing to the prime minister, he asked for Asman Jah's help in procuring a judge who was "an independent person" and a "perfect outsider." Mehdi expressed confidence in Hyderabad's own judiciary system but made the relevant point that his own connection as the former chief justice of the High Court made that venue unsuitable for the case. Furthermore, he described how his wife, a European lady "moving in respectable English society," was involved in the pamphlet, and thus Mehdi wanted a judge who was "European." He specifically asked for "some eminent European judicial officer of Her Majesty's British Indian Service."[41] By July, Mehdi seemed increasingly anxious to have some response from Asman Jah. He wrote, "Fully one month has passed away since the last of my petitions was presented to your Excellency, but I have not yet been favored with your Excellency's reply with reference to *any* of my requests."[42]

Mehdi indicated that the Nizam himself was reviewing the "whole matter." Because Server Jung was close to the Nizam (as his one-time tutor and a palace insider), the request to prosecute him would have gone to the Nizam for final consideration. Mehdi asked permission to make his case before the Nizam and explain his side of the story. This never seems to have occurred, probably because Server Jung prevented any such meeting from being arranged.

Behind the scenes, Asman Jah wrote to the Resident at Hyderabad, T. J. C. Plowden, asking whether Mitra might be deported from

Hyderabad State. As a princely state, it was within the government's power to deport people, but that in turn meant depositing them into one of the British presidencies. Plowden responded to Asman Jah's request by acknowledging that Mitra was "intimately concerned in the dissemination of anonymous correspondence with intent to obstruct and annoy the administration of His Highness' Government."[43] Plowden felt that the case against Mitra was very strong and that deportation was premature. In the view of the Residency, a trial should go forward.

Mehdi also faced a form of public pressure he was unable to deflect or ignore. He believed this pressure came partly from the general public, whose support he seemed to have had early in the summer but which would ultimately wither as the case went forward. He wrote to Asman Jah, "But all our friends and well-wishers have advised us that any further delay in taking action on our part would produce an unfavourable impression in the minds of the public and that thereby we would run a serious risk of losing that fair sympathy which we have hitherto enjoyed."[44] Asman Jah continued his silence, and Mehdi followed the one path left open to him: suing Mitra.

At the Residency, Plowden received a copy of the pamphlet. Because Ellen and Mehdi had visited Queen Victoria's court, an event to which the pamphlet gave considerable attention, it became necessary to investigate whether any or all of the allegations held some truth. Plowden began a correspondence with Mortimer Durand, foreign secretary and head of the Political Department, just days after the pamphlet was distributed. Plowden included a copy of the pamphlet in his letter to Durand and summarized its contents. He asked who knew of Ellen's background and when they knew it. From the pamphlet, Plowden opined, "It is asserted that Mrs. Mehdi Hassan's antecedents are perfectly well known to various high officials, and that

The main facade of the British Residency, as seen from the garden

a congratulatory telegram was sent by the Government to Mehdi Hassan and his wife on their presentation to Her Majesty—the insinuation, I suppose, being that the Nizam's Government were well aware at the time of Mrs. Mehdi Hassan's true position."[45] According to Plowden, a telegram was apparently sent on 9 June 1888, during the time of the couple's visit to London. In his diary Mehdi made no mention of the telegram.

In Hyderabad, Calcutta, and London investigations took place regarding the pamphlet's claims and Ellen's background. As copies of the pamphlet made their way from the Residency up the political chain, different threads of inquiry began to be woven together. First among these was a memo from A. S. Lethbridge regarding the pamphlet's author. He wrote, "it appears to be doubtful whether there is any such person as Mirza Bakir Hussain, though the Inspector-General of Police, in his letter No. 60 S.B., dated 28th May 1892, states that police authorities at Hyderabad allege that he is known to one Mirza Nisar Hussain, employed in the Judicial Commissioner's Court, but at present absent at Mecca."[46] Thus, some possibility was raised that one Mirza Nisar Hussain knew the pamphlet author, Mirza Bakir Hussain, but the former was "at present absent at Mecca" with an unknown date of return.

The second concern raised by the Government of India was the claim of marriage, or lack thereof, described in the pamphlet. This claim had come to the government's attention before, in 1889 and 1890, when the couple had been in England. The correspondence continued in June 1892 about eight weeks after the pamphlet's release: "With reference to the Secretary's query as to there being evidence of a marriage between Nawab Mehdi Hassan and the lady who passes as his wife, please see . . . [Colonel Henderson's reply] in which he gives his reasons for believing that there has been no legal marriage between the parties."[47] A response came a few days later from E. Berrill, the special assistant to the inspector general of police in the North-Western Provinces. Berrill's report was positive in that it indicated that Ellen had had a reputation of sorts for nearly three years. "Mr. Berrill's report is very positive, and it seems desirable to let the Resident know about it somehow. But much the same thing has been said about Mrs. Mehdi Hassan for the last 2 ½ years."[48] Thus, from the time of the couple's visit to London, the Government of India, the British government, and the Nizam's government were all aware of the rumors regarding Ellen's identity and the veracity of her and Mehdi's marriage claims.

As the response to the pamphlet shifted from shock to preliminary investigations, and then to the courtroom, Ellen was not in Hyderabad city. In July, Lethbridge again addressed the Government of India. Not only was he aware of Ellen's current whereabouts, but he also revealed information about alleged photographs of her, allegations that would become central to the trial.

> Mrs. Mehdi Hassan is still keeping away from Hyderabad, and there is a rumour that she is not on good terms with Mehdi Hassan. The case is being handled very judiciously here and the Resident is determined to see it through. No further action on the part of Government appears necessary at present. I met Mr. Berrill, the Special Assistant to the Inspector General of Police, North-Western Provinces, and he informed me that search was being made in Lucknow for well-known photographs of the two sisters which they had taken when they were prostitutes. These photographs represent them in the nude and in different indecent postures. There is some suspicions in Hyderabad that Mehdi Hassan's enemies have got hold of copies of these photographs.[49]

Lethbridge was likely correct in only some of his reportage. There is no evidence that Ellen and Mehdi were "not on good terms." Reading coverage of the trial in the newspapers, she wrote to Mehdi during its opening days, gently correcting him where he had made mistakes, all the while making her way back to Hyderabad where she would herself give testimony. That the Resident of Hyderabad and police of the North Western provinces were involved shows how seriously the Government of India took the evolving scandal. At the same time, the "well-known" photographs of Ellen and her sister in the nude never materialized. Perhaps Asgar Jan, the well-known photographer of Lucknow who had taken pictures of Ellen and her sister, destroyed them, lied about their existence, or perhaps they never existed at all.

What Lethbridge and others confirmed was that the Hyderabad pamphlet scandal was quickly becoming a sensation. Its content and contours rippled out from Hyderabad to Calcutta and beyond to

London, epicenter of the British Raj. The scandal brought to light the private details of one couple's life and made them public. That the couple was of mixed race and had climbed the social ladder at a dizzying pace made the allegations and rumors that much more shocking. Scandalous accusations of prostitution, pimping, and nude photographs contrasted with Mehdi's high rank in the Nizam's government and Ellen's presentation to Queen Victoria. The difference was startling. With recourse to legal action the only option available to Mehdi and Ellen, they would now embark on a nearly yearlong courtroom odyssey that would change their lives forever.

5

THE PROSECUTION'S
CHARGE

THE TRIAL BEGAN on 21 July 1892. The heart of the proceedings
took place in the Residency Bazaar Court in Hyderabad, but witnesses were also deposed at commissions held in north India at Lucknow, Allahabad, and Barabanki. Each side had a cast of lawyers who
handled much of the day-to-day arguments in court. The courthouse
had seating for spectators and members of the press, and newspapers
in India and Britain covered the trial proceedings, often printing large
verbatim sections of witness testimony.

Mehdi was in Hyderabad as the trial got underway and seems to
have attended court every day. He likely aided in his own case for the
prosecution by passing notes to his lawyers or whispering suggestions
in their ears. At the beginning of the trial, Ellen was in Kashmir. Over
the course of the first few months of testimony, she followed the case,
and in particular, she read newspaper coverage of Mehdi's testimony.
He made certain mistakes, and she wrote to him with corrections. By
mid-November, she was back in Hyderabad and made her appearance in court.

Central to the handling and outcome of the case was Oswald
Vivian Bosanquet, the presiding magistrate. Bosanquet served as the
second assistant Resident in Hyderabad, and in that capacity was also
the magistrate for the Residency Bazaar court. The pamphlet was

printed in the Residency Bazaar area, adjacent to the Residency itself, so matters that fell in this area came before Bosanquet as magistrate. Also, Mehdi chose to file his case in this court, both because he believed in British justice and wanted a British magistrate to hear the case, and because his former position as chief justice of the Hyderabad High Court made filing in that court more complicated. Despite a long career in India, Bosanquet's time in Hyderabad was short lived; he was made assistant to the Resident in 1892, and then left for a position in Rajputana in 1893.[1] Oxford educated, Bosanquet was admitted to the Indian Civil Service in 1855 and two years later received his first post as assistant collector and magistrate in the Madras Presidency. In 1890, he transferred to the Indian Political Service—the branch of the Government of India that dealt with India's princely states—and then went to Hyderabad. After his time in Hyderabad, he served as Resident at Indore and Baroda as well as holding various other positions, including superintendent for the Suppression of Thuggee and Dakaiti, a special assignment in the Foreign Department, and agent to the governor general of Central India.[2]

For the prosecution, several key themes emerged over the course of the trial. First, early questions focused on the printing of the pamphlet and a search for the actual author. Both the prosecution and defense seemed to recognize that Mitra was unlikely to be the sole author of the pamphlet, but with no one else to sue, much of the weight of the prosecution's case focused on him. A second major theme revolved around Ellen's character before her marriage and her age at the time of marriage. The prosecution argued that if she had been young at the time of her marriage, she would not have been sexually active in the years before. Moreover, the veracity of the marriage certificate itself was addressed: if the certificate was real, then the claim of a false marriage would be disproven. A final theme was the corruption of the prosecution, the defense, and nearly all the witnesses. From the start, each side accused the other of bribing witnesses, buying loyalties, and purchasing silences.

Witnesses described their memories, provided evidence, or gave statements about Mehdi and Ellen. Most were also asked about their recent connections and whereabouts in order to reveal undue influence from the prosecution or defense. For instance, when witnesses first provided depositions to one side, the opposing side of the case often contacted them and offered bribes to change their story. If their story changed, cross-examiners asked about any contact they had with the other side of the legal aisle.

The records of the trial proceedings were compiled and translated (where necessary) into book form, which would later be sold across north India. From this account, we can hear the voices of Mehdi, Ellen, and dozens of other witnesses. Yet the printed form belies the complexities of the case. Witnesses, lawyers, newspapers, and events all interacted and influenced one another as the case moved forward. This interplay demonstrates a fluidity in the process, whereby each was in dialogue with others, ultimately playing havoc with testimony and the search for the truth.

The book transcript shows the date on which testimony was given, the name of the speaker, and, where relevant, his or her caste and age. It records the answers given by witnesses, but does not always record the questions they were asked. As such, some of the testimony moves abruptly from one topic to another, so we are left to imagine the intervening questions that produced such responses. In a few cases, the record notes where an objection was raised or some other significant event in the trial occurred. Although the court transcript is a rich document, it remains one that has been edited before coming to us in its final form. Also present in the court was a shorthand writer. This unnamed individual was an employee of the court, and, at least once, his or her notes were openly referred to in court.[3]

Facing Bosanquet in the courtroom was a small army of lawyers employed separately by the prosecution and defense.[4] Mehdi's position gave him the means to hire his legal team, but Mitra was not so fortunate. How he covered his legal fees, and who might have helped him, remained a mystery and point of contention throughout the trial. During the case some lawyers worked in court examining and cross-examining witnesses while others were tasked with gathering evidence and attending the different commission hearings held across north India.

The chief lawyer for the prosecution was John Duncan Inverarity. Inverarity was forty-five years old on the opening day of the trial.[5] Before working on the pamphlet case, he had already developed a reputation as a successful Bombay lawyer, as well as being known for his adventures outside of the courtroom. In 1889, the *New York Times* reprinted an article from the *Bombay Gazette*. While in Africa, Inverarity and two Somalis had gone into the bush, where Inverarity shot a lioness. Failing to kill her on the first or second try, he set fire to the bush to flush her out. When she came out, he fired a third shot, but she made straight for him and attacked. The two Somali assistants were able to shoot her and subdue her with their rifle butts. Inverarity suffered a total of sixteen wounds but managed to take a photograph of his kill, dress his wounds, and take the six-hour journey back to Berbera in Somalia. He continued on to Aden, where a surgeon found him in good health.[6] During the trial, Inverarity was not present in court every day. He seems to have come to Hyderabad and the courtroom only sporadically, perhaps attending to other cases elsewhere. He returned to deliver the closing argument, but acknowledged his lengthy absence.

Handling the case in Inverarity's absence and playing a substantial role in the day-to-day work at court was A. C. Rudra. He had come to Hyderabad in the late 1880s and initially enjoyed a warm welcome in Hyderabad circles, followed by success in the courtroom. Mehdi even helped boost his career and social standing by securing his membership to the Nizam Club.[7] But Rudra ran into trouble when he seemed to set aside his legal career for one in journalism. He became a correspondent for the *Pioneer* and set about taking to task Hyderabad officialdom for what he saw as its problems and shortcomings. These officials and much of Hyderabad society then turned on Rudra. Those who knew him received something called the "*khanji* wink"—a kind of social blackballing of a person whereby no one was to associate with him or risk their own position. Rudra was turned out of the Nizam Club and even found difficulty renting a room. Hyderabad society went so far as to ostracize a friend he stayed with, forcing Rudra out. His writing no longer appeared in the *Pioneer*.[8] In a final blow, the Hyderabad High Court disbarred him for "offensive remarks" made during a different salacious case of the time.[9] Yet, though disbarred from the Hyderabad High Court, he was allowed to argue before Bosanquet in the Residency Bazaar Court. He served as part of the prosecution's team and played a central role in Bosanquet's court for the next nine months.

The trial opened with Mehdi's complaint against S. M. Mitra. In this short statement, Mehdi provided the facts of his life that were pertinent to the case and spelled out his specific charge against Mitra: defamation under the Indian Penal Code, section 500. This bit of legal code stated that one who defames another can be imprisoned up to two years, fined, or both. Challenging a major assertion of the pamphlet, Mehdi stated that he had married Ellen on 28 September 1873, when she was fifteen. Ellen's baptismal records, however, show that she was nineteen at the time of her marriage, which would have given her time to have been a prostitute in the years before marriage. As such, Mehdi's opening statement already weakened his case and damaged his credibility. Nevertheless, Mehdi argued vehemently that the pamphlet was both false and "grossly defamatory."[10] Mitra followed Mehdi's opening charge with a petition for adjournment, claiming he needed more time to gather his defense.

Before the court adjourned, Inverarity delivered his opening address. He began by outlining what he intended to prove over the course of the case. He would demonstrate that Mitra had printed the pamphlet in March and distributed it in April. He would show that there were two libels in the pamphlet: "The first was that Nawab Mehdi Hasan had never married her, and the second that Mrs. Mehdi Hasan was a common prostitute, and that Nawab Mehdi Hasan knowing her to have been such palmed her off as a respectable character on society."[11] Inverarity also outlined his attack on the supposed author of the pamphlet, Mirza Bakir Hussain, of Aminabad, Lucknow. He stated that such a person did not exist, and Mitra should be held accountable.

Inverarity also raised the question of motive. As Mehdi himself recognized, the pamphlet's aim was political. Inverarity asked why the pamphlet author had waited to disclose this "shocking" scandal if he had visited Hyderabad more than once? "If a person was actuated by pure motives there would have been no delay in publication—it ought to have been published two years ago. From this, it was evident that there had been a political motive for printing, that the pamphlet had been meant to be used as an instrument to pull down the present Government on suitable occasion, and it had nothing to do with public good."[12] The insinuation was that the pamphlet would ruin not only Mehdi's career in Hyderabad but also the careers of "alien" nonlocals who had assumed significant power.

Inverarity turned to the pamphlet's accusations against Ellen. Among them was that she was Eurasian, that is, a person of mixed parentage. Inverarity made clear he intended to argue otherwise. Drawing a distinction between racial descriptions, Inverarity stated, "She was the daughter of a European and not a Eurasian. Her father was Captain Donnelly belonging to an Irish family. From a Volunteer he rose to be a Captain. His brother was Surgeon-General with the Government at Madras."[13]

Inverarity concluded, explaining that, as the pamphlet was printed within the Residency Bazaars, it fell within the jurisdiction of the Residency Bazaar Court. This explanation would stymie any claim that the case should have been heard in the Hyderabad High Court. He also noted that Mehdi had applied to "prosecute another man who is in the Court of the Nizam." This was Server Jung, but Mehdi never had the chance. Mehdi needed the permission of the Nizam to prosecute a fellow member of the Nizam's government, especially someone so close to the Nizam himself. The Nizam never gave such sanction.

Having granted Mitra's request for more time to prepare his defense, the court had adjourned for a month. Now, on Monday, 29 August 1892, the court reconvened, and the prosecution called its first witness, Patrick Connor, described as Eurasian and the manager of the Record Press. Connor narrated how Mitra had visited him several times before asking him to take on the job of the pamphlet printing. For a pamphlet of six to eight pages in length, 300 copies, Mitra paid him fifty rupees. At the time of the actual printing, Connor was in the hospital and oversaw the job from there. When he saw a copy of the pamphlet and read its contents, "I took him [Mitra] to task about not having told me the nature of the printing. He told me not to be afraid. I refused to give him the pamphlets after they had

Chowmahalla Palace, home of the Nizams

been printed. He persuaded me to give them up, and said they were not intended for circulation here but in England where they were going by that [*sic*] mail." Mitra also told Connor that the pamphlet author's name was fictitious.[14] Inverarity called other witnesses involved in the printing process: Joseph Fischer, also described as Eurasian, the head examiner at the Residency Press, testified to meeting Mitra at the press; Cornelius Pereira testified to having helped physically print the pamphlet, as did Ramanjulu, Victor Hendricks, Durgaya, Venketasawmi, and Maslamoni. Finally, Inverarity called one Gopanna, whose sole job it was to stitch by hand 300 copies of the pamphlet. Some of the men received double pay for working on a Sunday. No cross-examination took place, so Inverarity called Mehdi to take the stand.

Mehdi began by narrating the details of his early life leading up to his marriage. In court, he produced the original marriage document signed by himself, Ellen, and witnesses. He noted that there were corrections on the document, specifically regarding Ellen's age. "The body of the document is in my hand-writing. The corrections in it are in my wife's hand-writing. The corrections are in the spelling of the names Donnelly and in the ages. The word fifteen in the margin in [sic] my wife's hand-writing."[15] For the marriage document to have Ellen's age as fifteen corroborates what Mehdi said in his opening statements but contradicts Ellen's baptismal record. Mehdi denied that his wife had called herself a "lady" while in England, denied that any scandal surrounded her presentation to Queen Victoria, and described the first time he saw the pamphlet when it was mailed to him at the Nizam Club.

During cross-examination by Eardley Norton—chief lawyer for the defense—and his team, Mehdi explained his sometimes imprecise memory of events and their timing by stating, "I keep neither private nor official diaries."[16] He had, of course, already published the diary of his visit to Europe, replete with his references to the "dirty intrigues of Hyderabad."[17] Answering questions concerning his whereabouts, he explained that he read the pamphlet at the club when he returned from Kashmir but left immediately for his shooting trip with the prime minister, Asman Jah. While on the trip, he took steps to vindicate his character through his correspondence with Yusuf-uz-Zaman and his offer of a 5,000-rupee reward.

Mehdi and others testified about photographs of Ellen and her sartorial choices. Did she make a conscious decision to adopt European-style clothing in Hyderabad rather than Indian dress? Why did she no longer wear Indian clothing or observe *purdah* as she once had in Lucknow? Expert witnesses testified to photographic technologies and their fallibility. Mehdi explained that Ellen had been photographed in 1873 to 1874 at the studio of Asgar Jan, the well-known photographer in Lucknow at the time. She was photographed in "Hindustani dress." Thus, the sole known photograph of Ellen, in which she is wearing Indian dress, likely comes from her teenage years. Mehdi described her transformation upon reaching Hyderabad. "She did not wear native dress after she came to Hyderabad, *i.e.*, in 1883. She did not wear native dress habitually in Hyderabad, but wore European costume. She wore native dress as fancy dress once or twice. She wore it when visiting native ladies here, after we came to Hyderabad, *i.e.*, in 1883. She did not wear native dress in European society at Hyderabad."[18]

As the questioning continued, under cross-examination the defense circled back to the marriage contract. Mehdi was asked about his contact with the Resident, Plowden, at the time of the pamphlet's publication. Had he shown the marriage contract to Plowden? Of course, the contract directly challenged one of the main accusations of the pamphlet: that Mehdi and Ellen were not married. Mehdi refused to provide answers to this line of questioning. Asterisks in the printed court transcript direct the reader to a footnote. "I refuse* to say whether I produced before the Resident the original of my marriage contract, on the ground that I can't disclose any conversation with Mr. Plowden without his leave, this being an official matter and Mr. Plowden my official superior." The footnote explained, "*Mr. Norton submits that such communications are not privileged. Court decides in the first place to enquire of Mr. Plowden whether he objects to the conversation being repeated."[19]

During the opening proceedings, beyond the courtroom walls, Mehdi and Ellen's affairs came to the attention of the Government of India again. In a correspondence with Plowden, Mortimer Durand, who was foreign secretary and head of the political department, hoped that the issue of privilege, which Mehdi had raised in court, would not escalate to higher circles. Plowden and Durand had crossed paths before. Durand had all but removed Plowden from his position in

Kashmir, calling him an "autocratic little beggar."[20] Thus, Durand could not have been too happy to receive missives from Plowden detailing what was fast becoming a messy affair.

The question of privilege referred to how, if at all, a conversation between Mehdi and Plowden might be a private and confidential one, unable to be discussed in open court. Plowden had already raised the issue, noting, "On the whole, as far as things have gone, public opinion seems to me adverse to Mehdi Hassan." In the course of his remarks, he added, "the question of privilege will doubtless have to be sent up to the Government of India later on."[21] The response from Durand was clear: "I must say I hope it will not. It would be an awkward question for us in various ways. If it must come to us it must, but don't send it up if you can avoid doing so."[22] From Durand's perspective, the fewer the repercussions from the case for the Government of India, the better.

During cross-examination Mehdi disclosed that he had asked for permission from the Nizam's government to prosecute Server Jung, whom he suspected of writing the pamphlet.[23] Yet neither Asman Jah nor the Nizam had granted permission, thus keeping Server Jung out of court as a defendant. Norton's cross-examination turned to Mehdi and Ellen's visit to London. While on tour, their entry into London social circles and ultimately to the queen's levée was made easier by their friendship with Morton and Clare Frewen. Mehdi was asked if he knew that Morton Frewen had in fact threatened to horsewhip him. Apparently, between the visit to London and the beginning of the trial, Frewen's feelings toward Mehdi soured considerably. Horsewhipping was no ordinary threat of violence: in late nineteenth-century Britain, it had the particular meaning of thrashing a scoundrel, that is, someone who has knowingly deceived others for their own gain. Mehdi's answer to the question regarding Frewen was, "It was never brought to my notice by persons that Morton Frewen was waiting in Hyderabad to horsewhip me, nor did I hear that he said he had a good mind to stop here to horsewhip me."[24]

Mehdi answered questions about Ellen's family. Since Ellen was the youngest of the Donnelly sisters, by the time of her marriage to Mehdi, the other two were already married and using their married names: Lucy Hodges and Esther Bigex. Mehdi noted that Lucy was living in Lucknow at the time of his wedding; that she was in "English dress" when he met her; and that "I thought her a woman of bad repute."[25] He offered no evidence to support this opinion. The statement about her dress referred to accusations that Ellen and Lucy had been prostitutes in Lucknow and were known to have worn Indian attire. As such, Mehdi's testimony that he only knew her to wear European dress helped defend his position. However, his comment that Lucy was of "bad repute" seemed to undermine the very case he sought to establish. When asked about Lucy's relationship to the princely family at Kapurthala in north India, Mehdi responded, "I had not heard that she had an improper intimacy with the Rajah of Kapurthala."[26]

Lawyers asked Mehdi about the extent to which his family accepted his new wife. These questions were designed to prove or shed doubt on his actual marriage. He testified as to the difficulty of an international marriage, partly because Ellen was European, partly because of her Christian faith. "I anticipated difficulties about my marriage that led me to get a contract in writing. I thought that being a foreigner, my wife might not, in case of my death, be recognized. I therefore took this precaution. I did not ask my relations living in Lucknow to the wedding as I wanted to keep it secret till it was over." After a few days, Mehdi broke the news to his family and friends. "[S]ome of my people were very angry at my marriage. My mother was very angry. She wanted me to marry among my own people; she didn't object on the score of Mrs. Mehdi Hasan's religion. The latter has become a Mahomedan."

Mehdi explained how Ellen converted to Islam. "I cannot recollect how long before the marriage Mrs. Mehdi Hasan apostacised. The discussion took some time. The discussions were between her and me. They were one of the reasons of the delay to the marriage. I can't say when or where she acknowledged the Moslim faith. It was I who converted her, and she would not accept the faith till she believed it to be the true one."[27] The questions then turned to Ellen's faith at the current moment. Mehdi seemed to suggest that while she was still Muslim, she frequented Christian places—a church, cemetery, or other such sites. "She goes to Christian places of worship, but she has never told me that she has reverted to Christianity. I did say in my preliminary deposition 'She is now a Christian.' By that I mean she goes to Christian places of worship. I personally believe she is a Christian."[28] The defense appears to have been trying to prove that either Mehdi was never legally married (or married at all), or that his marriage was in some way voided by Ellen's Christianity.

During Mehdi's lengthy cross-examination, the name Vasudeva Rao emerged. Rao was a low-ranking employee in the Nizam's government who had worked for Raja Murli Manohar and later under A. J. Dunlop. A rumor circulated that Rao was the pamphlet author, although a later claim suggested he took it under dictation from Syed Ali Bilgrami. Mehdi attempted to pay Rao for his testimony but does not seem to have trusted him much. In the transcript of the trial, this topic is one of the few moments where an objection is noted. "Q.—So you both distrusted each other, you refused to pay him ... (Mr. Inverarity objects). I did not intend to call him unless he came forward to give evidence for the truth and not for money."[29] Rao's name would reappear in connection with the pamphlet case years after its conclusion.

Mehdi was asked about the fact that he and Ellen did not start a family. "I never had any children by my wife. She has never been in the family way. When she went to Cashmir this year, Mrs. Mehdi Hasan did not tell me she was *enciente* [*sic*, pregnant]. To my knowledge my wife has never consulted any one here about her being *enciente*."[30] In later testimony, the suggestion was made that Mehdi was impotent, but no further explanation was offered for their childless state.

Norton briefly re-examined Mehdi over the next few days. Mehdi provided some clarifications concerning his earlier testimony and added a few details. When repeated questions arose concerning Ellen's oldest sister, Lucy Hodges, Mehdi expanded on his knowledge of the family she married into. "I know that the Raja of Kapurthala had married Miss Hodges, the sister of Mr. Hodges [Lucy's husband]. She was known as Lady Randia Sing. The Raja of Kapurthala is converted to Christianity."[31]

Early in the trial, Eardley Norton, the lawyer for Mitra, had sent a telegram to Mortimer Durand requesting information about Ellen. On 2 September, he wrote again: "Am defending in prosecution by Home Secretary for defamation. Would you kindly inform me whether as fact Indian Government instituted enquiries, any time since 1889, regarding Mehdi Hassan's marriage? Information urgently needed personally."[32] Before a response was sent, the deputy secretary from the Government of India wrote to Durand, "Take care how you answer. He is a dangerous man to deal with." In developing a response to Norton's request, further details about the Government of India's investigation of Ellen became clear. "It was in July 1889 that Foreign Secretary wrote to Sir Asman Jah with reference to presentation of Mrs. Mehdi Hassan and unpleasant rumours in England on that subject. Foreign Secretary wrote in hope that Sir Asman Jah would be able to give him satisfactory assurances as to the lady's position. Sir Asman Jah's reply of 17th August was considered satisfactory, and no further action was taken."[33] The correspondence continued by revealing that the Government of India maintained a file about Ellen and, in particular, her questionable antecedents. A lengthy correspondence then ensued within the government echelons as to whether or not to reply to Norton. Some suggested that he be "simply ignored," while others suggested a formal response that denied any enquiries.

On the same day that Norton telegrammed Durand, Faridoonji Jamshedji, the respected private secretary to the prime minister, took the stand. Faridoonji testified that he had heard rumors in 1889 concerning the validity of Mehdi and Ellen's marriage. The heart of the rumors was that the couple was not married at all. Faridoonji considered raising it with Mehdi, but did not, claiming, "I should have felt a delicacy about speaking to a man about his wife. I did not look on it as an act of friendship to speak to my friend Mehdi Hasan about his wife. It is only a fool who meddles between husband and wife."[34]

Inverarity continued to call witnesses, who offered brief testimony on a range of topics and events related to the prosecution's case. A man named Shujat Ali, who knew Mehdi from Lucknow, testified that he had attended Mehdi and Ellen's marriage. Inverarity also called Sadullah, who claimed to be Mitra's teacher. Mitra, according to Sadullah, could not read or write Urdu, but understood it orally. He testified, "First, in the beginning of March, Mitra gave me a copy written in Urdu by Rajab Ali. He told me to read it out, and he (Mitra) would put it into English."[35] While this connected Mitra to the pamphlet, it did not necessarily link him to its authorship or to its printing. Sadullah also named Vasudeva Rao as involved in the pamphlet's authorship and printing.

Prosecution witness Amir Mirza, a resident of Lucknow, knew Mehdi in 1873—the year of the marriage in dispute. He testified that he was not physically present at the exact moment the marriage took place, but arrived about two hours later. He testified to recognizing the signatures on the wedding document. After him, Mahomed Husain and Moulvi Ikbal Ali both gave testimony. The former described how, in local Lucknow circles, Mehdi introduced Ellen as his wife, while the latter stated that Ellen was "always received as his wife in Mahomedan circles in Partabghar."[36]

Amir Mirza had one other connection to the case, although it was never proven. When Ellen and her sister were living in Lucknow, they apparently came under suspicion of being prostitutes. If true, they would have had to register themselves as such with the Lucknow police. Allegedly, when the police came around to insist on the registration, the girls played a sort of cat-and-mouse game by hiding, with Mirza's help. Ellen's life before her marriage continued to be a contested part of the story as each side in the court case tried to provide evidence and produce witnesses who would confirm or deny her (and her sister's) actions at the time.[37]

Inverarity called a final witness, Shaik Buran, described as a "peon of Mr. Connor" (the manager of the printing press), who testified to having taken a bundle of printed pamphlets from Connor to Mitra's home.

The trial paused in Hyderabad as two commissions in north India took up the task of deposing witnesses. Although court testimony ended at the beginning of September, the first commission did not convene until a month later, beginning on 3 October. This allowed Mehdi and Server Jung to speak with, and possibly influence, potential witnesses. In these commissions, the prosecution and defense both deposed witnesses to help their case.

The assistant commissioner of Barabanki presided over the first commission.[38] The first to give testimony was the elderly Sheikh Mohammad Husain, a petty official in Bilouli. The sheikh was Mehdi's cousin on his paternal side, and his name also appeared on the marriage document. How it got there and what Mehdi's state of mind was when he asked the sheikh to sign it were areas of inquiry. Apparently, Mehdi brought the document to the sheikh, who could not read it since it was in English but signed it anyway. In addition, the sheikh cast some doubt on Mehdi's nuptial happiness. Mehdi read the document, and then, according to the sheikh, "He said with the document in his hand,—'I have committed a fault (khata). I cannot speak out before you as you are an elder, but I say this much that my fault is that of having married an English woman.'" The sheikh further described that Mehdi "besought and coaxed me, and I affixed my signature to the deed."[39] This testimony did not contradict Mehdi's claim that he was legally married to Ellen, but it suggests that at one point, perhaps, the newlywed was not entirely happy or that he recognized that his marriage to an Englishwoman would result in disapproval from his family.

Sheikh Mohammad was not the only person to sign the marriage document *post facto*. The next witness called before the Barabanki commission was Fazl-ul-lah, the son of a local *hakim* who had known Mehdi since their childhood. He testified that, at about the same time as Sheikh Mohammad Husain had signed the document ("18 or 19 years ago"), he had done so as well. Fazl-ul-lah recounted that Mehdi said he had married a "mem" (a *memsahib*). In their conversations, Fazl-ul-lah brought up the possibility of Mehdi taking a second wife, an Indian Muslim woman from within their community. But Mehdi had promised his wife that he would not take another and said he would keep that promise to his death.

The Barabanki commission further heard short testimony from two other witnesses, Munshi Ihsan Ali and Ahmad Husain. Ali was a neighbor to Mehdi and his mother in Fatehpur and would occasionally bring messages to her from him. Ahmad Husain was a local *zamindar* who testified to knowing Mehdi and hearing about his marriage but could provide no further details.

The case then moved to Lucknow, where a different commission deposed witnesses. The first was Michel Johnson White, the principal of Canning College, called on 10 October. White brought with him the lists of students who had attended Canning College in 1872 and 1873, the supposed time of Mirza Bakir Hussain's attendance. He stated categorically, "There is no such name as Mirza Baker [sic] Hussein." White, however, did have the record for Mehdi's entrance into the college on 3 August 1867 at the age of fifteen. White was followed by William Roe Hooper, a British doctor. Hooper testified to having recently treated Mehdi for problems with gout. He said he had met "Mrs. Mehdi Hasan" when they overlapped in London.[40] His testimony suggests he regarded Mehdi and Ellen as a respectably married couple.

Munshi Sajjad Husain, a twenty-nine-year-old *zamindar*, was important to the prosecution. In addition to his landholding duties, Husain founded and edited the Urdu newspaper *Oudh Punch*, which was published in Lucknow. He wrote several articles critical of Mehdi in *Oudh Punch* about the pamphlet case. Mehdi's friend Wajid Ali took umbrage, arguing that the pamphlet was an attack on a "co-religionist." In a letter to Husain in August, he wrote, "Whether right or wrong you ought to have supported him [Mehdi Hasan] at this juncture and ought to have written articles against the pamphlet. If you cannot agree to this in every case you are to keep silence."[41] In Hyderabad and Lucknow alike, the pamphlet case was fiercely discussed in ever wider circles, with individuals lining up on either side and using English as well as Urdu newspapers to vent their opinions.

At the Lucknow commission, Munshi Sajjad Husain provided some details of Ellen's early life before her marriage. She socialized with a local family, the Evanses, who were also friends with Husain. The Evanses had known Husain's father through business dealings, and, as such, he came to know them and met Ellen in or around 1872. Husain testified that he had had conversations with Mr. Evans, who spoke poorly of Ellen. "I am very sorry that this girl used to be well-conducted, and now she has got into bad society, that she has come to know such people [a list of names of boys], and her sister Mrs. Hodges who [sic] conduct is bad has corrupted her (kharab kya)." Evans also noted that "their father takes no care of them and drinks." Husain also testified that Mrs. Evans had said much the same thing: that Ellen became a prostitute because her sister (Mrs. Hodges, Ellen's oldest sister Lucy) had led her down this path. Husain claimed that "Mrs. Hodges was a prostitute, and it was also notorious that she had had a child by a Punjab Raja and got Rs. 100 a month from him."[42]

Husain also recalled seeing Ellen in a "compromised situation" with a guest of the Evanses, Mr. Money. As Husain describes it, he went to see Mr. and Mrs. Evans, but they were not immediately available. Walking through the house to the sitting room, he passed a room with the curtain partially drawn and glanced in. He testified to seeing Ellen and Mr. Money "caressing each other" on a bed.[43] Husain's testimony so far—his opinions in *Oudh Punch*, his conversations with the Evanses, and his eyewitness testimony of Ellen in a compromising situation—were all fodder in the case against Mehdi and Ellen, but he had one more bit of damaging testimony to reveal.

From his testimony, we learn that Husain collected photographs. His tastes included European *carte-de-visites* as well as more titillating photos, including those of local prostitutes. He was asked how he came to have a photo of Ellen dressed in Indian clothing. Husain described how he had met Ellen at the Evans' home. He complimented her preparation of betel leaf (combined with areca nut to make *paan*), to which Mrs. Evans responded that Ellen was "very fond of native things" and that she had even had herself photographed in local dress. Husain asked to see this, so the next day Ellen showed it to him. He complimented her on the picture, and when he wished to have it for himself, she acquiesced. When asked in court, Husain said, "The photo of Gertrude Donnelly was apart [kept separate] among the photographs of the prostitutes. The names of some of these are Mooshtari, Hyder, Imami, Abadi, Barodawali Piarey, &c., also Allen Booney and also a M. Ml. Lota who came with a circus."[44] He described how he classified his photo collection into categories: prostitutes, renowned poets, *taluqdars,* rajas, native chiefs, and renowned Europeans. However, Husain stated that he did not keep Ellen's photograph with those of the known prostitutes, and only came to consider her as one after hearing of the case in which he was now a witness.

Questions by the defense turned to Husain's writing about Mehdi and Mehdi's command of English, in an effort to discredit him. In *Oudh Punch* Husain had written about the pamphlet case as well as Mehdi's views of the Indian National Congress. Husain dismissed Mehdi's criticism of the Congress: "I think his opinion in Congress matters utterly worthless."[45] The next day Husain was again on the witness stand, where he called into question Mehdi's ability to write a letter to the editor that criticized the Congress. "I myself take a deep interest in the Congress. I have seen a letter in the English *Times* attacking the Congress and signed Mehdi Hasan. I read the leading article in the same paper complimenting him on his power over the English language." Norton then asked, "From your knowledge of Mehdi Hasan, is he capable of writing such a letter.[?]" Husain answered, "No, he is not capable."[46]

Asgar Jan, the photographer and brother of the well-known Lucknow photographer Mushkur-ud-dowla, took the stand next. He testified that he had photographed Ellen in Indian and in European dress. The questions put to him revolved around two issues: first, had he been offered bribes or otherwise influenced by either Mehdi or Server Jung in his testimony? Throughout the case, defense and prosecution lawyers questioned several witnesses as to whether the opposing side had influenced them, planting the troubling idea that widespread witness tampering was infecting the case.

The second line of questioning concerned the style of Ellen's dress in the photograph, and whether it was the same or a similar style to those of known Lucknow prostitutes. Here, Asgar Jan provides us with a window into the norms of photographic portraiture for the time. "I have photographed many respectable Mohamedan ladies. I have never photographed one with her *dopatta* completely taken off. They sometimes cover head and shoulders, sometimes their shoulders only, but always their shoulders." In an exception to this, he recounted having taken a photograph of Geti Ara Begum of Delhi, whose photo showed her *dupatta* arranged in such a way to reveal her covered breasts. Husain was then asked, "Except for Geti Ara Begam [*sic*] and Gertrude Donnelly can you give me another instance of a respectable married Mahomedan lady being so photographed?" Husain could not, adding, "Prostitutes are photographed as they please, and also in this way."[47]

On 20 October, twenty-five-year-old Joanna Rostan took the stand to recount a shocking detail of Ellen's past. Rostan was in Lucknow in the 1870s and knew Ellen's father, but only by sight. She testified that Ellen had a mixed reputation at that time—some people believed that she was good, others that she was "very bad," and some thought she was to be pitied. Rostan testified that she had provided John Edgelow—a lawyer for the defense along with Norton and J. B. Boyle—with the name of James Lauchlin, who, she claimed, had been engaged to Ellen.

Edgelow had scrambled to find Lauchlin and secure his testimony. Both Lauchlin and Rostan were in financial straits at the time of the Lucknow commission. Since they knew each other, and since each was being courted by both sides of the case, they discussed whether they might be able to make money from their testimony. Rostan testified, "Neither Mr. Norton, nor Mr. Edgelow, nor Mr. Boyle offered me any inducement to give evidence. I told the Counsel for the defence that Lauchlin had commented on the fact that money was to be had from the prosecution [Mehdi Hasan's side], but not from the defence."[48] Attention momentarily turned to Rostan's financial condition, and the extent to which she could have been paid to give testimony.

As it happened, just days before her testimony, she had been arrested. Three "decrees" had been issued for her, that is, collectors were seeking payments for three debts. For a young married European woman, being arrested was no small affair. She testified, "This arrest has annoyed and disgraced me, and I feel it a great deal because it was unjust. I have lost confidence in the gentlemen for the defence entirely."[49] Rostan then recounted her conversations with Lauchlin, who claimed that the defense had been doling out compensation for testimony favorable to their cause, in other words, testimony that would denigrate Ellen. When Rostan told Lauchlin that no money was to be had from the defense and that she had given information to the prosecution, he apparently became very angry with her, saying, "It's through your being so stupid Mrs. Rostan that I have lost it [money for testimony]." In revenge, Rostan claimed, Lauchlin made a sworn statement that she was intending to flee Lucknow and her creditors, resulting in her arrest. After giving this testimony, Rostan stepped down from the witness box.

During the Lucknow commission, Mary Gill—a onetime younger schoolmate of Ellen at the Lucknow Girls' School—testified that Ellen's mother worked as a matron at the school. It was at school where Ellen began to acquire a sullied reputation. Gill noted that Ellen's mother left her position shortly after a visit from her other daughter, Mrs. Hodges. Gill explained that at the time of this visit, in 1866, "We heard that she was a Rajah's wife. We girls ran out from School to see her and we were punished for it. Mrs. Hodges had a little boy with her."[50] As for Ellen's reputation, Gill testified that she fraternized with young men who lived near the school. "Her general conduct was not right, the way she used to go on with young men. There were a lot of young men living near our house. It was in connection with some of these men that Gertrude Donnelly got a bad reputation."[51] On further questioning, Gill was asked if Ellen had been "seduced" in a storeroom on the school grounds, which the girls of the school had dubbed the "haunted chamber." "Did you intend the Court to believe that Gertrude Donnelly had had sexual intercourse with any man in that haunted chamber, when you said she came out of it?" Gill's answer was not conclusive, saying only she thought it "looked bad" that Ellen had gone into the room.

Gill was the first to testify about Ellen's mother. The senior Mrs. Donnelly had died suddenly in Kanpur from illness. None of her family was with her at the time, and the exigencies of death in India required a hasty burial. However, questions hung over the death that cast Ellen in a poor light. Gill claimed that Ellen's sister Lucy arrived in Kanpur after the burial and ordered the body disinterred. Gill recounted what Ellen had told her after the fact: "Gertrude said her mother's body was found lying on her face with the tongue protruding, and Gertrude said she might have been buried in a trance."[52] The specter of being buried alive was as profound a fear then as it is now. What happened at the graveyard and in the hours and days after would be hotly contested.

Gill then introduced a bombshell. In her testimony, she suggested that Ellen had been a victim of incest with her father. She claimed that Gill's mother had spoken to the young Ellen, who was grieving the loss of her mother. Gill testified to overhearing their conversation: "My mother spoke to Gertrude about the life she had been leading, and Gertrude began to cry and threw her arms round my mother's neck, and said she was sorry to have to live this life, but her father made her. My mother had talked of her living in adultery, Gertrude Donnelly said her father had taken liberties with her which a father ought not to take. They used to drink together, father and daughter."[53] Such liberties supposedly took place immediately after Mrs. Donnelly's burial. By this point, Michael Donnelly's drinking was becoming an established part of the story. The charge that a young Ellen joined him in drink—and perhaps in bed—added to the aura that something was terribly wrong in the Donnelly household before her marriage to Mehdi.

After Gill, Dominic Braganza, a sixty-year-old piano-tuner and pensioner, took the stand. His family name suggests an Indo-Portuguese origin. Braganza had known Ellen when she was a young girl of twelve or so. In an early deposition, he stated, "I know nothing against her character."[54] Later, however, he testified to knowledge of a mole on Ellen's knee, the inference being that he could only know of such a body mark if he had seen her undressed or otherwise compromised. Nothing further came of his testimony about Ellen's body. However, Braganza was caught up in the swirl of accusations on both sides about witness bribing. He stated that he was in debt about 1,000 rupees and that, when he first met with the prosecution's lawyers, they offered 300 rupees for his willingness to testify. He added, "The money was to come from Mehdi Hasan's pocket."[55]

Like Gill, Lauchlin, and Rostan, Braganza was a representative of the relatively poor, ethnically white or Eurasian underbelly of the British Raj.[56] The opportunity to earn several hundred, if not thousands, of rupees for giving testimony about a woman none knew particularly well would have been nearly irresistible. The question that both the prosecution and defense wrestled with was this: Who had offered money first?

In October, some drama unfolded outside of the courtroom in Hyderabad. Mehdi Hasan was suspended from his position as home secretary of the Nizam's government. Four months earlier, in July, Prime Minister Asman Jah had asked Mehdi to turn over any evidence he had concerning the pamphlet, as any scandal that touched him also touched the prime minister and the Nizam himself. Asman Jah sought to better understand the nature of the pamphlet and Mehdi's evidence before he himself headed into court.

Mehdi delayed his response to the request for nearly two months, however, and by October, matters took a more serious turn. With no reply from Mehdi, the Nizam sanctioned an order, published on 21 October in a *jarida* that formally suspended him from his position as home secretary. A Bombay paper, the *Deccan Budget*, ran the full text:

> Orders by H. E. the Minister. "To Fateh Nawaz Jung, Home Secretary to H. E. the Minister, an order from His Highness, dated 17th July, was issued that he should submit for His Highness' perusal all the proofs in his possession in refutation of the accusations contained in the Pamphlet. At that time the complaint had not been filed against Mr. Mitra. On the 31st August,— that is, after one month and a half—the reply of Fateh Nawaz Jung was received declining to execute this order of His Highness notwithstanding his ability to do so. Even this was by means of a document so wanting in subordination and humility that it can never be pardoned, nor, in the interest of good Government, be overlooked. But as the case is at present *sub judice* in the Residency Courts, having regard to justice and equity this much punishment only is now awarded that he may be suspended from his office of Home Secretary from the 15th October. After the termination of the case, appropriate orders will be issued as to the future retention of his services. In his stead for the present until further orders, Nawab Imad Jung Bahadur, Chief Justice of the High Court, will officiate and look after the duties.[57]

The suspension canceled his salary and threatened Mehdi's ability to pay his team of lawyers and other costs associated with the case. It was also a deep blow to his professional reputation, made worse by the wording of the *jarida* that spelled out Mehdi's offense. From this point forward, Mehdi and Ellen's finances would become increasingly strained.

Back in court, three days after the *jarida*, witnesses for the defense continued to paint an increasingly turbulent picture of Michael Donnelly. On 24 October, Richard Grant took the stand to testify about the character of Ellen's father, saying, "Mr. Donnelly was very fond of his bottle."[58] He also asserted that neither side had made any financial inducement to him, but that he had shared a "peg"—a shot of liquor—with the defense team: Norton, Boyle, and Edgelow. Concerning Ellen, the wizened Grant could only offer rumors that he had heard about her in the early 1870s: "The rumour was that Gertrude had gone bad with a native in the station, and gone away with him afterwards."[59]

George Edwin Archer, aged fifty-seven, followed Grant on the witness stand. He had been police inspector in Lucknow and Unao. After leaving the service, he worked in the nascent ice business of north India. In early depositions given to both the defense and prosecution, Archer had nothing negative to say about Ellen, stating, "I have known Miss Gertrude Donnelly at Cawnpur during the year 1869–70, and during the period of our acquaintance found her to be a respectable and virtuous young lady."[60] He described Ellen as a "nice plump handsome girl." But Archer's later testimony in court contradicted the image of Ellen (and his own) as respectable and virtuous. He claimed, "I on one occasion paid Gertrude Donnelly fifty rupees for the night, but she was not in a fit state to co habit as she was suffering from her monthly course. I supplied her father with many bottles of brandy and Gertrude with many bottles of scent. I gave her the fifty rupees before I found out that she had monthlies. She came in the evening, and I satisfied myself that she was not in a fit state to co-habit." Later he said, "I did not ask for my fifty rupees back. I should be ashamed to."[61]

In the Residency Bazaar courtroom in Hyderabad more witnesses took the stand. Ram Pal Singh, Raja of Rampur Estate, testified regarding Ellen's reputation. Before taking the stand, Singh had corresponded with Yusuf-uz-Zaman, explaining that he had not read the pamphlet itself but had followed the court case in the *Pioneer*. Since the case had been widely covered by the press, he understood that it had already damaged Mehdi and Ellen long before Bosanquet delivered any judgment. "You are quite right to say that they will never be able to make their appearance in society whether the case is for or against them."[62] In a second letter to Yusuf-uz-Zaman, the raja explained that Norton had asked him to go to Lucknow and make a statement, but he had ignored the request. In part, his hesitation came from his and Norton's shared participation in the Congress—Singh did not want to mix his politics with the scandal—but also he felt that taking the witness stand was not in accordance with his rank in society. He stated that, "to run up [to Lucknow] at the telegraphical message to revile the character of a married couple (rightly or wrongly) does not behove [sic] a conscientious man."[63] Yusuf-uz-Zaman responded, "The pamphlet has, no doubt, done its service very truly now. They may hang Mitra or his efigy [sic] but M. H. can never regain the position or raise his head in Society. I wonder with what object he was advised by his friends (?) to institute this case?" He concluded his letter, alluding to Mehdi's own "folly" in the entire matter: "There certainly was a row in 1889 but the matter was hushed up and suppressed and the fire though smothered for a time, was not wholly extinguished. It blazed this time through folly of the man himself."[64]

When Singh appeared in court, he had a vested interest in this case, given that he himself had married an English woman. Ellen had been introduced to him as Mrs. Mehdi Hasan, and Singh testified that he all but mistook her for an Indian, commenting more than once on the quality of her Urdu. "I never surmised that she was a European, her Urdu was so correct," he said, adding "I will swear I did not take her for a European."[65] Singh explained that his politics were squarely in line with the Congress, and that Mehdi's were very much anti-Congress, but that he (Singh) held no animosity toward him.[66]

A final commission of investigation held at Allahabad included two additional witnesses who gave depositions, Thomas and Mary Evans. H. Fraser was the magistrate who presided over their testimony on 5 October. Thomas Evans gave a brief account of his knowledge of the Donnellys. He spent much of his time denying any knowledge about what had happened or the reputations of those involved. He did remember Michael Donnelly, calling him a "respectable man" and having no reason to think that father and daughter were leading "an immoral life."[67] Mary Evans came next. Her testimony added even less than her husband's, only verifying that at one point Ellen had stayed with them.

In mid-November, the case momentarily stalled. The problem was Mitra, who had become ill and failed to attend the court on 14 November. According to India's Criminal Code (Sections 205 and 353), the case could not continue if the defendant was not physically present. In his ruling on that day, Bosanquet wrote, "The Court understands that accused is too ill to attend at the Court house, and therefore as the parties are anxious to proceed with the case, the Judge will sit at any other convenient place to which the accused can be moved."[68] The next day Mitra again did not appear in court. Bosanquet adjourned the proceedings, noting, "The Resident will be addressed with a view to securing the use of Colonel Marshall's bungalow for the Court, as it is understood that the accused can safely [sic] moved there."[69]

It is unclear exactly where the trial continued, but within a few days, the proceedings resumed. Several witnesses who had testified earlier were cross-examined, beginning with Faridoonji, the prime minister's private secretary. He confirmed that Asman Jah participated in a confidential inquiry regarding the couple's marriage, as requested by Durand. Mehdi himself also took the witness stand again. The first questions to him addressed the possibility of an apology and withdrawal of the charges. Mehdi asked that Mitra apologize and then go away from Hyderabad. Mitra refused.

During testimony so far, Ellen had not been physically present in the courtroom. However, from Mehdi's testimony, it is clear that she was actively following the case through the newspapers, which assiduously printed the daily testimony of witnesses. For instance, regarding the timing of Michael Donnelly's death, Mehdi testified, "I said in my examination-in-chief that my father-in-law died before my marriage. When my wife, read the statement, she told me it was wrong." Thus, Ellen read his statement as the newspapers reported it. We also know that by this point, 19 November, Ellen was back in Hyderabad. "Mrs. Mehdi Hasan is here. She came with me on Sunday last," said Mehdi.[70]

Under cross-examination, the defense entered into evidence Ellen's baptismal record. This document recorded her birth as 3 June 1854. This would have made her nineteen at the time of her marriage, not fifteen. If she had been only fifteen at the time of the marriage, as written on the marriage certificate, she could not have led an "immoral life" prior to marriage, the prosecution claimed. The prosecution's logic seems shaky at best: a young woman of fifteen is old enough to be sexually active. When presented with the document, Mehdi answered, "I would be surprised to hear that she was 19 and nearly 20 at the time of the execution of exhibit B (Defence files the certificate of Gertrude Donnelly's birth). Beyond my wife's statement, I can't point to a single source to corroborate the fact that she was 15 in 1873. I swear that I did not intentionally put her age at 15 in 1873, so as to make it impossible that she should have been a prostitute before that date."[71] Mehdi could offer no stronger rebuttal to the presentation of the baptismal record.

Mehdi's final testimony returned to earlier themes in the case. His large withdrawals of cash, he claimed, were needed to pay his lawyers. He testified that while the case was proceeding, Server Jung was interfering with his ability to speak with potential witnesses, as well as interfering in Mehdi's work as the head of the Court of Wards.[72] Frustrated, he explained, "Owing to Sarver Jung, I can't even see my witnesses or any one . . . I know that Sarver Jung is trying to find some fault against me in the Court of Wards."[73] Mehdi denied knowing Lauchlin, and, responding to his deposition, said, "If Mr. Lauchlin swears to certain marks on my wife's person, I will undertake to have her medically examined to contradict him." Mehdi recounted a conversation he supposedly had with Lauchlin, who apparently boasted, "Well, sir, I swear that I know nothing about Miss Gertrude Donnelly, but money makes a person know everything in this world."[74]

For the final stage of the prosecution, Inverarity called for Shujat Ali, Zaki Ali, and Amir Mirza to be re-examined. Their brief testimony simply confirmed aspects of Mehdi and Ellen's life. With this, Inverarity and the prosecution's case rested.

The contours of the case were now established. With Bosanquet presiding as magistrate, and with depositions collected from north India, the prosecution—under Inverarity's command—made the case that Mitra had published the pamphlet and that it was libelous on two fronts: that Mehdi and Ellen were not married, and that Ellen had been a prostitute who was now passed off as a respectable married woman. Arguably, Mehdi's case was off to a weak start. He himself bumbled questions regarding the time of his marriage and the details surrounding the wedding certificate. Outside of the courtroom, Mehdi had all but lost his job, and the couple's finances began to spiral downward. In court, Ellen's age proved problematic for the prosecution. Evidence leaned in favor of her having been older at the time of marriage, not younger as Mehdi claimed. If she had been older, then she would have had time to lead an immoral life before marriage, so argued the defense. Finally, the prosecution's witnesses presented a poor front against charges of perjury, corruption, and inconsistency. As the prosecution rested its case, the defense was preparing a list of witnesses who would testify against Ellen in particular, leveling sexually detailed and graphic charges against her that—true or not—would be impossible to recover from.

6

I HAVE SEEN

THIS LADY BEFORE

On 18 November 1892 the defense in the pamphlet trial took the stage. As magistrate, Bosanquet read aloud the "charge sheet" against Mitra, who pleaded not guilty. Eardley J. Norton now rose to address Bosanquet. He not only outlined his critique of the evidence already presented but laid out his plans for the defense of the printer. He began to unleash a carefully plotted attack on Mehdi, eviscerate Ellen's character and reputation, and impugn the credibility of the prosecution's work. His strategy was to target Ellen while at the same time demolish Mehdi's credibility. The pamphlet accurately described her past—so argued Norton—thus it was for the public good that the truth be confirmed. Truth in the past and truth in the courtroom at times clashed as Norton leveled the charge of perjury against the prosecution witnesses. And, his own star witnesses would deliver graphic details about Ellen's sex life and raise fundamental questions about her morality.

Beyond the details of the case, it is entirely possible that Norton's fervor was driven by personal animus derived from political differences with Mehdi. Not only did the two men disagree over the details of the court case and the politics of Indian nationalism, but both appear as prideful and stubbornly wedded to their own superiority.

Norton had come to India from Britain in 1879 at the age of twenty-seven to practice law, having studied at Merton College, Oxford, and Lincoln's Inn. He practiced law at the High Court in Madras and became involved with the Indian National Congress, established in 1885. He participated in the 1887 annual meeting of the Congress held at Madras. Owing to his outspoken support of Indian nationalism, Congress leaders asked Norton to join the committee that drafted its constitution. Norton was also instrumental in helping create a British-based wing of the Congress. In 1889 he visited Britain to attend the inaugural meeting, although it unclear whether his time in London overlapped with Mehdi's stay there.[1] Like Mehdi, Norton expressed his opinions through the newspapers. Neither Norton's pro-Congress sentiments nor Mehdi's criticism of the Congress ever surfaced in court. It seemed the court case was an unspoken proxy for the future of Indian nationalism.

Norton's opening address was a masterful piece of legal prose: eloquent, wide-ranging, and wickedly devastating. Like Inverarity, he began by stepping back from the minutiae of the case and looking at the two broadest charges brought by the prosecution: that Mitra had published the pamphlet and that what it said was untrue. From the outset, Norton claimed that the contents of the pamphlet *were* true and thus not defamatory. He first argued that the truth needed to be made public. It was for the "public good" and "public benefit" that the very private nature of Ellen's life be revealed. Norton added, "I shall go further and plead that the statements in this pamphlet, by whoever they were made, were made in good faith, within the pleaded exceptions of the Penal Code and for the good of society at large."[2] Second, Norton addressed the idea of publication. He argued that Mitra had not in fact published the pamphlet, saying, "there is no evidence of the publication of this pamphlet—and I am speaking within the facts—to any living person except to Nawab Mehdi Hasan

Eardley John Norton

himself."[3] Norton took a technical view of publication whereby printed matter needed to be distributed to constitute publication, and since only Mehdi had testified to having received the pamphlet, that could not be called "publication." It involved printing, yes, but not publication. Norton also assailed the couple's character. He said that Mehdi "is not a man who has any right to complain, because he has no character himself. He has no character to lose, and Gertrude Donnelly has less."[4]

In addition to the issues of the pamphlet's truth and publication, another line of attack employed by the defense was to charge prosecution witnesses with perjury—none more so than Mehdi. Norton outlined no fewer than thirteen points on which Mehdi had perjured himself: the timing of Michael Donnelly's death; the date on which he and Ellen signed their marriage contract; the destruction of the photographic negative held by Asgar Jan; the accounting of 6,000 rupees supposedly used for legal expenses; the claim that the transaction of that 6,000 rupees was legal; the assertion in previous correspondence with the prime minister regarding the status of his marriage; the statement regarding Ellen's age at the time of their marriage; professed ignorance concerning the Durand inquiry into Mehdi's marriage; the suggestion that he never heard rumors about his own marriage; ignorance about the government inquiry; the statement that he never received a letter from Yusuf-uz-Zaman; professed ignorance of Colonel Ludlow's service in the case, and, finally, Mehdi's claim that Server Jung forbade the Nizam's government officials from speaking with him.[5] Norton argued that Server Jung had every right to be involved in the case, since Mehdi had named him as the quasi-defendant, and suggested that Server Jung was trying to avoid being prosecuted himself by aiding in Mitra's defense.

Norton then turned his attack to Mehdi's background and his claim to have been able to support Ellen before their marriage. As to Mehdi's assertion that he was the son of a *zamindar*, Norton scoffed,

"Any one can be a Zemindar in Lucknow, and the less Mr. Mehdi Hasan says about his being the son of one of those gentlemen the better for himself."[6] Many individuals held this title, which did not necessarily denote affluence. Norton suggested that Mehdi did not have the means either to marry or to support Ellen for any length of time before they claim to have been married, contradicting Mehdi's statement that he had provided Ellen with a month of housing, food, and amenities before the marriage. Norton chastised Mehdi for going on a hunting trip just days after the pamphlet was released, questioning his loyalties at a moment of crisis. "Instead of proving his character is good, instead of staying at home and trying to find out whether his wife is his wife, instead of trying to hunt down his two-footed maligner, Mehdi Hasan is a man who prefers to go out on a shooting tour to shoot four-footed game."[7]

Norton asked why, if Ellen had adopted Islam and was a woman of good character, did none of Mehdi's family attend the wedding, especially his mother. He asked why Mehdi did not call his mother to testify at the Barabanki Commission. Rudra, a lawyer for the prosecution, challenged Norton on this line of inquiry. Norton, knowing that Rudra objected for a specific reason, laid a verbal trap. He said Mehdi "had a mother and one of the witnesses of the Barabanki commission said she was too old and ill to appear as a witness." To which Rudra replied, "She has since died." Norton sprung his trap: "Then I congratulate her on her happy release from such a son."[8] Norton pointed out that no witness had testified to Ellen's acceptance into Muslim households. Mehdi had claimed that she remained in *purdah* after their marriage, and did not socialize much outside of their home. Norton suggested such a claim was ridiculous, as relations between Indians and Europeans had actually been better at the time of their supposed marriage than they were at present. He paused, acidly remarking that in his testimony, "Mehdi Hasan appears to have been pushed forward by circumstances from lie to lie and not to have had time to draw breath amid the waves in the ocean of his perjury."[9] For Ellen, after the initial "hot flush of Mahommedanism" had faded, as Norton described it, she returned to visiting Christian places of worship, and then began her intimacies with Salar Jung II.

Norton now shifted away from Mehdi's status as the son of a *zamindar* and his role in Ellen's keeping *purdah* to his more recent alleged role in witness tampering. He argued that, beyond perjuring himself, Mehdi was guilty of bribing witnesses: some he bribed to testify in support of his own position; others, planning to testify for the defense, might have been encouraged by Mehdi and his "bags of money" to change their testimony in Mehdi's favor. Statements like this were peppered throughout Norton's remarks. "I charge him [Mehdi] upon the evidence that he did bribe Asgar Jan and that through Ali Abbas, a pleader in Lucknow."[10] This particular charge was especially damaging, since Ali Abbas was a member of the Lucknow legal milieu, so such an accusation would undoubtedly hurt his reputation. Norton questioned Asgar Jan's testimony about the negatives he had or did not have of Ellen: When were they first created, and how old was she in the images? Asgar Jan was caught in a difficult position, according to Norton: "He was anxious to help Sarver Jung, but could not resist the continued application of money by Mehdi Hasan."[11]

Norton returned to Mehdi's finances and the large checks he wrote after the trial had started. Norton alleged that most, if not all, of that money went toward bribing witnesses. He declared that Mehdi tampered with or destroyed the original checks so a direct match with their receipts could not be established. Yet Norton did not deny that his own defense team had also paid money to witnesses. Here, he cleverly avoided implicating himself in any wrongdoing. "I admit that we did pay money to these witnesses, but mark the difference: we paid the money and did not use the statements, whilst Mehdi Hasan used the statements and did not pay the money." He continued, listing the witnesses Mehdi had bribed: Dominic Braganza, Joanna Rostan, and George Archer, of whom Norton said, "I think of all the specimens of human biped I have ever had the misfortune to encounter, he is one [of] the very worst and most discreditable." He also listed those Mehdi had attempted to bribe: James Lauchlin, who held out to testify for the defense; Richard Grant; Fanthom (a minor character who worked at the Lucknow post office); and Pundit Ratannath.[12]

Norton meticulously dissected Ellen and Mehdi's marriage document. He began by claiming that the document, and thus the marriage, was a fraud. Norton charged that Mehdi had created the document in the current year, 1892, as part of his evidence for the case, rather than presenting an actual record from the time of the alleged marriage in 1872. Norton first pondered why Mehdi had provided no "reasonable excuse" for the absence of his relatives at the ceremony. He argued that if Ellen were a woman of sound moral character, as Mehdi claimed, then his family would have had no aversion to attending the wedding. Norton suggested that not only was Ellen of poor moral character, but the wedding itself never occurred.[13] He then focused on the five supposed witnesses to the wedding: Himayat Ali, Shujat Ali, Mirza Mehdi, Mahomed Husain, and Fazl-ul-lah. One by one Norton demolished the credibility of the signatories. Only Shujat Ali and Himayat Ali were physically present at the wedding; the other three individuals signed the document hours or days later. By the time of the trial, Himayat Ali was dead. Norton did not contest that it was Shujat Ali's signature on the marriage document but discredited him for his statements regarding the other signatories, especially the deceased Himayat Ali. Mirza Mehdi refused to give evidence in the trial based on his poor health (corroborated by a doctor). Norton demonstrated that Mahomed Husain's testimony contradicted itself: Husain said, on the one hand, that he had signed the marriage document a short time after the event itself, and on the other, that Mehdi had never even told him about the wedding. Norton suggested such contradictions could not come from a reliable witness. Further, he proposed that the confusion stemmed from the recent creation of the entire document, and thus Husain had struggled to concoct a reliable lie about the past. Fazl-ul-lah's testimony Norton discredited for his inconsistencies and poor memory.

Norton addressed the absence of Mehdi's mother at the wedding. Fazl-ul-lah, who had signed the marriage document, was also a doctor and had testified earlier to having examined Mrs. Hasan and found her to be very sick. Norton mocked, "All that this gentleman could tell us of old Mrs. Mehdi Hasan was that he had felt her stomach through a *purdah*. They put forward this witness to say the old lady could not come into court. I asked him if he had seen her, and he replied, 'I have seen her stomach.' Why, how could he know her stomach? Any stomach might have been behind that *purdah*. The identity of that portion of her person is wanting."[14]

Norton next spoke to the inquiries made concerning Mehdi and Ellen's marriage at the time of their presentation to Queen Victoria. He asserted that, when Durand had asked Asman Jah to find out if the rumors were true, the prime minister and his personal secretary, Major Gough, participated, willingly or not, in a conspiracy to hide the fact that the couple were not married. Norton supported his claim by saying, "But did Sir Asman Jah make enquiries as they ought to have been made, from the persons most competent to give evidence, namely Mehdi Hasan and his so-called wife? No."[15]

By the late nineteenth century, new interest in the scientific analysis of evidence reached even into the courtroom in Hyderabad, where Norton—with forensic flourish—honed in on such details as the marriage document's ink and paper. Before the trial began, Mehdi had gone to the Residency and shown Plowden a printed copy of his wedding document. Norton focused on the fact that Mehdi did not show him the original. He charged that Mehdi either did not have the original or was in the process of creating it at that time. He then alluded to the ink of the signatures in the original wedding document Mehdi produced, noting that Ellen's signature was in a different ink: "Hers is signed with darker, richer, thicker ink, with Kashmir ink."[16] Ellen had been in Kashmir shortly before the trial began. Norton pressed his case by arguing that, after she added her signature to the document in Kashmir, the others followed suit in Lucknow and Hyderabad. In Mehdi's own testimony, Norton pointed out, he had stated both that he came to the wedding ceremony with the document drawn up, and that the events of the ceremony were transferred afterward to paper. Norton pilloried Mehdi over the conflicting statements: "I say he has perjured himself in his alternative statement that the document was signed after the corrections were made, and that he brought the document ready signed to the ceremony, before the corrections were made."[17] He concluded his attack on the marriage document by asserting that Mehdi had intentionally entered the wrong birthdates for himself and Ellen. The prosecution, Norton asserted, wanted the court to believe that the later date of birth would have made it impossible for her to have been sexually active with a variety of men, let alone "have been kept by Yusuf-uz-zaman, or have had intercourse with Rufi-ud-deen, or have been the mistress of Syed Husain Belgrami, or have submitted herself to practically all comers."[18]

In his testimony, Shujat Ali had suggested that Mehdi and Ellen had used a wedding document because Ellen feared Mehdi would take a second wife. Norton noted that there was no legal precedent for any form of contract that would bind Mehdi to Ellen alone. In a theatrical way, Norton wondered aloud about Mehdi's decision making. He wondered why Mehdi had not clarified in his own mind the order of events regarding his marriage and the signatures on the marriage document, he wondered why Mehdi would launch a court case without having been clear in his own mind the order of events that had transpired, and he wondered about the folly of Mehdi's decision to go to court based on an event—the marriage—that had never happened, a fact which Norton believed Mehdi knew as well.

Norton also questioned Mehdi's wisdom in filing the case when the outcome could jeopardize his pension. Norton said, "But I say it is impossible to reconcile those two statements, for he must—before he launched himself upon a case of this sort, involving issues of life and death—for it possibly involves his retention in the British Service and his pension—have given some attention and consideration to the facts he had to prove, and have endeavoured to make his mind clear."[19] The question of Mehdi's pension would come to have far-reaching implications for the couple.

Norton laid out the testimony James Lauchlin—who claimed to have been engaged to Ellen—would give as a star witness for the defense. Among the several charges Lauchlin would bring, by far the most shocking was that of incest. Norton prepared the court for what was to come: "He will tell you as a matter of fact that after he had actually arranged to marry her, improper intercourse had taken place between them, and also prove this, the most fatal charge against this woman's character, that the reason why Lauchlin broke off the engagement was, that he actually found her on incestuous terms with her own father." Gasps and tittering must have swept through the courtroom as Norton unveiled this bombshell. Knowing what he said was at the edge of propriety, he continued, "That is an extraordinary and terrible statement to make, if it were uncorroborated, but it is corroborated by the statement made on oath of Mrs. Gill."[20] In her earlier testimony, Mary Gill had first raised the possibility of incest as well as an improper burial for Ellen's mother. Norton added, "there was a fear that the unfortunate woman had been buried alive."[21]

Norton turned to the Durand inquiry of 1889, which had investigated unsavory rumors in London about Ellen. Mehdi denied any knowledge of the inquiry, but Norton argued that he was lying.

Norton suggested that Asman Jah had perhaps mismanaged the affair. "The Minister stands in an awkward dilemma. He either consciously abstained from tapping the only true source of information, in which event he is guilty of grave neglect of duty. Or, he let himself be manipulated by a set of interested practitioners, without checking what they did, in which event his Ministerial fitness for offices becomes questionable."[22] Having cast aspersions on the prime minister's office, Norton had another prominent figure of Hyderabad to castigate: Seymour Keay, a close ally of Mehdi. Norton charged Keay with being eager to find ways to influence the case and argued that Mehdi had fed him information during the Lucknow commission.

> He did so with the object that Seymour Keay should endeavour to gag the proceedings by terrifying if he could the Resident, the Nizam, and yourself. I shall be able to prove that Seymour Keay has endeavoured to influence people in this case and I publicly charge him with a gross abuse of his position as a member of Parliament in his efforts to stifle justice. I will say nothing more about Mr. Seymour Keay in this case, but I give him timely warning that if he goes on like this, he will burn his fingers and burn them badly.[23]

Norton now shifted his approach, charging Mehdi with prostituting Ellen to the young Salar Jung II. He drew on written evidence between Mehdi and Salar Jung II in which the former invited the latter to his home. Norton provocatively suggested that this was an invitation for intimacy, Mehdi inviting Salar Jung II "not with the sober excitement of a cup of tea but with the bribery of Gertrude's voluptuousness."[24] Norton read descriptions of the "arrangements" Mehdi had made for Salar Jung II, paying special attention to the arrangement of the rooms and bedrooms to insinuate that the visit was not for tea but for sex. In his conclusion, Norton stated, "I think,

Sir, we may believe that if a woman of bad character is seen to enter with a male companion a stable and to close the door, I think we may safely conclude that they have not gone there for the purpose of saying their prayers."[25] Norton then ended his opening address to the court, ushering in the next phase of the trial.

Both the prosecution and defense called a variety of people—some were well known, while others appear and disappear into obscurity. Broadening our focus, we can see that, overall, the defense witnesses included several well-known and respected members of Hyderabad society, whereas the prosecution called upon more individuals not known in Hyderabad, many seemingly plucked from the streets.

For the defense, Syed Mahomed Akbar Khan, superintendent of His Highness the Nizam's Police, began the testimony. Khan testified to Rafi-ud-din and Yusuf-uz-Zaman's life in Lucknow, where he had known both men. According to Khan, they were "fast boys" with money to burn. On his second day of testimony (30 November) he was describing the ways in which Rafi-ud-din and Yusuf-uz-Zaman would frequent the Donnelly home, when, suddenly, he was momentarily interrupted by the arrival of the most anticipated member of the pamphlet scandal.

For the first time through the courtroom doors entered Mrs. Ellen Gertrude Michel Mehdi Hasan. Undoubtedly a round of shuffling and whispers broke out as people turned to see the woman at the heart of the pamphlet case. In the printed and published court transcript, the event is noted rather prosaically: "Mrs. Mehdi Hasan enters the court.* (*Counsel for prosecution asks the Court to note that Mrs. Mehdi Hasan entered the Court alone to be identified, and that the three witnesses Mohamed Akbar Khan, James Lauchlin, and Atta Hasain were all in the Court at the same time when they identified her.)"[26] As Ellen took her seat she must have felt the eyes of the entire courtroom on her. She would have her day as a witness, but for the moment she had to withstand a parade of witnesses for the defense who would reveal the shocking and graphic details leveled against her.

At the end of November, James Lauchlin took the stand.[27] Because he was the onetime fiancé of Ellen, his testimony carried with it the scent of credibility. From 1857 to 1858, Lauchlin had served in the army as a volunteer at the rank of private. He had been a professional wrestler, training for several years at Mathura and Baroda (under the sponsorship of the Maharajah Khande Rao) before coming back to Lucknow and Kanpur. He spent some time as a horse dealer, where he had first met Joanna Rostan, and then worked as a church clerk. Norton had introduced Lauchlin in his opening statement, but Lauchlin had prepared his own: "I have seen this lady before. I saw her first in the Memorial Gardens at Cawnpore in 1869. I knew her then as Gertrude Donnelly. In 1869 I was engaged to marry her as such." Wasting no time, Lauchlin described details of their sex life. Recounting his first time with Ellen, he said, "She was quite a willing victim, and I had no difficulty with her; there were no struggles; she pulled me in herself. I was the victim. This happened in her own bedroom." He continued, "It was she seduced me" and "I had connection with her so often that I can't remember the number of times."[28]

Lauchlin related the final days of Mrs. Donnelly's life. This narrative was critical for the defense in discrediting Ellen before she ever took the stand. Lauchlin's testimony included a description of Mrs. Donnelly as "Eurasian"—a suggestion that she had Indian blood in her veins.[29] Moving to the events surrounding Mrs. Donnelly's last days, Lauchlin claimed he and Ellen had had a fight when she accused him of being "no man." Offered in the heat of an argument, this comment could have referred to Lauchlin's character and norms of manliness, or to his lack of sexual prowess. While Ellen complained to her mother, Lauchlin, feeling snubbed, went to nearby Kanpur.[30] The concerned Mrs. Donnelly followed her prospective son-in-law and met him at the Telegraph Office in Kanpur. Lauchlin returned to Lucknow that same evening, but Mrs. Donnelly, now not feeling well, remained behind. Two or three days later, the telegraph operator, a man named Thomas D'Souza, sent two telegrams to Lucknow. The first stated that Mrs. Donnelly was very ill, and the second, a few hours later, reported that she had died at 9 A.M. and was to be buried later that same day. Mrs. Donnelly's death now brought Ellen, her father, and Lauchlin all to Kanpur. According to Lauchlin, he, Ellen, and her father arrived at the telegraph office at dusk of the same day. A sudden widower, Michael Donnelly, perhaps emotionally spent and already beginning to drink, stayed at the office where his wife had died. Lauchlin and Ellen set off for the graveyard. She wanted to visit the grave, and, upon seeing that it was not yet fully covered, she wanted to see her mother's face one last time. Lauchlin testified, "Gertrude was set upon seeing her mother's face. The coolies were still only filling in the grave; we stopped them and pulled the coffin up, unscrewed it and showed her mother's face to Gertrude; when the coffin was opened Gertrude stooped to kiss her mother, but started back at seeing that her mother's tongue was hanging out."[31]

Lauchlin described how the rest of the evening unfolded. "Donnelly was drunk when we got back. Gertrude went to her father. I subsequently found Gertrude and her father together that night. They were in the very act of adultery. That was the termination of our engagement, as I determined not to marry her after that."[32] Ellen and her father had decided to spend the night in the guest room of the telegraph office. Lauchlin described exactly what he witnessed: "The Donnellys were lying facing me. They were uncovered, but she had her *chemise* on, and he had his pants on and shirt. They were on top of the bed."[33] This description seems far from an "act of adultery." Ellen and her father, who had been drinking, were mostly clothed and lying on top of the bed as the weather was hot. Perhaps they were less dressed to keep cool and Ellen went to her father to console him, or the Donnelly family had a less stringent view of attire within the family.

Yet despite his seeming revulsion at the sight of Ellen and her father, Lauchlin acknowledged that he continued to visit Ellen for sex. But he did not tell her the marriage was off. In secret, he had become engaged to another woman named Rebecca Orman. Ellen knew nothing of this and allegedly continued to welcome Lauchlin into her bed. When she discovered his new plans and new fiancée, she was understandably distraught. Lauchlin had intentionally told Ellen the wrong time of day for his wedding so that she would not appear and cause a sensation. The trick failed, and Ellen showed up on Lauchlin and Orman's wedding day. Lauchlin stated, "Gertrude Donnelly went to the clergyman who married us, a Mr. Ellis, and said I had committed bigamy, and Mr. Ellis came to the Ormans and taxed me with it."[34] Rebecca Orman seems to have not known anything about Ellen, or Lauchlin's connection to her, until after she had married him. Lauchlin stated during testimony that he and his wife were living apart, and he blamed Ellen for ruining his marriage.

Months earlier, in his opening testimony, Mehdi had recounted an exchange with Lauchlin that might have compromised his testimony. Now, on the stand, Lauchlin had the opportunity to refute Mehdi's account. "I did not tell Mehdi Hasan that 'I knew nothing about Gertrude Donnelly,' nor did I say 'money makes a person know everything in this world.'"[35] Having raised the possibility of incest, Lauchlin portrayed Ellen as sexually aggressive, described himself as a ruined man, and suggested that Mehdi perjured himself. Then James Lauchlin stepped down from the witness box.

Perhaps the second most important witness for the defense was Yusuf-uz-Zaman. His testimony was critical because he was mentioned in the pamphlet itself and had corresponded with both the prosecution and defense; now he was about to further portray Ellen as a woman of poor moral character. Zaman's testimony also sheds light on how ordinary Indians and Europeans met, mingled, and sometimes formed close relationships outside the purview of elite circles of government or royalty. When he took the witness stand, he was forty-three years old and both a *zamindar* at Banda and an honorary magistrate. In his youth, he had attended Canning College and the Wards' Institute along with Mehdi.

In his opening statement, Yusuf-uz-Zaman testified that he knew Ellen and her family in 1872. He stated, "During that period I had sexual intercourse with Gertrude, both at her own house and at my own house."[36] Yusuf-uz-Zaman said that he paid her—and paid her often—in amounts of ten, twenty, or thirty rupees, adding up to between 200 and 300 rupees. He explained that the money was intended as a present, not directly as an exchange for sex. "I gave her money as presents. Sometimes she asked for money, and sometimes I gave it her myself. I paid her because I cared for her. She used to ask me for money, if I did not pay her. I paid her on the quiet; no one saw me pay her."[37] Zaman's testimony clearly complicates understandings of prostitution or concubinage. No clear one-to-one relationship between money and sex existed in his claimed relationship with Ellen. Although the money was given around the time of sex, it was not so clearly linked to the act, and, as Zaman testified, he considered the money a "gift" rather than a transactional payment.

Zaman described where the Donnellys lived and how he came to know Ellen. Mutual friends introduced him to the family, but by the third visit, his relationship with Ellen had become physical. In that first intimate encounter, Zaman went to the Donnelly home in the evening. A servant met him at the door and told him to go upstairs to the roof, where Ellen was waiting. The roof had a small edge around it, enough to shield it from the road. It was the beginning of the month, so Zaman and Ellen had only a sliver of moonlight to see by. She arranged a carpet for them to sit on. He narrated what happened next:

> The events of that night are impressed on my mind: it was the first time that I had had intercourse with a European girl. I first asked if she would have a drink . . . The bottle I took was brandy, and I took it as I knew European ladies drank. I had not met any European ladies before, and I had not seen European ladies drink before that. I stopped on the roof for the whole of that visit, and I did my work very quietly.[38]

Zaman testified that he and Ellen followed a similar pattern of rooftop trysts no fewer than fourteen times. Adding to his boast of virility and machismo, Zaman stated that he also frequented prostitutes in and around Lucknow, describing himself as "rendibaz," one who frequents prostitutes.[39]

Before the case began and during its proceedings, Zaman had corresponded with both the prosecution and defense—Mehdi on one side and Server Jung on the other—and in open court, he made clear his sentiments. "I am not interested in Mitra, and I don't care what happens to him. I am certainly interested in Server Jung, and so far as Server Jung is affected, I would sooner see Mehdi Hasan lose this case than win it."[40] Thus, Mehdi's earlier correspondence with Zaman and attempts to influence him were all for naught.[41] The defense juggernaut was rolling; it had testimony from members of both the European and Indian community concerning Ellen's sexual liaisons.

In addition to Yusuf-uz-Zaman, other witnesses for the defense made the journey from Lucknow to Hyderabad. Among them was Thomas D'Souza. D'Souza was forty-nine years old and described as "Eurasian." He was also the telegraph operator present on the night Mrs. Donnelly died. Complicating his presence at the trial was the fact that D'Souza had married Lauchlin's sister Olivia in 1866. D'Souza confirmed much of Lauchlin's testimony as to the events of mid-June 1869, when both Donnelly parents, Ellen, and Lauchlin had been in Kanpur.

The telegraph office and its employees were a vital part of British rule in India. They staffed their stations twenty-four hours a day in order to accommodate communication from across India and around the world. Telegraph operators usually had some living accommodation at or near their office, and Kanpur was no different. D'Souza had tried to make the best of a difficult situation when the Donnellys visited, arranging two beds for Ellen and her father to use the night of the funeral. D'Souza added one further detail about the Donnellys' visit at Kanpur. The morning after, his servant had complained to D'Souza's wife that she was unable to clean the bedroom. "My wife said that the sweeper woman on entering the Donnelly's bed room found Mr. Donnelly uncovered (langta) and she therefore could not sweep the room."[42] One can imagine the senior Donnelly, prone to drink and stricken with grief over the loss of his wife. Having had too much the evening before, he passed out, naked, on the floor. Although this vignette did nothing to confirm or refute the charges swirling around the case, it contributed to an overall sense that the Donnelly family was coming undone.

Like nearly all the witnesses, D'Souza followed the case in the newspapers. He testified, "I have been aware of the proceedings of this Court from the public papers since about October last."[43] He had read of the case in the *Deccan Budget*. "Before being called as a witness here, I knew that Lauchlin was going to be called for the defence. I read his evidence in the paper."[44] To what extent D'Souza or any of the witnesses in the pamphlet case changed their testimony to conform to or contradict what they read in the papers is impossible to say. At the very least, it is clear that the court proceedings, the newspapers, the witnesses, and the general public were all engaged in conversation with each other—suggesting ways in which justice, even British justice, was far from bound by the courthouse walls.

The pamphlet case in Hyderabad reached the highest echelons of power in the Government of India as well as the British government in London. Two men, the viceroy of India, Lord Lansdowne, in Calcutta, and his immediate superior, secretary of state for India, Lord Kimberley, in London, exchanged secret correspondence regarding the case. Although the personal fate of Mehdi was of little concern to them, they did discuss how the pamphlet case concerned the Nizam, how British citizens were involved, and what the future of India's premier princely state might be.

For the moment, their central concern was Seymour Keay, an active member of Parliament named in the trial proceedings. Lansdowne wrote to Kimberley, "Matters are made worse by the interference of English adventurers of the Seymour Keay type. That worthy is now in Hyderabad taking up the cudgels for his ally, Mehdi Hassan, whose name is familiar to you, and who is now figuring prominently in an unsavoury *cause celebrè*. It is universally believed here that Keay has made very large sums of money out of the State."[45] Writing from London, Kimberley was in a weaker position to assess the state of affairs in Hyderabad. However, he shared Lansdowne's concern over the role of "adventurers," both Indian and British:

> I read your speech at the Nizam's banquet with much interest. I have been told that the abuses of his Government arise largely from his being in the hands of corrupt and intriguing foreigners (I mean men not his own subjects), and that it would be much to his advantage if he had more of his own people in his service.

Whether there is any truth in this, I have of course not the means of knowing.[46]

Lansdowne wrote back, outlining his sympathy with affairs in Hyderabad but recognizing the limits of colonial power, unless the Government of India increased its "interference" much more than it had previously done. "You are quite right in believing that Hyderabad suffers greatly from the presence of 'corrupt and intriguing foreigners,' and I am sorry to say that some of them are fellow-countrymen of our own; but it is very difficult to deal with such people unless we interfere to a much greater extent in the domestic affairs of the State than we have hitherto been in the habit of doing."[47] Where interference in the princely states had once been a policy of the East India Company, especially in the years before 1857, a more measured response now came from the two highest officials of British policy in India.

In court, attention shifted to early police investigations regarding the pamphlet. On its release, Asman Jah had asked Colonel E. S. Ludlow, inspector general of police in the Nizam's government, to investigate its veracity. He sent telegrams from Hyderabad to the district superintendent of police at Lucknow asking about the existence of the pamphlet's supposed author, Mirza Bakir Husain in Aminabad.[48] Ludlow now took the witness stand. He said, "I understood my instructions to be to find out the author and publisher of the pamphlet. It necessarily formed part of the enquiry which I had to undertake, to make enquiries as to facts mentioned in the pamphlet, so as to help me in discovering the author by perhaps giving me a clue."[49] Working under Ludlow was a man named Stevenson. Mehdi testified that he had not been in contact with Ludlow, Stevenson, or another policeman named Hugh Gough. In response to Mehdi's testimony,

Ludlow was categorical: "Mehdi Hasan's statement of 31st August 1892, that 'before Colonel Ludlow sailed for England, I did not place myself in communication with him or he with me,' is not true." He further referenced a letter he received from Mehdi on 12 April, shortly after the pamphlet was distributed.[50]

Next to testify was Rafi-ud-din. Of the names mentioned in the pamphlet, Yusuf-uz-Zaman and Rafi-ud-din were supposedly at the center of the "joint-stock company" created to keep Ellen in their possession. In his youth, Rafi-ud-din had attended Canning College with Yusuf-uz-Zaman, Mehdi, and Server Jung. At the time, the college principal wrote of Rafi-ud-din, "His success at these examinations will show that he is by no means deficient in natural ability. He has displayed, however, during the past year, while studying for his BA degree, a want of steadiness and perseverance in carrying on studies that are in any way distasteful to him."[51] Now he was a crucial witness in the trial. He introduced himself as the son of Mirza Afsur Beg, and as clerk at the Session Court, Raebareli. He described himself: "I am an Urdu poet, and one of my favourite themes is adversity."[52] Early in his time in Hyderabad he had served as tutor to the sons of Salar Jung I and, later, as an assistant tutor to Nizam Mahbub Ali Khan. Rafi-ud-din was also first cousin to Server Jung, who had twice found employment for his relative.

Rafi-ud-din corroborated the pamphlet's claim that he had had sex with Ellen. Years earlier in Lucknow, he said, he met Ellen when she visited the home of his uncle, Mirza Abbas Beg. In his introductory testimony, Rafi-ud-din said that he introduced Yusuf-uz-Zaman to Ellen after having sex with her. He stated, "I knew Yusuf-uz-Zaman at the Canning College. I introduced him to Gertrude myself. At that time I often had sexual intercourse with Gertrude Donnelly. When I first knew Gertrude in 1869–70, she seemed to me to be about 16 years old. During these visits of mine to Gertrude I fell rather in love with her."[53] Ellen's baptismal record is in accordance with Rafi-ud-din's estimate of her age. Rafi-ud-din testified that he first began having sex with Ellen in early 1872. The relationship lasted six or seven months and then faded later in the year. He noted that Ellen's servants told him she was a "common prostitute."[54] In subsequent testimony, Rafi-ud-din somewhat contradicted himself when he stated, "I did not fall in love with Gertrude, but I liked her and she me. The sexual intercourse was the result of mutual liking."[55] According to Rafi-ud-din, after her relationship with him ended, Ellen took up with Yusuf-uz-Zaman, and after him, she went to Hyder Hussain (Mehdi's relation, mentioned earlier by Server Jung), and then finally to Mehdi himself.

Rafi-ud-din ended his "connection" with Ellen in part because he found her with Yusuf-uz-Zaman. This alone might have strained or broken their mutual relationships, but it was even worse that he found her at Yusuf-uz-Zaman's home; going to a client's home rather than meeting elsewhere was an intimacy usually bestowed by local prostitutes. Further aggravating the situation, she was in "native dress." Rafi-ud-din explained, "In taxing Gertrude I told her I would not have thought her so bad as to come to Yusufuzaman's [sic] house in native dress like a common prostitute."[56] When asked how he knew that Ellen's dress was like a prostitute and not a respectable woman, he described typical Lucknow dress and bragged, "I knew the prostitute's dress well in those days from personal experience."[57]

Rafi-ud-din testified that, in subsequent years, he and Lucy Donnelly had also been having sex. He explained that his time with Lucy was in exchange for money, perhaps distinguishing his feelings and relationship between the two sisters: with Ellen, it was affection and attraction; with Lucy, it was sex for cash. He admitted in further testimony to having visited with other women of European descent for sex. In addition to the Donnellys, the Gillmans and the Howes lived in Lucknow in the early 1870s. Rafi-ud-din testified, "I did not visit the Gillmans for the purpose of making love to Ellen Gillman. I might have visited there for that purpose. I think I did make love to Miss

Howe, but not to Miss Gillman. I don't remember Miss Howe's Christian name. I did not succeed in my suit with her."[58]

Rafi-ud-din returned to a previous element of the story. He testified that the city superintendent in Lucknow asked Ellen and Lucy to take out licenses as prostitutes. He claimed that Mehdi had wanted the girls "to play a game of hide and seek so as to save them."[59] Finally, Rafi-ud-din claimed that the Lucknow city magistrate, Captain Noble, had given Ellen and Lucy twenty-four hours to leave the city, which they did, going to Meerut. This revelation—if true—would mean that there might have been a paper trail kept by the Lucknow authorities concerning the Donnelly girls' behavior. Thus, rather than relying on the testimony of witnesses who had their own motivations, let alone possible bribes, the police records would reveal details of the past. However, no such records ever surfaced. Possibly the warnings of the city officials were made orally, leaving no written record, or they were not made at all. Rafi-ud-din later testified that Mehdi helped protect the Donnelly sisters from the police, and Amir Mirza ultimately "watched out and saved" Ellen from needing to register as a prostitute. According to Rafi-ud-din, Amir Mirza also had a sexual relationship with Ellen.

Since Rafi-ud-din's name appeared in the pamphlet itself, he—like Yusuf-uz-Zaman before him—testified to its accuracy. He said, "When I read the pamphlet it struck me as being partly right and partly wrong about myself." The two areas in which he felt the pamphlet was wrong were the creation of the joint-stock company to keep Ellen and the claim that the keepers' adoration had ceased. Otherwise, for Rafi-ud-din, the rest of the pamphlet was correct.[60]

Near the end of his testimony, Rafi-ud-din revealed two further allegations. Throughout the case, questions swirled over photographs of Ellen and her sister. Did she pose in local dress? Did she pose like a prostitute? Did she pose with her sister? Were the sisters nude or partially nude? When might have any of this have occurred in relation to their marriages? Rafi-ud-din answered one of those questions when he said, "I have seen a naked photo of Gertrude Donnelly." Up to this point, questions had revolved around the ambiguous meanings of a photo showing Ellen's left breast covered only by her *choli*, and whether this was akin to the way prostitutes posed. No one, however, had mentioned they had seen a photograph of Ellen nude. Although this might have been a surprising revelation, neither Norton nor Inverarity pursued it. Perhaps both sides realized that, once the words were spoken, the newspapers would propel them far into the public sphere. For the defense this would further undermine Ellen, and for the prosecution, no sooner had the words left Rafi-ud-din's lips than the damage had been done. Yet this was not all; in almost the same breath, Rafi-ud-din made another shocking revelation. He had earlier testified that he believed Mehdi and Ellen did not have a sexual relationship. "The reasons why I said that I believed Mehdi Hasan did not have intercourse with Gertrude, though his mistress, are that I believe Mehdi Hasan to be impotent. This was always his reputation at school."[61] Again, he appears not to have been questioned further about this revelation—having asserted it was damaging enough. With that, Rafi-ud-din stepped down and the court adjourned for the winter holidays.

The trail resumed on 3 January 1893 with a *munsif,* Mohamed Ali-ud din Hassan, taking the stand. Ali-ud din Hassan served at Paithan, a small town south of Aurangabad. Part of his role in the events leading up to the trial was to be Mehdi's messenger. Mehdi sent Ali-ud din to see Yusuf-uz-Zaman and obtain information and letters from him regarding his knowledge of the pamphlet's contents. For instance, Ali-ud din was able to convince Yusuf-uz-Zaman to write that he did not know Mehdi's wife, but he did know Ellen Donnelly. When asked about Mehdi's wife, Yusuf-uz-Zaman could honestly reply that he did not know her. Ali-ud din testified to telling Yusuf-uz-Zaman things such as, "I told him to write in such a way as not to be called as a witness."[62]

While Ali-ud din was travelling on Mehdi's behalf, another individual, Mirza Sajid Beg, also went to Lucknow to do the bidding of his older brother, Server Jung. His purpose was to collect photographs of Ellen from Asgar Jan. Sajid Beg had extensive meetings with Asgar Jan, trying to acquire photographs and other materials to aid in Mitra's defense. According to Sajid Beg, Asgar Jan was not immediately willing to come forward with materials or to testify in the pamphlet case. Sajid Beg warned him "that if he did not speak the truth he would be sent to the Andaman Islands [a British penal colony]."[63] Sajid Beg heard about other possible photos of Ellen, one apparently hanging in the room of a Lucknow prostitute named Hyder Jan. However, he did not pursue the lead, preferring to obtain photos from Asgar Jan directly.[64]

Sajid Beg also informally interviewed a variety of people in Lucknow, all of whom apparently spoke ill of Ellen. The list of individuals included various Lucknow elites, such as Choudri Mahomed Husain, Choudri Murtuza Husain, Choudri Kazim Husain, Mir Ahmed Husain, Ladlay *sahib*, Yakub uz-Zaman, and Mahomed Miah. Sajid Beg provided one additional name that would appear in the postscript of the pamphlet case: Ganga Prasad Varma. As we shall see, Varma was a local printer in Lucknow and a supporter of Congress. He would be responsible for printing the entire court transcript in book form. At an early date in the trial, Varma had participated in a conversation with Sajid Beg and members of the defense team—Norton, Boyle, and Edgelow.[65]

The photographs that Sajid Beg sought would be subjected to intense scrutiny. The very nature of the medium required specialized knowledge and witnesses who could provide technical details. Before calling Rafi-ud-din's brother to testify, Norton called C. Polacek. This man came from Simla, but hailed originally from Austria. He provided technical details about the photographs produced in court—which ones were likely printed from original glass negatives and thus dateable to Ellen's youth in Lucknow, and which were more recent photographs of photographs and less conclusive.

Witness by witness, piece by piece, the defense chiseled an image of Ellen as a woman of loose morals and behavior in line with that of a prostitute. After Polacek, Mirza Mahmud Beg, Rafi-ud-din's brother, testified. Mahmud Beg served as a deputy collector in Basti, a town about 150 miles east of Lucknow. He provided another account of Ellen's reputation and a characterization of his own friendship with Syed Husain Bilgrami. The two were very close friends, Mahmud Beg stated, when "our respective wives appeared before each of us."[66] Bilgrami had told his friend Mahmud Beg how Ellen had "created quite a sensation in the town by her good looks, that people were after her, and that she was quite accessible."[67]

Sheikh Gulam Mohammad Kadri had been in Hyderabad less than three years when he was called to testify. He explained that he had come to Hyderabad to present a petition to Mehdi. In doing so, he befriended Mehdi's servant, Bairam, who lived in a small house behind Mehdi and Ellen's home. Kadri was skilled at numbers and also in mediation. When Bairam had to do the household accounts or came into conflict with other members of the staff, Kadri would serve as an outside mediator to return peace to the premises. He regularly visited the home and became friendly with Bairam, and thus, on occasion, saw Mehdi and Ellen in more intimate settings, or so he testified. One day Kadri was going to Mehdi's home when he met Syed Jaffer Hussein, a young and good-looking employee in the home secretary's office. At this particular moment, according to Kadri, Hussein was drunk. The two men went to Mehdi and Ellen's home. Upon entering the main hall, Ellen came out of a side room. She spoke to Hussein in English (which Kadri did not understand well). Kadri testified, "She then threw her arms round Jaffer Husain's neck, and he put his arms round her waist. They met in the hall at the top of the steps, and then lifted the 'chick' and went into the room beyond."[68] The chick was a rattan door covering, sometimes lined with cloth for privacy, used to allow air circulation in homes.

A major accusation in the pamphlet concerned Ellen's supposed intimacies with Salar Jung II. This was scandalous on several fronts. For a government prime minister—and son and successor to the beloved Salar Jung I—to be involved with a European woman of dubious character was unseemly, but, if done discreetly, considered within the rights of a man of power. Indian princes and noblemen occasionally had European wives or mistresses, although by the late nineteenth century, the practice was less common. If Mehdi and Ellen were married, however, any relationship between Salar Jung II and Ellen would be adulterous. Given the accusation that the couple was not in fact married, the additional allegation that Mehdi had pimped this woman to the young prime minister made the matter simply outrageous. In court, servants of Salar Jung II testified in detail as to the comings and goings of Ellen, Mehdi, and Salar Jung II.

Abdul Karim was the *khansamah* of Salar Jung II, and thus in an excellent position to testify on the veracity of such claims. In his opening remarks, he described how, one evening, Salar Jung II had gone to Bolarum Palace and invited Mehdi and Ellen to join him for dinner. Karim testified that, after the meal, "Mrs. Mehdi Hasan slept in Sir Salar Jung's room that night." How had such a connection been accomplished? After a long meal, Salar Jung II, Mehdi, and Ellen retired to the verandah and continued their conversation. At about 11 P.M., Mehdi rose, excused himself, and went to bed. He sometimes pitched a tent off to one side of the palace. Karim continued, "The other two stopped and talked for a long time. They then got up and went straight to Salar Jung's bed-room, from whence they called me to shut the door." Karim closed the bedroom doors while Mrs. Mehdi Hasan "lay in bed with the sheet up to her neck."[69] He added that, during those years before the pamphlet case, Ellen had "often" spent the night in Salar Jung II's bedchambers.[70]

Like several other witnesses in the case, Karim testified to Salar Jung II's relationships with other European women. In particular, he mentioned the Stanley Company girls, some of whom Salar Jung II fancied.[71] "I never saw any other European woman sleep with Salar Jung except members of the Stanley Company. I saw Salar Jung sleep with members of the Company. Many people must have known about it. When he slept with the Stanley Company girls, he sent them to his room and he himself went round to the room by the back way."[72] Karim added that when the company was in town, it was Mehdi who brought them to Salar Jung's palace.[73] Such an accusation began to show Mehdi in a new light: procurer of European women for the young prime minister.

The next witness was Major Percy Gough. He served as the military and miscellaneous secretary in the Nizam's government, a respected position. Gough handled the inquiry made by Durand when Ellen was presented to Queen Victoria. He testified that he had secured letters from Saiyid Ikbal Ali and Shujat Ali, who attested to Mehdi and Ellen's marriage, and to Ellen's sound reputation in Hyderabad. Gough showed letters to Asman Jah and believed they would satisfy Durand as well. When questioned why he did not ask Mehdi and Ellen about the rumors, Gough responded, "I felt a delicacy about examining Mr. or Mrs. Mehdi Hasan on the point, and I believed that the two letters from Ikbal Ali and Shujat Ali had satisfied the Minister and would satisfy Sir Mortimer Durand." Gough also claimed that he was explicitly told to mention that Mehdi did not know of the inquiry.[74]

After Gough, another respected member of the Nizam's government, N. Hormusji, testified. He was on the railway station platform in April, the day after the pamphlet appeared and the morning that Mehdi and the prime minister left for their shooting expedition. The Nizam's government had placed Hormusji at Mehdi's disposal. The two men met on the platform, where Hormusji told Hasan, "I had just heard of the appearance of the pamphlet, and that its contents were very scandalous, and I sympathized with him."[75]

During the trial, Asman Jah wrote to Durand, seeking the letters from Ikbal Ali and Shujat Ali.[76] It is unclear how Asman Jah had used these references when Durand made his initial inquiry but no longer had the documents in his possession. These letters would have shed light on the inquiries made in 1889. Durand was trying to stay clear of the case as best he could. In response to the prime minister's request, the correspondence within the government bureaucracy urged restraint. It also questioned Bosanquet's handling of the case. Behind Bosanquet's back, doubts began to rise. An assessment from an official in the foreign department states:

> I venture to think we should not send these letters—and as a matter of fact that Mr. Bosanquet should not have allowed this enquiry into the correspondence of 1889 at all. Up to now he has taken a lot of oral evidence as to the contents of that correspondence which under the Indian Evidence Act* was quite inadmissible, and now at the eleventh hour the Minister comes and asks us for the originals to produce in Court. Mr. Bosanquet has not only acted irregularly in allowing all this oral evidence, but he has forced our hand for whether we send the letters or not, the fact that there was correspondence and the general contents are now matter of notoriety. All the same

I would not send them, because the clearer we keep of all connection with this case the better. [*This Act is not in force in
Secunderabad, but that fact simply gives Mr. Bosanquet larger
powers to refuse the evidence if he chooses.][77]

The official response to Asman Jah came from Durand at the beginning of February, stating that the prime minister must have made his
request based on "some misapprehension of the wishes of the Court."
It explained that it would be "undesirable" for the Government of
India to release the letters "without very special reasons."[78]

In court, witnesses continued to provide detailed accounts of sexual
liaisons with Ellen. Among them was Mir Mustafa Ali, a relative of
Salar Jung I who worked for Salar Jung II. Through his testimony, a
picture emerges of cosmopolitan Indian men having multiple intimate
relations with European women, both in India and beyond. At the
"high noon" of the British Raj, an intimate, although hidden, set of
connections existed between ruler and ruled. Ali recounted the initial meeting between Ellen and Salar Jung II. Ali had met and spoken
of Ellen to the prime minister, who suggested that she be invited to
his palace for one of the many entertainments he gave. When Ali
made this offer to Ellen, according to Ali, she "replied that as she had
never been in high society it would not look well for Sir Salar Jung to
invite her to big dinners, but that she would come to his private parties if Sir Salar Jung liked."[79] In her first few years in Hyderabad, Ellen
remained out of its highest circles, in part because Mehdi had not
risen in rank yet and, perhaps, because she was worried about her past
catching up with her. Before his cross-examination, Ali made one
more statement: he himself had had sex with Ellen. He reported,
"I did not have her a hundred times. I may have had her two or three
times. I had her in the Salar Jung's palace in the city, but I don't

remember if I had her there on every occasion."[80] He added further details of their trysts: "there [in the hallway] we had intercourse . . . I had her once at a pic-nic . . . I once had her at her own house . . . I had her standing up."[81] He later changed the last account to being "on a couch" rather than standing up.

During cross-examination, details of Ali's life came under scrutiny as the prosecution attempted to discredit him. Ali had been in England before coming back to Hyderabad, as Mehdi was rising in power. While in England, it seems he fathered a child with a young English woman. He proposed to her, but her father rejected the offer. The woman carried the child to term, but Ali testified that the child had since died. In his own defense he said, "I did not leave the mother and child unprovided for and in misery and disgrace."[82] He later claimed he was a man of honor, and that blame fell on the parents for breaking off his engagement to the girl. By way of further proving his honor, he denied accusations that he left a large bill unpaid at a club.

While Mustafa Ali was finishing his testimony, Mehdi was completing a memorandum addressed to Asman Jah.[83] This memorandum was his response to the request by the prime minister and Nizam for an explanation of the pamphlet's contents. When the Nizam initially asked for this response, Mehdi delayed and then replied that his lawyers advised him not to respond, since the trial was ongoing. His delay and incomplete answer, as we have seen, resulted in his suspension. Mehdi wrote to Asman Jah in October and again in December asking whether he should submit a response while the trial was in session.

Mehdi received no answer from the prime minister, so on 21 January 1893, he sought advice and assistance from the British Residency. In his letter, Mehdi called the pamphlet "scandalous" and wrote, "I became convinced of the fact that the person who was really responsible for it was the Nawab Server Jung, and that the printer, a man named Mitra, was merely his tool."[84] Mehdi described the charges against Ellen in the pamphlet as "hideous allegations." He painstakingly recounted his efforts to sue Server Jung, rather than Mitra, and how those efforts—in the form of requests put to Asman Jah and the Nizam—were met with silence. He addressed the matter of his suspension, noting that the *jarida* contained "more than one fundamental mistake of fact." In particular, he claimed that he never received any official notice requesting him to make a statement regarding the pamphlet, only an unofficial letter from Faridoonji asking for some sort of response. Mehdi claimed that, after explaining it would take time to compile evidence and write a reply, the "Minister was perfectly satisfied" with the reasons given for the delay. Believing he had acted in good faith and done nothing to displease the prime minister or the Nizam, Mehdi described his reaction upon hearing that he had been suspended:

> It was in consequence of my full belief that my conduct in this matter was open to no blame that, while I was engaged in attendance on the Commissions which were sitting in the North of India, I was completely surprised and dumb-founded to read a telegram in *The Pioneer*, about 24th October, stating that I had been suspended from my post on the ground that I had sent an evasive and disrespectful reply to an order of His Highness the Nizam.[85]

Mehdi felt that he had taken the necessary precautions in explaining the delay to Asman Jah. Yet he missed the fundamental issue at hand: the Nizam had requested something from a subject, and no excuse was sufficient for not fulfilling that request.

Mehdi believed that if the Nizam himself could clearly hear all the facts of the case, he would surely restore justice. He passionately explained, "I repeat that I do not for one moment believe that His Highness has hitherto had the least idea of the widespread character and unparalleled cruelty of the conspiracy which has been laid against me, and I have the fullest hope that, when the facts now put forward reach the ears of His Highness, full and ample redress will at last be afforded me."[86] Turning to the trial itself, Mehdi's criticism acquired a decidedly classist tone. He suggested that the defense called individuals whose class status made them untrustworthy witnesses. He wrote that, in a city like Lucknow, "amongst the dregs of the community," it would be possible for the defense to pay anyone to give false testimony. He accused Edgelow of having found such witnesses, and Norton of "stooping" to use this class of people desiring financial compensation to testify against Ellen. To reinforce his point that the defense chose to rely on witnesses from a certain class background because they could be bought, he observed that more upstanding witnesses were never called. "From the number of witnesses actually summoned, the names of all those persons who possess status and undoubted character have been carefully excluded."[87]

In closing his letter to the Residency, Mehdi proclaimed his faith in the court system. "I have no doubt that, when the case has terminated, it will be proved to the world that she [Ellen] has passed unscathed through the frightful ordeal and the foul conspiracies which have been prepared against her."[88]

In the courtroom, the defense called more witnesses. For instance, Captain D. J. Finglass testified that in speaking with Mitra about the pamphlet, the name Vasudeva Rao came up. This name again surfaced during the testimony of John Norton, head master of the All Saints' Instruction. Norton—who admitted that he was a relation of the defense lawyer, Eardley Norton—described how Vasudeva Rao was mentioned in his conversation with Mitra. "I went back alone to Mitra, and he then told me that Vasudeva Rao was at the bottom of the whole matter."[89] Long after the trial's conclusion, newspapers reported much the same thing. Additional testimony was given by Fakrud din (Fakhrudeen) Hasan, who asserted in court that he was Mehdi's cousin. This is the same cousin who escorted Ellen to Bombay, and who would once again be involved in Mehdi and Ellen's life years after the trial concluded.

Apparently, early drafts of the pamphlet were written in Urdu, and some questioned Mitra's ability to understand these. If he could not read Urdu, how could he have read and translated the pamphlet into English? Among the witnesses who testified about this, Dr. Aghornath Chatopadyaya (the respected father of Sarojini Naidu) explained that not only was the account of him in the pamphlet false (that the Chatopadyayas and Ellen socialized together), but that Mitra had a solid understanding of Urdu and would not need a tutor. Mirza Kazi Namazi also testified to Mitra's Urdu competence, and a clerk at the Hyderabad Club named Amraya (no surname given) testified to Mitra's linguistic knowledge. An illiterate baker named Sayanna swore that Sadullah, who had claimed to be Mitra's teacher, had come to his home and read about the case in the Urdu paper *Mashir*.[90] According to Sayanna, Sadullah read the paper to help himself craft false testimony that would put Mitra in jail so he could collect 500 rupees from Mehdi. A later witness, the barrister James Henry Nelson, supported Sayanna's testimony when he claimed, "Sadullah certainly admitted that he had lied in this court in the Mehdi Hasan case."[91]

On 27 January, Norton deposed Asman Jah at the Saifabad Palace.[92] He began by confirming the existence of the Durand inquiry, violating Durand's request that the inquiry be kept confidential. Asman Jah revealed that he and Mehdi had spoken not about the inquiry, but only about rumors circulating in London concerning Ellen. Norton asked,

"What rumours did you hear on Mehdi Hasan's return from England?" Asman Jah told him, "Mehdi Hasan came and spoke to me after his return from England and told me about the rumours about his wife, but I do not remember the detail. The rumours attacked the status of his wife."[93] The prime minister's testimony suggested that he had turned the investigation over to Mushtak Hussain, one of Mehdi's close allies. At the end of the investigation, Asman Jah explained, "Mushtaque made enquiries then drafted a reply and brought it to me. Mushtaque also brought Ekbal Ali to make statements, and I was satisfied that they were sufficient to show that the statements made against Mehdi Hasan were false."[94] Because it appeared to be a legitimate inquiry, turning up nothing unseemly regarding Mehdi or Ellen, Asman Jah signed off on the report and sent it to Durand where—he thought—the matter ended.

At the end of February, a series of rebuttal witnesses were called by both sides. They were cross-examined either to discredit them or to bring out details that would support the prosecution's case against Mitra. The first witness called back to testify was Faridoonji Jamshedji, private secretary to the minister. Like Gough, Hormusji, and Chatopadyaya, Faridoonji was a respected member of Hyderabad society. Before working for the prime minister, he had worked for Salar Jung II, and so he could describe the visits between Ellen and Salar Jung II. He testified that he had never seen Mehdi stay in tents on Salar Jung II's property—a key point that would have allowed Ellen to spend the night with Salar Jung II while Mehdi slept outside. He also categorically denied that Ellen—as the pamphlet had claimed—had become Salar Jung II's nurse or paramour.[95]

Faridoonji also testified to an altercation between himself and Mehdi. The issue was the precedence given to Ellen at formal events. By the late 1880s, Ellen emerged from her secluded life and began mixing with Hyderabad's local and British elite, something Mehdi's friends had warned him against allowing. A picture of Ellen comes into focus: she moved into Hyderabad society slowly, her background and status unclear, and her place, literally and figuratively, within Indo-British society was under negotiation. Faridoonji recalled, "Mehdi Hasan asked me why I had not told off his wife to go into dinner. I replied that the Aid-de-Camp at the Residency generally arranged that and I reported the occurrence to Sir Salar Jung, who addressed the Resident, and Mrs. Mehdi Hasan's position was finally settled."[96] Faridoonji added, "I think that by November 1889 Mrs. Mehdi Hasan was received at garden parties at the Residency. The late Mrs. George Palmer did protest against Mrs. Mehdi Hasan's precedence. Mrs. George Palmer was a respectable European married lady." He continued, "Mrs. Palmer protested against Mrs. Mehdi Hasan's taking precedence of her, as it was decided that she should. Mrs. Palmer protested unofficially to me. The matter did not go further than myself."[97] This vignette alludes to the possibility that some members of Hyderabad's European community were less than welcoming of Ellen.

Next on the witness stand was Syed Husain Bilgrami. He denied a charge by one Atta Hossain that he had been intimate with Ellen and denied Mahmood Beg's accusation that Bilgrami had referred to Ellen as having a "bad moral character." He also refuted any charge that Salar Jung II had had an improper let alone immoral relationship with Ellen.[98] However, he admitted under cross-examination that he was not with Salar Jung II at all times, and that Ellen and Salar Jung II "may have been together at all hours of the day or night without my knowing it."[99]

Toward the end of his testimony, Bilgrami was asked about the rumors he had heard regarding Ellen's marriage and prior status. He seemed to distinguish one type of rumor ("bazaar rumours") from other types and considered rumor from a printed work as a different form.[100] Thus the credibility of the information was mediated through the form. He considered early information as "bazaar rumours" of which he took no notice. "I maintain that the existence of bazaar rumours do not constitute 'a breath of scandal.'" He added that, "I did not believe the bazaar rumours current in 1889. I don't remember having ever mentioned them to Mehdi Hasan or he to me. I draw a distinction between the rumours of 1889 and the pamphlet of 1892, because the latter was printed."[101] He further stated that in conversation with Vicar-ul-Umra, the prime minister who succeeded Asman Jah, both men agreed that the pamphlet was "scandalous."

Nawab Tuffal Ali Beg Nadir Jung Bahadur and Abdul Kader testified, lending minor support to the prosecution's rebuttal. Bairam, the *khansama* of Mehdi, followed them. Bairam largely rebutted the earlier testimony about Syed Jaffer Hussein: he (Hussein) never came into Mehdi's home, and Bairam never saw him engaged in anything improper with Ellen. He also testified that Ellen had been *gosha*, or secluded, while at Raebareli, but she was not when he worked for her again at Hyderabad.[102]

An angry Syed Ali Bilgrami followed Bairam on the witness stand. He testified that Ellen had visited with his wife from time to time. The defense had tried to establish that Ellen was not considered a proper Muslim woman and thus was never in the company of other Muslim women. Bilgrami was clearly not happy to be giving testimony. He and Mehdi were not on good terms, as he explained: "I am hostile to Mehdi Hasan at this present moment. I have been hostile to him since the beginning of the case. I did not resent the allusion of my name in the pamphlet: what I resent is Mehdi Hasan's insinuation that I am privy to the publication of the pamphlet."[103] Bilgrami explained that his argument with Mehdi was about the authorship of the pamphlet. He had no other issues with him.

Ellen's enigmatic background, her embrace of Islam and Christianity, and her varying sartorial choices mystified some of her Indian acquaintances. Although the fluidity of her choices suited her, they were less easily understood by others, such as Bilgrami. Under cross-examination, Bilgrami described the visits between Ellen and his wife. As he explained, Ellen's visits followed neither an Indian style of socializing nor a European one but rather something in between:

> When Mrs. Mehdi Hasan came to call on my wife, she particularly asked that the servants might be sent aside, and I sent them [away] before she came in. She can hardly be said to have called in *gosha* fashion, but she did not call in European manner. I did not ask her to come and call, nor did my wife. I was not responsible for that call. Mrs. Syed Ali Belgrami has never been inside Mrs. Mehdi Hasan's house. She did not object to Mrs. Mehdi Hasan visiting her in so many words, but she did not quite like the acquaintance.[104]

Percy Gough returned to the stand to restate that he had never witnessed anything improper between Ellen and Salar Jung II. When he stepped down, Syed Jaffer Hussein came forward. Hussein testified that Ellen had visited his home, calling on the women of his home: his stepmother, sister, and wife. He categorically stated that he had never had "undue familiarity" with Ellen, saying "I treat her as my own sister."[105]

The next witness was Edward Quieros, from Lucknow. Quieros served in the Lucknow police at the time that two of the Donnelly sisters, Ellen and Lucy, were suspected of being prostitutes. His testimony was very clear: he never knew the Donnellys to be prostitutes or even considered them as such.[106] He admitted knowing another immoral woman named "Donohoe" but did not believe it was the same person as Ellen or her sister. When cross-examined, Quieros provided a detailed description of what—in his policeman's mind—constituted a prostitute:

> If Gertrude had been in the keeping of one man, I should say she was leading an unchaste life, but she would not be a prostitute in the eyes of the police. A woman in the keeping of one man would not be subject to police surveillance. If a woman were visited by only one friend quietly, without any disturbance, she would not be considered a prostitute by the police. Prostitutes were women who carried on prostitution as a trade. If she carried it on quietly with one or two men she would not be a prostitute. If she carried it on quietly with two or three men without make a disturbance, she would not be a regular prostitute, i.e., a registered prostitute. If a woman were to carry out on prostitution quietly and without disturbance, she would not be considered by the police as a regular prostitute.[107]

In this description, Quieros allowed room for Ellen to be "kept" by one, two, or even three men without falling under the stricter definition of prostitution followed by the police. If a woman qualified as a prostitute, she would be required to register under the Contagious Diseases Acts.[108] Quieros' definitions also explain why no paper trail of Ellen or Lucy having been prostitutes in Lucknow ever materialized: they were not considered as such by the police, and thus were never registered.

Had Ellen and her sister been prostitutes? Had Ellen had sex—for love, money, or both—with the men called by the defense? What of the wedding document, suspicious "Kashmir ink," and other physical evidence? How could any of the prosecution's witnesses—including Mehdi—be credible if Norton and the defense had shown they perjured themselves? In court, the defense had revealed lurid details about Ellen's sex life and intimacies of her body while calling into question her morality, even accusing her of incest. Witnesses portrayed Ellen as a woman of questionable moral character, and in doing so, sometimes revealed hidden and intimate relations that took place between Indians and Britons. The case touched the highest echelons of British power as officials looked on, concerned about the involvement of established men like Seymour Keay in a *cause célèbre*. And Mehdi, trying in vain to contain the damage, increasingly fell victim to a manipulated bureaucracy that stripped him of his position and made his path forward more difficult. Led by Norton and likely funded by Server Jung, Mitra's defense had provided a stirring rebuttal to the prosecution. The testimony of the final two witnesses would be even more complicated and more fraught as a result.

7

STAR WITNESSES

AND A VERDICT

THE TRIAL WAS now in its ninth month. Two witnesses at the center of the scandal remained to testify: Server Jung and Ellen herself. Server Jung was first, taking the stand on 7 March. He confirmed his acquaintance and friendship with Mehdi, Rafi-ud-din, and Yusuf-uz-Zaman from their Lucknow days. He described how the latter two would share with him news of their sexual conquests of the Donnelly sisters. He described Ellen's reputation as "a very loose woman."[1] When the pamphlet appeared, Server Jung stated that Asman Jah asked him to write a report on the veracity of its contents. Server Jung "entreated him not to press me to answer it," because the honor of a member of the government was at stake. He appealed for more time but was pressed into writing something immediately. Because Server Jung did not publicly denounce the pamphlet or deny its claims, a rift was created between him and Mehdi. Rumors that he had even privately validated it deepened that divide. In the weeks after the pamphlet's release, as rumors of Server Jung's possible role as author circulated in Hyderabad, the rift between the two men opened into a chasm. Mehdi retaliated first by asking the prime minister and Nizam for permission to prosecute Server Jung, but that permission was never granted. Server Jung said, "Mehdi Hasan had been a very great friend of mine up to that time."[2] Indeed, all the evidence suggests this

Server Jung

was true. Under threat of legal action, Server Jung responded by sending his brother to north India to procure evidence in his own defense. Server Jung recounted how the local paper, the *Hyderabad Record,* run by a man named Solomon, had pushed the rumors circulating in 1889 to the front pages. Mehdi apparently "snapped his fingers and said the [*sic*] Solomon was a rascal."[3]

In his testimony Server Jung portrayed himself as an ally of Mehdi, trying to help and protect an old school friend. When Mehdi returned from England and rumors regarding Ellen's presentation to the queen were circulating in and around Hyderabad, Server Jung claimed he tried to help Mehdi stem their flow and protect their "secret" of the nonmarriage and Ellen's questionable past. "I warned him that the secret was leaking out. He [Mehdi] said to me you don't know the manner and customs of England. The lords and great nobles there keep mistresses and take them to her Majesty's *durbar.* He seemed quite content with what he had done, relying on the English precedent."[4] If these were in fact Mehdi's words, he made the crucial mistake of believing that he was accepted as an Englishman in England with an English wife. In other words, the liberties enjoyed by Britons at home were not equally available to their colonial subjects. The consequences of such a mistake would be catastrophic for him and Ellen both. Server Jung added one further vignette in his testimony: that Mehdi's nickname in Lucknow had been *bhadwa* or "the pimp." This morsel went unchallenged in court, but as the newspapers reported each witness's testimony, such accusations immediately began to do damage.

The next day, Wednesday, 8 March 1893, the last witness in the pamphlet case began her testimony. The trial transcript indicates that in a sworn affidavit she identified herself as Mrs. Ellen Gertrude Michel Mehdi Hasan, age thirty-four, resident of Chadderghat, Hyderabad.

Wearing a western-style dress, and perhaps taking a minute to eye her allies and enemies alike in the courtroom, Ellen took her seat. From the beginning, her testimony was shaky. For instance, her stated age of thirty-four would have her birth year in 1859, but her baptismal record shows her birth four years earlier, in 1854. This was likely strategic: by giving her age as 34, she aligned herself with the prosecution's narrative that she was too young to have done the things she was accused of in the pamphlet.

At the beginning of her testimony, Ellen described her family. Her father had been a retired pensioner from the Commissariat Department and had gone home to Ireland at some point during her childhood. Her mother had worked in some capacity at the Lucknow Girls' School. Much of her testimony contradicted what earlier witnesses had said about her. Ellen categorically denied knowing Mary Luckerstedt—who claimed to know Ellen from their Lucknow school days—and said that all her statements were false. She rejected ever knowing Lauchlin, Archer, Kidd, Anthony, or D'Souza. In a single statement she refuted the evidence of five men who all claimed to have intimately known her. "I never saw a man named Lauchlin there [in Kanpur], nor Archer, nor Kidd nor Anthony, nor Do'Souza [sic]." Lauchlin's story of the grave came into question. In addition to denying even knowing Lauchlin, Ellen said that only she and her father went to Mrs. Donnelly's grave. "At the cemetery we only looked at the grave. I did not have the grave opened, the coffin dug up and opened, and my mother's face shown to me, nor did any one else have it done in my presence."[5] She speculated as to why Lauchlin had given evidence against her and Mehdi. "I think that bribery by our adversaries was Lauchlin's motive for coming forward and swearing to all the details which he has deposed to in this Court."[6] Ellen renounced the incestuous connection laid out by Lauchlin as "absolutely false." She flatly denied what others had alleged about her knowing Yusuf-uz-Zaman or Yusuf Mirza, Shujad Husain, Earnest Anthony, or Mary's mother, Mrs. Lucherstedt. She admitted knowing Mehdi's relation, Hyder Hussain, but rejected ever having any sexual relationship with him. She rejected ever having a relationship with Syed Husain or knowing Atta Husain.[7] She rebuffed claims made by Mustafa Ali and Abdul Karim as well. Ellen was asked about Braganza's testimony of their intimate relationship, proved by his knowledge of a birthmark on her left knee. Ellen acknowledged the mark, but suggested an alternative way in which Braganza might have come to know about it. "I may have some birth marks about me. I have heard what Braganza says about me. It is true that I have a mole on my left knee. I don't know how Braganza is aware of that fact. I have not shown this intentionally to any one, male or female. My 'ayah' may have seen it."[8] Ellen insinuated that her *ayah* may have told Braganza about it. That Ellen's *ayah* could have seen the mole reflects the sometimes intimate relationships between master and servant. These relationships could include help with bathing and dress, allowing ample opportunity to notice something like a mole.

Ellen detailed her early life before her marriage. She spent about four years, from 1869 to 1872, living with her sister Lucy (Mrs. Hodges) at Jalandhar. She painted a drab scenario from which Mehdi's marriage proposal might have seemed like an opportunity to change her life. Jalandhar, she said, "was very dull. I had no companions. Mrs. Hodges led a most lonely life as a native lady."[9] By the time Ellen stayed at Jalandhar, Lucy's husband had died. Lucy, it appears, chose to live as a "native lady" while Ellen continued to be a young woman of the British Raj. The insinuation of the defense was that Lucy— once having been a prostitute in Lucknow—now either continued that trade in Jalandhar or took up with a local man who supported her. Lucy's choice, as Ellen relates in her testimony, suggests an alternative for a young woman living without a husband in British India.

Ellen described in court how she met Mehdi in 1872, about the time she returned to Lucknow. After a mutual friend introduced them, he began to woo her. "He came frequently to our house after that and paid his attentions to me. He declared his love both orally and in writing. He was the first man who ever made love to me."[10] Here, the expression "made love" means courted, rather than the modern meaning of sexual intercourse. Mehdi asked Ellen's father for permission to marry her, but apparently Mr. Donnelly laughed at the idea. Ellen turned Mehdi down, perhaps bowing to her father's wishes, but then changed her mind and agreed to marry him. "I personally liked Mehdi Hasan's offer. I personally liked Mehdi Hasan very much better than any one I had met up till then. Before leaving Lucknow that time I had accepted Mehdi Hasan and agreed to marry him."[11] Ellen testified that she never had her father's consent to the marriage, and that her sister Lucy did not approve of it either: "Mrs. Hodges showed by her manner and the coldness of her reception of Mehdi Hasan, that she was averse to my marriage."[12] Perhaps Lucy and her prospective brother-in-law did not get along, perhaps her experience in Jalandhar had left her recently embittered, or perhaps the loss of her own husband soured her views on marriage.

Ellen answered questions about the marriage itself. She testified to having converted to Islam a few days before the ceremony. In earlier testimony, Mehdi had stated that her father was dead at the time of the marriage, and that is why he was not present, but Ellen had corrected her husband via a letter written to him during the early days of the case. "I read Mehdi Hasan's statement [in the newspapers] that my father was dead at the time of my marriage. I was in Cashmere or Allahabad, or at all events not here, when he made that statement, and I at once wrote and told him of the mistake he had made."[13] Ellen, Mehdi, and the truth were all in conversation with each other as the trial continued. It remains unclear where Ellen's father was at the time of the marriage, but it seems he was not in Lucknow.

Ellen addressed the question of her faith. She converted to Islam for two reasons. First, in case anything should happen to Mehdi, her sharing his faith would more likely ensure she would inherit whatever wealth he possessed. She recalled, "We had discussions about our creeds . . . Recollecting what little experience I had had of the world, it is probable that Mehdi Hasan suggested the expedient of my conversion with a view to getting rid of the above difficulties."[14] Those difficulties included appearing before a magistrate where questions might arise concerning Ellen's age, conversion, or other unpleasantries. Second, conversion to Islam meant that the marriage could be conducted privately, not before a member of the clergy. The latter path did not require addressing her age, whereas a marriage before a church official might have raised the issue. She testified, "I am a Christian now, though I only see a difference in the name. I am no longer a Mahomedan. I have been to Church for some years past. The cardinal difference between the two faiths is I consider that Christianity believes Christ to be the son of God, and Mahomedanism does not. I believe Christ to be the son of God."[15]

Ellen turned to an explanation of the photographic evidence used against her. She seemed to move freely between dressing in Indian or European styles of clothing, defying any easy categorization of her as "purely" Indian or European in her cultural identity. From her testimony, she explained the when and where of her appearance in Indian dress, but not the why. "I got photoed in native dress at Lucknow, two or three days after I was married. I was photoed once again in English costume, during that month in which Mehdi Hasan and I stopped at the Collector's house."[16] Ellen chose to go back and forth between Indian and European dress during her everyday life as well, not just for the photographer's lens. This choice was somewhat remarkable. Most women of her time and situation would have likely identified as either Indian or European in their everyday practice. It was also increasingly unusual to move between cultural milieus in the later nineteenth century when racial identities were hardening. "During that period, *i-e.*, at the Collector's house, I habitually wore native costume when at home, but European dress when I went out driving. I used native costume at Partabghar [Pratapgarh] and Rai Bareili [Raebareli]."[17]

Ellen described her social life in Pratapgarh and Raebareli. The visits she received from Muslim women and those whom she visited would have bestowed on Ellen a degree of social respectability. She explained that, while at Pratapgarh, she called on the wives of Bakir Husain and Syed Jaffer Hussein, the sister of Mohamed Hussein, the wife of Kadir Buksh, the wife of Mumtaz Ali, and the wife of Ali Baksh. While living at Raebareli, she did not visit any male company. "I lived in strict seclusion at those places as a native lady."[18] Later she explained that she kept strict *purdah* except when she traveled. "My purdah was strict according to my ideas, but the ideas of Mahomedan ladies differ on the subject of purdah."[19] She explained that, after her marriage, she saw nothing wrong with being photographed in both Indian and European dress, even though a "typical" Muslim married woman might have chosen otherwise.

Ellen denied any knowledge of unpleasant rumors circulating in London and Hyderabad after her presentation to Queen Victoria. "I never heard of the scandalous reports in 1888 or 1889 about my relations with my husband. My husband did not tell me of them. When in London I was once in the room when Sir Gerald Fitzgerald was talking with my husband, about a scandalous annonymous [*sic*] letter that had been received . . . My husband never told me of the contents of the letter, but he said that it was a most disgraceful anonymous production with reference to my presentation."[20] Mehdi and Ellen crossed paths with Fitzgerald on several occasions during their time in London. Mehdi mentions three encounters where such a conversation might have occurred: in March 1888 at the India Office, during their day out to Epsom, and during a function at Cambridge University.[21]

Ellen had begun her testimony on a Wednesday. By the following Monday, she was nearing the end and must have been exhausted. At this point, she made a comment that did not help her case. She stated, "I agree that my husband's English Grammar is very bad."[22] Although made in passing, her comment throws some doubt on Mehdi's authorship of his many letters to the press regarding English social customs, politics in England, and Hindu-Muslim relations. Some of his enemies had attacked him not only for his ideas but for his poor English skills. Many suggested he could not have written and published so many letters. Was Mehdi entirely truthful in his claim of sole authorship? Whether Ellen helped her husband with those letters, whether he had another source of assistance, or whether he managed to write them himself remains unknown.

As testimony concluded and the two chief lawyers for the prosecution and defense prepared to return to the courtroom and deliver their closing remarks, Mehdi tried one last time to gain the attention of the Residency and have Server Jung's out-of-court machinations investigated. In a letter of 9 March 1893, Mehdi wrote to the first assistant Resident, George Irwin, "The power and influence of Nawab Server Jung have risen to arrogant and irresponsible heights."[23] He stated that Server Jung had received large contributions to the Mitra defense fund from a variety of nobles—even from Asman Jah, who had given a *lakh* of rupees to Server Jung. Mehdi referred to all of these contributions as "extorted." This became known as the *lakh* bribe scandal, yet another significant scandal that was the talk of the town in Hyderabad during the pamphlet trial and widely covered in the newspapers.[24]

If Mehdi's accusations in his first letter were tentative, those in his next, sent three days later, were conclusive. Mehdi wrote, "I am now in a position to state that the payment of this sum to Server Jung is to be found in black and white in Sir Asman Jah's private treasury account." If only the Resident, Plowden, would investigate the matter, Mehdi asserted, he would know of Server Jung's abuses of power.

Breakfast at Bashirbagh palace. Mehdi is seated fourteenth from the right. Prime Minister Asman Jah and the Resident, Dennis Fitzpatrick, are eleventh and twelfth from the right, respectively.

Mehdi then linked Plowden with Server Jung's abuses and his own difficulty in the pamphlet case. Plowden, he wrote, with his "long and intimate acquaintance" with princely states, would best be able to ascertain "the effect produced on the extent and quality of evidence made available for the defence in this case, by the enormous increase to Server Jung's power during the pendency of the case, while I, the prosecutor was suspended, stricken down, and deprived of all resource and facility for prosecuting my case."[25] Plowden perused these letters and wrote to Asman Jah. He revealed alarm over Mehdi's correspondence: "The allegations in these letters are of so remarkable and so grave a character that it is impossible to leave them unnoticed, incredible though they appear to me."[26] As we will see, large sums of money did pass between Asman Jah and Server Jung, and whatever action Plowden chose was not enough. The end result only further eroded Mehdi's standing in Hyderabad and hastened his demise.

Norton presented his closing arguments for the defense first. Most of his closing address to Bosanquet and the court has been preserved verbatim in the printed book of the trial, but his initial remarks were summarized by an unknown editorial voice. Unlike his remarks at the opening of the trial, which took days to present and occupied pages of the printed transcript, his edited closing address was relatively short—only seven printed pages.

Most of Norton's address consisted of denigrating the prosecution's rebuttal witnesses. Norton said of Faridoonji Jamshedji, "He has not helped the case for the prosecution by one single iota."[27] Norton dispatched the testimony of Bilgrami, Hussain, Ali, and Gough with equal disdain. Concerning Syed Jaffer Hussein, Norton suggested that the prosecution strove hard to find someone who could speak well of Ellen. "The other side had been obliged, in their desperate attempts to reinstate Mrs. Mehdi Hasan, to descend for support to a stratum from which Jaffer Hussain sprang."[28] Norton's comment here is a reminder of the ways in which class permeated the trial and scandal; the value of some witnesses, like Syed Jaffer Hussein, was attacked in part because of their class status. Norton also attacked the prosecution's calling of Quieros, who, in addition to his considered definitions of who could be called a prostitute, admitted knowing about an immoral woman named "Donohoe" who lived near the Lucknow ice pits. Norton demolished the prosecution's attempt to separate "Donohoe" and "Donnelly," deriding the choice of Quieros as a rebuttal witness: "It would have been much better if his learned friend had allowed Mrs. Donohoe to have been suffocated in the ice-pits at Lucknow."[29] Norton concluded by naming the thirteen men who had allegedly been intimate with Ellen—twelve were Indian and the thirteenth was her father. Near the end, he contemptuously summarized Ellen's life: "She started life with a mistake as to her age and ended it with a mistake as to her chastity."[30]

The lead prosecution lawyer, John Duncan Inverarity, now returned to the court. He had been silent since his opening statement, delivered months earlier. His colleague, A. C. Rudra, had been handling most of the examination and cross-examination. But now, when it came time to present his reply to Norton and have the last word before Bosanquet, Inverarity boldly sallied forth. In careful and measured detail, he went through the entire case and all its witnesses. He moved forward and backward, shifting from one witness to another and then returning to add a missing or forgotten detail.[31]

Inverarity began on 18 March with a brief address to Bosanquet. "I am not only under the disadvantage of not having been present when the bulk of the evidence was given in the case, but I am also in the position of having to address your Honor at a time when your patience and attention must be almost exhausted, and am in the position of being considered the last straw which breaks the camel's back."[32] He continued, painting a broad outline of the case: Mitra had defamed Mehdi and Ellen; a charge was made about the two never having been married, and Mehdi was accused of using his wife for self-promotion. Because so much of the defense testimony revolved around Ellen's supposed life as a prostitute, Inverarity had to address this as well, although he professed a desire not to do so. He raised the concern that much of the evidence presented was not germane to the suit at hand and thus should be dismissed. He railed, "I say in this case the evidence should have been directly confined to the matter in the pamphlet and should not have been spread over the whole of Mrs. Mehdi Hasan's life or any allegations not even hinted at in the pamphlet."[33] However, it was too late. Ellen's past *had* been discussed in great detail, and Inverarity—while hoping that all of the oral testimony as such would be dismissed—nevertheless went on to challenge its veracity as best he could.

Early in his address, for instance, he referred to the testimony of Munshi Sajjad Husain, who claimed he had heard of Ellen's immoral behavior but could offer nothing more substantial than that. Inverarity pounced on such weak testimony, saying, "I have yet to learn that a woman's character is to be taken away because a man comes forward and says he heard some one else, whom he could not recollect, say that she had been guilty of a certain thing."[34]

When Server Jung testified near the end of the trial, the evidence he presented included a letter written to Asman Jah stating what he knew about the pamphlet and its allegations. Inverarity noted how in his testimony, Server Jung admitted not knowing Ellen personally in their Lucknow days, so "what he knew was hearsay, and that is not much." Inverarity claimed that what Server Jung wrote in his letter to the prime minister was knowingly false, and in support, pointed to Server Jung and Kurshed Jah, a Paigah nobleman, as the main backers of Mitra.[35]

Inverarity asked how Mitra could possibly afford employing Norton, Edgelow, and Boyle for almost a year. Who provided the money to secure evidence and witnesses, let alone cover the lawyer's fees? Inverarity pointed his finger directly at Server Jung, who had testified that he had been procuring evidence to defend himself from a possible suit by Mehdi. Yet, Inverarity argued, in doing this, Server Jung discredited his May 1 letter to the prime minister, in which he claimed to know nothing about the case. In April, the month before, he was already knee deep into making inquiries toward his own defense.[36]

Inverarity also suggested that Server Jung and Kurshed Jah had a plan, which would explain why they were so invested in the pamphlet case. This plan had political ramifications that went far beyond the issue of Ellen's character, but its success was deeply connected to proving her guilt. By linking Ellen's notorious past and her presentation to the queen with Asman Jah and his office, the latter would come under such criticism that his career would be ruined. With the prime minister's position vacant, Kurshed Jah would move into that role, securing a vital position for himself and reaffirming his alliance with Server Jung.[37] Inverarity said, now stating the obvious, "I say the publication of the pamphlet which led to this case was the offspring of political intrigue."[38]

Throughout the trial, lawyers and witnesses on each side liberally tossed accusations of bribery at the other. Inverarity was careful to say that he was not accusing Norton, Boyle, or Edgelow of wrongdoing. Rather, he referred to agents who procured information for these men but kept them clean of any direct and "dirty doings." "The real persons were the agents behind them, and they were particularly careful not to let professional gentlemen [the three defense lawyers] know the source from which it came."[39] Such agents, Inverarity claimed, included Server Jung and others who provided the defense with material. Inverarity explained how both the prosecution and defense had engaged in "dirty doings" and came to witnesses with bags of money to entice them to change their story. Such a situation, Inverarity argued, was dangerous and undermined the entire court proceedings. "The defence says we were also there with our money bags. Accept that condition of things as being established—both sides being there with their money bags—, and what more dangerous atmosphere could you have. Witnesses say that they do not know to the defence, and then come to the prosecution and say they made a statement, but will make a contrary statement if they are paid. It is a most dangerous atmosphere—both sides being prepared to purchase and buy up witnesses."[40]

Truth in the pamphlet case, it seemed, was available to the highest bidder.

Inverarity also noted that the defense had originally submitted a longer and different list of witnesses than they actually called. Many of those on the list were never called, and the defense strategy, according to Inverarity, changed during the trial. First, he charged, the defense sought to control the damage they had incurred by the loss of some witnesses; second, they put forth contradictory plans to confuse the prosecution; and third, they pursued a campaign against Mehdi and Ellen that, regardless of the outcome, would ruin their reputations. In that, they were entirely successful. Using somewhat racially charged language, seven times Inverarity referred to the defense tactic to "blacken" Ellen's reputation.[41] Inverarity charged that "at the time the case they intended to make has crumbled to pieces and the defence have resorted to another case altogether."[42] He suggested that Server Jung, operating behind the scenes, funded most of the evidence used against the couple.

Throughout his closing address, both directly and indirectly, Inverarity commented on individuals' class status and its bearing on their testimony. He singled out Gill and Lauchlin to suggest that their testimony was malleable, given the financial inducements. "Mrs. Gill is also acquainted with Lauchlin, who I don't think disappears from this case with the best character possible, and it shows that all these witnesses are in the same social scale at Lucknow and belong to a class usually influenced by direct pecuniary considerations."[43] He commented more broadly on the trial witnesses: "One often lives in a fool's paradise with reference to witnesses, more especially in the mofussil [countryside], where one is not acquainted with the people instrumental in bringing witnesses, and counsel are entirely in the hands of people who are really the persons who get up the evidence. A solicitor must trust to his subordinates, and we know the people working under Mr. Edgelow and Mr. Norton on this occasion were not particular in what they did."[44] Inverarity noted how Rafi-ud-din, another key witness, was also in financial straits, yet once he began to testify, his pay doubled and he received a promotion to an appointment in Kurshed Jah's Paigah estate.[45]

As Inverarity methodically worked through the evidence, Norton periodically interrupted him. In regard to Archer's testimony, Norton pointed out that a particular piece of information was given not in a deposition but under cross-examination. Inverarity responded, "I hope my learned friend will not interrupt me unless I make a mistake, and I am not making a mistake here. He [Norton] appears to feel the force of my argument."[46]

A major theme of the defense had been to portray Ellen as having led an immoral life before her marriage, and Inverarity seized on several inconsistencies in the testimony. For instance, Mrs. Gill and James Lauchlin presented diametrically opposing views of Ellen's early life: Gill said she was an upright and virtuous woman, but Lauchlin portrayed her as sexually promiscuous and morally challenged. Inverarity detailed the inconsistencies of character and chronology. In Lauchlin's case, Inverarity wondered aloud what type of man would continue to have sex with a woman he had seen in an incestuous connection with her father. He quipped, "I would rather have thought that a sight of that sort would have disgusted any one, that he would have left the house and never returned again. That is the natural thing for a man to do even in the lowest class of life."[47] Inverarity continued by demolishing key chronologies in Lauchlin's testimony, demonstrating how connections with Ellen were not possible due to their mutual whereabouts. In particular, he showed how the supposed incestuous moment after Mrs. Donnelly's death at Kanpur could not have happened, as Lauchlin's testimony about when he was in Kanpur contradicted itself and that of D'Souza. Lauchlin identified a different room where the supposed incest was committed, and he claimed to have had the room for three days, whereas D'Souza testified that the party left after just one. Lauchlin, contradicting himself, remembered the act occurring two or three days after the funeral, whereas, if D'Souza was to be believed, the group had already left Kanpur by that time.[48]

Inverarity argued that Ellen's actions before she was married were not consistent with those of a prostitute. She was never registered by the police as such, never caused a disturbance by her actions, was a guest at several Indian and European homes, and, for all practical purposes, seemed to have married out of love. Inverarity points out, "You do not find a common prostitute have [sic] connection with a man out of pure love, and you do not find a common prostitute visiting respectable houses."[49] Inverarity wondered aloud if anyone in the court could see in Ellen's demeanor any sign of her former life. His suggestion was that if Ellen had been a prostitute in her earlier life, there would be some evidence of this in the present. None of this, argued Inverarity, was visible. "It is almost impossible that a person could have led such a life as she is said to have led without it leaving some trace in her speech and appearance. I say there is nothing of the kind in her manner and voice and her general appearance is entirely against the theory that she has led for years and years mind you, a life of that kind."[50]

The defense had brought Braganza to the witness box, where he testified to having known Ellen nearly twenty-five years earlier, in Lucknow. His testimony seemed particularly convincing for its detail— he remembered that Ellen had a mole on her knee, suggesting that he had seen her naked. Ellen herself admitted to having moles on her body, seeming to confirm Braganza's memory. But Inverarity cast doubt on the integrity of Braganza's memory. He wondered aloud how a man could remember such a detail years later, planting the idea that the defense had told Braganza about the mole.[51] Other witnesses, including crucial ones like Yusuf-uz-Zaman, came under Inverarity's scrutiny. He noted that Yusuf-uz-Zaman's deposition differed from his oral testimony. Inverarity suggested he had been coached and changed his story. Norton objected, but the sea of damaging evidence Inverarity presented to rebut the defense was having an effect.[52]

Much testimony revolved around the photograph of Ellen dressed in Indian clothes, with her *dupatta* revealing her left breast cupped by her blouse. Most of the testimony argued that it was an indecent or prostitute-like pose for an Indian woman, but Inverarity stressed that Ellen was European. "They [the defense] forget that the person who was photographed was a European girl, and a European girl, according to our case, would know nothing about the manners and customs of native women of bad character. A European girl, perfectly decently attired in native costume, might arrange the folds of her dress in a way that was indelicate for a native, without having any knowledge of the fact."[53] Inverarity pointed out that Norton's lengthy remarks "would lead people to believe that there was something in the photograph that was indecent." In other words, Norton's language did not draw a distinction between Ellen's breast being clothed but uncovered by her *dupatta* and being completely nude.[54]

Inverarity moved to the topic of the wedding and the evidence given by Himayat Ali. His signature appeared on the original marriage document, but he was dead by 1892. Inverarity argued that if the wedding document were forged in 1892, as the defense had argued, how could a dead man's signature appear on it?[55]

Mehdi and Ellen's wedding not only joined them as husband and wife but also required each to put in writing their age at the time. The record used for Ellen was that of her baptism. Inverarity first claimed that the record was not really a record at all, because it was not an "official" record as defined by the rules of evidence. Second, even if the record remained as evidence in the case, Inverarity suggested there was ample ground to question its veracity. He noted that the name of the child is misspelled—written as "Gertrude Eliza Michel" on the baptismal record—and that there was confusion between the "Michel" on the baptismal record and "Michael" her father.[56] Inverarity also questioned Lauchlin's testimony that, when he met Ellen, she looked about nineteen years old. Lauchlin had testified, "Gertrude Donnelly I took to be 19 or 20 at the time I was engaged to her. She was a full-grown girl. She looked very much older than 15 in 1869."[57] Rather than adding weight to the baptismal record's validity, Inverarity suggested that this diminished Lauchlin's credibility, as he mistook the difference between a girl of fifteen and a woman of nineteen or twenty.

A further point made in the prosecution's closing argument was to note Mehdi's handwriting and, in particular, his letter "m." Inverarity showed how Mehdi's letter "m" appeared one way in the marriage document from 1873, and a different way in 1892. He asked how it would be possible for Mehdi to forge a handwritten document in a writing style so different from that of the past. "It would be impossible for a man to have made a sudden alteration in his hand-writing for the purpose of fabricating a document."[58] Inverarity challenged the defense claim that Mehdi had only produced a printed copy of the original marriage document to present to Plowden, implying that no original copy ever existed. To this Inverarity replied, "No one would be such a fool as to produce to the Resident a document bearing copies of signatures which it might turn out afterwards he was not able to procure."[59]

Inverarity noted how there was no dispute as to Ellen's keeping *purdah* from the time of her marriage in 1873 up to her arrival in Hyderabad in 1883. He argued that this was entirely consistent with the proper behavior of a woman married to a Muslim man and living as a Muslim.[60] In the same vein, he raised the question of Mehdi marrying again. Inverarity argued that it would be "extremely unusual" for "a native" not to marry at all. So, the fact that Mehdi claimed he and Ellen were married and that he never took another woman as his wife could be seen as further evidence of their actually being married.[61] The prosecutor further noted that Rafi-ud-din had testified to a rumor that Mehdi was impotent, which prompted Inverarity to sneer, "who ever heard of an impotent man keeping a mistress."[62] The defense had also argued that Ellen's return to Christianity rendered her marriage, if one had occurred at all, void under Islamic law. To refute this, Inverarity found evidence that a marriage of an Akbhari Shia (like Mehdi) to a Christian or Jewish woman was in accordance with that sect of Islam, and thus Ellen's choice of faith did not annul the marriage.[63]

Inverarity took up the evidence of Ellen's supposed trysts with Salar Jung II at his palace, which Mustafa Ali and Abdul Karim had testified to seeing. Inverarity raised inconsistencies, contradictions, and impossibilities in the testimony of each witness. For instance, he attempted to discredit Mustafa Ali by noting that he was in debt and had "seduced his landlady's daughter in England under promise of marriage."[64] He also wondered why Salar Jung II, as prime minister, would talk about his intimacies with a low-level servant earning only fifteen rupees—the insinuation being that Abdul Karim testified on the payroll of the defense. Inverarity questioned the trustworthiness of his testimony, claiming that both men's testimony had been "absolutely demolished." Inverarity was not shy about such declarations, as if needing to add emphasis at the end of his careful rebutting of testimony. The pamphlet indicated that "the two—Salar and Gertrude— were seen together at all hours of the day and night."[65] To counter this, Inverarity recalled testimony by the prime minister's private secretary, Faridoonji, who claimed no knowledge of any such relationship. Inverarity argued that the lack of evidence describing it as a well-known affair should be given considerable weight. He added, "I say it is impossible that she could have been there day and night without his knowing of it."[66]

The defense had used a letter Mehdi sent to Salar Jung II in which Mehdi said that he had made all the "arrangements" necessary for Salar Jung II to visit his home. The defense suggested that "arrangements" (underlined in the original letter) implied that Salar Jung II would have easy sexual access to Ellen. Inverarity thought the defense had twisted this letter and wording into a sinister plot. Rather, he portrayed the wording as indicating Salar Jung II was a "man's man" who preferred to have some time and space whereby he could relax in male company and not need to keep up appearances before women.

This particular explanation of the arrangements for Salar Jung II was made to Bosanquet by Inverarity as a fellow man. His appeal reveals a hidden side of being male in nineteenth-century India: the kind of constricted (literally and figuratively) manner that men, Indian or British, had to adopt in mixed company. In this portrayal, Inverarity displayed a somewhat typical Victorian male attitude toward women. Addressing Bosanquet, "There are many people," he said, "who are not shy amongst ladies but have an objection to wasting an afternoon in their society. I hope I won't incur the anger of the ladies, but your Honor knows what I mean. Many people prefer smoking their cheroots with their legs in the air and brandy and soda by their side than to be tightly belted and with shoes and stockings on talking pretty nothing to members of the opposite sex."[67] Inverarity suggested that Salar Jung II would have preferred to "let his hair down" in a male-only setting that Mehdi's arrangements offered.

Inverarity finished his closing statement on 23 March, nine months after the trial began. The case was adjourned until Bosanquet came back with his decision almost a month later.

Bosanquet returned to court on April 19. He began with a brief review of the charges against Mitra, then launched into a careful analysis of whether or not Mitra had "printed" the pamphlet. He reviewed the testimony of Connor, Fischer, and Hendricks—witnesses who all testified to the physical printing and binding of the pamphlet. Bosanquet chided the prosecution, "The real weakness of the case for the prosecution lies in the contradictions made by the discrepancies between the witnesses when cross-examined."[68] The magistrate declared that if the prosecution witnesses who testified about the printing of the pamphlet had been cross-examined early on—which he claimed they had a right to do under the Section 256 of Criminal Procedure Code—instead of after some delay, the case would have never moved forward.[69] By focusing on the printing, Bosanquet did not address the actual content of the pamphlet in his public verdict. Bosanquet announced his verdict and sealed the reputations of Ellen and Mehdi: Mitra was acquitted.[70] Requests by the defense to pass judgment on the contents of the pamphlet could not be accommodated. The allegations made in the pamphlet "and their truth is therefore a question outside the province of this Court to decide."[71]

Bosanquet's public verdict in April at the end of the long court case was awkward by its brevity, but he penned another internal Government of India memo (forty-three typeset pages long) akin to an elaborated judgment later in August. This took place when Mehdi had reapplied for employment in north India. His application triggered an investigation of sorts by Government of India officials who wanted to know why he had been dismissed from the Nizam's government, and what his conduct during the trial had been. As such, Bosanquet was asked to write anew regarding the case. It might also be seen as a way for Bosanquet to shield himself from further criticism. For all the brevity of his judgment in the case's verdict, here at last was a full-throated explanation of the case from the man responsible for its outcome. The stated purpose of the memorandum was to decide what the early lives of the couple had been and to show how Mehdi conducted himself throughout the case.

In the lengthy August memo, Bosanquet recounted the allegations made in the pamphlet, portraying the chronology of events in three periods: Ellen's life before marriage; the marriage ceremony; and her life in Hyderabad. Bosanquet began with the testimony of Lauchlin. He considered Lauchlin "the most important witness" for the early years, "if not in the whole case."[72] Lauchlin's testimony, if believed, would support a number of allegations made for the defense: Ellen's older age at the time of her marriage; her incestuous relationship with her father; the story of her mother's grave being disinterred; and the accusations of drinking and overall immorality before she married Mehdi. For Bosanquet, Lauchlin lent greater credibility to the accusations in the pamphlet.

But Lauchlin's testimony had to be evaluated against that of D'Souza. Both men were at the telegraph office but provided different accounts, as the prosecution had noted. Lauchlin and D'Souza differed on which rooms of the telegraph office the supposed incest had occurred, and they also disagreed on when the gathering broke up. Bosanquet found Lauchlin's testimony more credible than D'Souza: "Lauchlin, on the other hand, if he really saw what he describes, would remember the room till his dying day."[73] Thus, in Bosanquet's mind, the significance of the event made Lauchlin's testimony more believable than D'Souza's.

Bosanquet clearly favored Lauchlin as a witness. Lauchlin initially testified that he had sex with Ellen when her mother and father were elsewhere in the house, but later testified he did not have any "connection" with her until after her mother's death. How to explain the contradiction? Bosanquet said that the later statement was most likely true. "He must have known the contradiction that it would cause, and if he had not been a truthful witness he would have refrained from making it, since there would be nothing more improbable in his having Gertrude before her mother's death than after it."[74]

Turning to the photographic evidence from the case, Bosanquet sympathized with the plight of Lucknow photographer Asgar Jan. It mattered less to the magistrate whether or not Ellen had been dressed like a prostitute; he was more interested in the sale and distribution of the photographs. Presumably Asgar Jan would have profited from the sale of such images. Bosanquet argued that, since the photographs of her had been in some demand at the time of their production, the appeal would have been her status as a prostitute, regardless of her dress. He wrote, "But then why should there have been a sale of Gertrude's photograph to strangers unless she were notorious in some way? The suggestion by the prosecution that she was an object of interest by being a Christian convert to Mahomedanism is hardly sufficient, and the only other way that I can think of is that she was a well-known prostitute."[75]

Nearly midway through his memorandum, Bosanquet dropped all pretense of being an impartial seeker of the truth and stated that he firmly believed the defense. "Their witnesses have given a clear and corroborated account of the events which they allege occurred, they have successfully sustained a severe cross-examination, they are all in respectable positions . . . and there is no evidence, I consider, that they have been bribed or had any improper inducement not to speak the truth."[76]

Examining the details surrounding the marriage document, Bosanquet pointed to the contradictions in both Mehdi and Ellen's testimony. For instance, Mehdi's recollection of the marriage contract and wedding ceremony changed between his deposition and his courtroom testimony. In one account, he recalled arriving at the ceremony with the contract in hand while in another, he said he wrote the contract after the ceremony. Added to this were the errors on the document itself and subsequent corrections regarding Ellen's age and the spelling of her name, which made Mehdi's testimony look increasingly weak. As Bosanquet notes, Ellen herself remembered Mehdi bringing the contract to the ceremony, not writing it afterwards.[77]

Bosanquet recognized that some aspects of the prosecution's case might be valid but found ways to dismiss them. For instance, the prosecution had argued that Mehdi and Ellen were a married couple because, in part, Mehdi had never taken another wife. While this might be seen as a testament to loyalty or love, Bosanquet felt otherwise. "[I]t is only his refusal to marry that is relevant as showing the probability of his being already married. The evidence is therefore weak. But it is further weakened by the many inconsistencies and improbabilities to be found in it."[78] Among the inconsistencies were Mehdi's statements about Michael Donnelly's whereabouts at the time of the marriage. Mehdi testified that the senior Donnelly was dead at the time of their marriage, but Ellen testified that, in fact, her father was not dead but living in Ambala, although too ill to attend the wedding. Bosanquet questioned why Mehdi could not get this right and why he seemed to have made an elaborate attempt to support his mistake. Bosanquet opined, "there is, therefore, no excuse for an inaccuracy on such a material point. The fact that it would tell considerably in his favour, besides being hard to detect, raises the suspicion that it was intentionally made."[79]

Bosanquet now circled back to a key piece of evidence: Ellen's baptismal record. For Bosanquet, the document "proves nothing beyond the date of the baptism," although it also recorded information about her parents and her birthdate. The magistrate believed that the correction to her age was made on the marriage document in 1889 at the time of the initial inquiry, or in preparation for the 1892 trial. He argued that Mehdi and Ellen had gone through "a form of marriage" and that they created the document after the fact.

Bosanquet further dismissed many of the witnesses who had offered titillating but otherwise uncorroborated evidence about Ellen's trysts with Hyderabad nobility, including Salar Jung II. As to the allegation that Mehdi had pimped his wife, he quipped, "I consider that it must be entirely neglected."[80] He addressed the initial investigation that Asman Jah had asked Colonel Ludlow, inspector general of the police, to conduct in the days after the pamphlet was released.

Mehdi claimed he knew nothing of this and had not asked for or received any government assistance. Yet here an error of judgment proved embarrassing for both Mehdi and the Nizam's government. In his investigation, Ludlow not only inquired into the authorship of the pamphlet—his initial and only charge—but extended his investigation into the truth of the pamphlet, thus asking some very personal questions about Ellen through telegrams addressed to multiple locations across north India. In a letter from Faridoonji to Major Gough, the mistake of extending the investigation and the necessity of fixing it came to light. Faridoonji wrote,

> His Excellency regrets to find that this inquiry has been extended beyond the authorized limits . . . Even admitting, for the sake of argument, that it was necessary to enquire into the past conduct of the lady referred to, it was necessary that this should have been done by confidential letters, explaining the reasons why this information was required. Telegrams are necessarily brief, and they would not explain why this information had been called for.[81]

Mehdi's contradictions about government involvement immediately after the pamphlet's release stamped him, in Bosanquet's words, as a "thoroughly perjured witness."

Toward the end of his memorandum, Bosanquet summed up his impressions of Mehdi and Ellen. "As Gertrude Donnelly Mrs. Mehdi Hasan was a woman of absolutely no morals, having descended even to incest. She married Mehdi Hasan in 1873, and since then has not been shown to have committed any act of immorality. Prior to the institution of this case, Mehdi Hasan must have been aware of his wife's past immorality." A cover-up ensued, he asserted. Mehdi, having most likely known of his wife's antecedents before marriage, "has been guilty of a gross outrage to Her Majesty the Queen by conniving at this woman's presentation at Court."[82] Bosanquet neatly dodged any blame that could have been placed on the Frewens or the British government.

Bosanquet's initial judgment and his subsequent memo illuminate the heady mix of sex and politics the pamphlet case embodied. For him, the central questions regarding Ellen revolved around her sexual conduct. Prostitution, multiple known partners, incest, and a marriage to cover up her immoral past were all part of the mix. Mehdi's offenses were much more political in nature: perjury in the court case; insulting the queen by presenting Ellen at court, and participating in a web of political intrigues within Hyderabad that shifted power to himself and his allies in direct opposition to Server Jung, the Nizam, and their allies. Since Bosanquet's August memo was to be used to assess Mehdi's "fitness" to return to work in British India, the attack on Mehdi was designed to bar him from readmission to service. The attack on Ellen only served to confirm her immorality.

8

PINK AND YELLOW

ACCUSATION

AFTER BOSANQUET ANNOUNCED the verdict, the Residency Bazaar Courthouse surely erupted in gasps of shock, shouts of victory and despair, and excited conversation as the prosecution, defense, witnesses, and the press all made their way out of the courthouse into the April sun. Eardley J. Norton, chief lawyer for the now victorious defense of Mitra, would later compile a photo album of his time in Hyderabad. One photo is taken in front of the courthouse, with its low, flat roof and four-arched portico. Norton, several Europeans, and dozens of Indians pose in a semicircle as the long shadows of the afternoon stretch across the ground before them. Though much is unknown about this photograph of those who won their case, the apparent smug satisfaction of the participants stands in stark contrast to what Mehdi and Ellen were likely experiencing.

The photograph recorded the end of the pamphlet scandal for Norton and his legal team as well as for the witnesses on their side. Yet for others, a final and painful chapter was about to unfold. Mehdi and Ellen would again move between "pink" and "yellow" India, returning to Lucknow to live out the rest of their lives. Plowden and Server Jung would continue to wield power in their respective circles before that relationship soured, and then Server Jung—like the other nonlocals who had dominated Hyderabad politics for a decade or

Post-trial victory gathering of the prosecution outside the Residency Bazaar Court. Norton, wearing a pith helmet, is in the second row, between the fifth and sixth figures from the right in the front row, both with canes.

more—would also return to north India. John Seymour Keay would spend years criticizing Plowden and Server Jung. The Nizam, Mahbub Ali Khan, would oversee changes to his administration that would bring an end to an era of scandal in Hyderabad. His reforms paved the way for his son, Mir Osman Ali Khan, to succeed him and usher in a new and prosperous era for India's largest princely state. The pamphlet case and its participants would linger on in occasional newspaper reports but would soon be a topic more likely hushed up, ignored, or swept under the rug of history.

Just days after the verdict, Mehdi wrote to George Irwin, the first assistant Resident at Hyderabad. His letter puts some distance between himself and recent questions about the procedures followed in the trail raised in Parliament by his longtime friend and ally, Keay. With the pamphlet case concluded, it seems that Mehdi still felt that his loyalty to the Government of India was well placed. The feeling would not last long. Mehdi wrote:

> I also take this opportunity to assure the Resident that I have had nothing to do with the questions recently asked by Mr. Seymour Keay in the House of Commons, nor with the articles that have from time to time appeared in the "Morning Post". I have always laid my grievances and complaints before the Resident, and I sincerely thank him for the help and support which he has accorded to me, notwithstanding the difficulties which he has to encounter. It is due only to his indirect help that I was able to conduct my case at all. I beg to assure the Resident that I am grateful to him, and that he will always find me loyal to him and to the Government of India.[1]

With the verdict in the case delivered and reported, the press paused in the immediate aftermath and passed judgment on what had transpired.[2] For instance, from the *Madras Weekly Mail* came this summation:

> The case was one of the most unsavoury description and had occupied the attention of the Court from August last until March this year. It was practically the outcome of the ceaseless intrigue for place and preferment of which many Native States are veritable hot-beds, and Hyderabad more than any other . . .
>
> As we said before, it was an unsavoury case—how unsavoury only those know who, like ourselves, have been compelled to look through pages upon pages of M.S.S. containing perhaps the most abominable allegations that have ever been made in

an open Court. The extraordinary part of the case was the extreme latitude which was allowed to both sides in calling evidence to rebut or prove the allegations made, and a regrettable feature that occasion was taken to besmirch the reputation of people who have been placed by death beyond any possibility of vindicating their character from the foul charges made against them ... [The verdict] leaves the matter, as far as Nawab Mehdi Hassan is concerned, exactly where it was before.[3]

Reactions continued to come in, including a scathing critique of Bosanquet from the *Indian Jurist*, a respected journal that covered legal cases in India and was followed by British and Indian lawyers alike. The anonymous article began, "In the horrid Hyderabad *Pamphlet Case* the penny press has been cheated in pitiable fashion of its legitimate prey, by a magistrate of whom better things might have been expected."[4] It continued, lambasting the length of a trial that involved relatively obscure individuals, and then noted the brevity of Bosanquet's public judgment, complaining that "lo, we have no more for our waiting than the 'mouse' of a judgment of acquittal for want of proof of publication." Bosanquet had "done his work so far with admirable tact, patience and dignity,"

> but the public, stupefied and dismayed by an unparalleled forensic fiasco, wants to know why the magistrate spent nine months in finding out that there was no publication and he could not try the case; and lawyers who have made a study of procedure will be asking one another, what can have induced the magistrate to inquire into the merits of the accused person's special plea and the truth of the defamatory statements unless and until he was satisfied upon the question of publication.[5]

In a stern voice, the author of the article suggested that Bosanquet should have examined the witnesses himself at the beginning of the trial and decided if there was a case to be brought at all. He held this power, according to the article, under Section 252 of the Code of Criminal Procedure. This bit of legal language clearly stated that the magistrate should hear the complainant (in this case, Mehdi) and gather witnesses and evidence to see if the complainant has a legitimate case. Had Bosanquet done this, he would have seen the weakness of the "publication" charge and likely dismissed the case, sparing Mehdi and Ellen from ruin. Bosanquet may very well have "committed a blunder" and held some "dim perception" that he had made a mistake. The author surmised that Bosanquet "has not yet grasped the meaning of the provisions of Chapter XXI of the Code." This part of the code, which Bosanquet himself had cited in his verdict, was the *old* code, which had subsequently been revised. The new code, so the *Jurist* pointed out, made it *obligatory* for the magistrate to examine evidence himself before proceeding to trial. In other words, the very section of the code Bosanquet had chided the prosecution for failing to utilize was one he himself had misunderstood. The article concluded, "The greatest sufferer, perhaps, is the general public, whose mind has been unhealthily stimulated, surfeited and debauched by a feast of extraordinary richness and variety. Never in our experience has there been in India so scandalous a trial so foolishly and wickedly conducted as that of the Hyderabad *Pamphlet Case*. May we never look upon its like again."[6]

One person who seemed unable to let go of the whole affair was Keay. So we must momentarily pause here, leaving Mehdi and Ellen in their Hyderabad bungalow to hurriedly pack their life's possessions and make plans to return to Lucknow, leaving Bosanquet to suffer the scorn of the press, and leaving Mehdi's enemies to revel in their victory. Whereas the trial had been a public spectacle, the British government was more concerned with possible political repercussions and how the scandal might reveal deeper problems with the politics of British India. Keay was central to their concern. He was among a few powerful Britons who supported Mehdi and Ellen, consistently raising their plight with other government officials. And, Keay's position in Parliament gave him a platform from which to interrogate his colleagues within Government of India service. Finally, Keay's critiques show that the scandal was as much about politics as sex.

By mid-June 1909, Keay had reached the age of seventy and was near the end of his life. He might have looked back and felt that his accomplishments were many.[7] In 1862, just five years after the uprising of 1857, he left Britain for India as an employee of the Bank of Scotland and later worked for the Government Bank of Bengal. His financial acumen caught the attention of Salar Jung I in Hyderabad, who hired him to work in the Nizam's government.[8] By the 1870s, Keay saw the opportunity to build a fortune by working in the private sector. He began by opening a private bank and then founded the Hyderabad (Deccan) Spinning and Weaving Company. While working in Hyderabad, he married Nina, second daughter of William Carne Vivian of Penzance. The couple had two daughters.

In recognition of his birthday, *Vanity Fair* in its 8 October 1892 issue portrayed Keay in caricature. The illustration shows a man of medium height and slender build. Gray hair is tucked under a black felt hat. The eyes are fixed, and a large nose provides protection to a modest mustache with turned-down corners. The sketch portrays a man resolute in his beliefs and, as the caption reads, fluent in "prosy facts & figures." His birthday rhyme from the magazine summed up his travels and India connections.

October 8th, in 1889—three years ago this ever-blessed day—
at Westminster there suddenly did shine a luminous effulgence
known as Keay. John Seymour was the name whereby was
christened this man of many a fearsome fiscal fad; and Members sat, and rubbed their eyes, and listened; for he had learned
finance in Hyderabad.

St. Andrews claims the glory of his training; his rough-
hewn ends a Scottish bank had rounded. In later days, intent
on fortune gaining, in gorgeous Ind a money-shop he founded.
Wily Hindoos and Parsees well-affected did business with this
keen and canny bairn; then home he sailed, and straightway was
elected M.P. for Elgin and likewise from Nairn. He talked of
sinking funds and cash reserves (he once had served the subtle
Salar Jung) until he shattered Mr. Goschen's nerves with dogged
density and tripping tongue.

His aim in life is one: to do his duty by crushing Chan-
cellors when they are shifty. His high-heeled boots are
things of boundless beauty. His age—to quote from "Dod"—
is three-and-fifty.[9]

In writing about one of Keay's prepared memorials to the Government of India, a note summed up Keay as such: "Mr. Keay, who
prepared these memorials, appears to be a most zealous and able
person, but I have come to the conclusion that the memorials which
he has prepared do not present some of the principal points in the
case, and that they lay too much stress on weaker points on which
there is room for much dispute and difference."[10]

Since his election to Britain's Parliament four years earlier in 1889,
Keay had been a vociferous critic of Plowden, Server Jung, and the
general administration in Hyderabad. His criticisms grew as Server
Jung's power increased, and he was particularly incensed by the
Residents' practice of receiving Server Jung as a kind of intermediary

Caricature of John Seymour Keay from *Vanity Fair*, 1892

between the Nizam and Resident. When the scandal broke, Keay supported Mehdi and pilloried Plowden for continuing to receive Server Jung at the Residency. As a member of Parliament, he had a public platform from which to question the actions of the Government of India, and specifically Plowden's role as Resident. We have no direct correspondence between Keay and Mehdi, but the two were in Hyderabad together over several years, and it is likely that they met in London as well.

Throughout the pamphlet scandal, Keay's favorite target was Plowden. He attacked the Resident's handling of the pamphlet case, his reception of Server Jung at the Residency, and his overall management of Hyderabad affairs. Keay made these attacks in voluminous letters to viceroys, secretaries, and his colleagues in Parliament. Plowden, in turn, responded through many of the same channels, but the men carried out their frequently acrimonious relationship on paper and seem to have avoided each other while in Hyderabad. In fact, Keay had been banned from the Residency by Plowden's predecessors, suggesting that he was something of a nuisance before Plowden even became Resident.

Of the pamphlet case, Keay wrote to Mortimer Durand, "The case has, however, been most seriously prejudiced, if not prejudged by the Resident himself, in a way which, in my judgement, demands the prompt consideration of His Excellency the Governor-General in Council, in the interest of the administration of justice."[11] He argued that Plowden's relationship with Server Jung, who was implicated in the pamphlet case and opposed to Mehdi, made Plowden partial to the defense. Making matters worse, he believed that Bosanquet could not remain impartial as long as he served under Plowden as an assistant Resident.

Because Plowden continued to entertain Server Jung, Keay felt the Resident was creating nothing less than an atmosphere of political chaos. He wrote, "By these means he has succeeded in impressing the whole population of Hyderabad, the officials, and the Nizam himself, with the conviction that he is strongly in favour of the defence, with the necessary consequence already mentioned, namely, the total demoralization of witnesses favourable to the plaintiff."[12] During the trial, Keay had implored the Viceroy, Lansdowne, to intervene on Mehdi's behalf. He also urged Lansdowne to make necessary changes to Plowden's supervisory role of Bosanquet, on one hand, and his role as host to Server Jung, on the other. In an attempt to help his friend Mehdi, Keay specifically suggested to Lansdowne that he use his power to remove or restrain Plowden as Resident, "for the purpose of ensuring that the interests of justice shall be secured in the further stages of the case."[13]

The Residents in Hyderabad had a practice of communicating with the Nizam through a trusted intermediary. Keay lambasted Server Jung in his role as a go-between, and Plowden for choosing him. As Keay described it, the intermediary was usually of "unimpeachable character and veracity, whose antecedents are absolutely untainted . . ." Keay was unequivocal in his condemnation of Plowden for violating customary practice in choosing Server Jung as a go-between. "I have no hesitation whatever in saying that the whole of the present difficulties in Hyderabad have been brought about by the complete departure which Mr. Plowden has made from the wholesome tradition mentioned above."[14]

Server Jung did not tolerate Keay's attacks without defending himself. For instance, after Server Jung obtained a copy of one of Keay's letters, he too wrote to Durand. As would be expected, he denied the charges made by Keay, threatened legal action, and lumped Keay into a cabal with Mushtak Hussain and Mehdi:

> Sir, I last night perused with extreme surprise a letter dated 2nd of November from Mr. J. S. Keay addressed to you bringing several charges against me.
>
> I beg to state that there is also lately no truth to any of those charges and that they have been penned for sinister purposes

of his own by Mr. Keay, and for which I will immediately demand redress in a court of law.

Mr. Keay has introduced the Resident—Mr. Trevor Plowden's name in the above calumnious letter with the sole object of attracting the notice of the Government of India to me, as is shown from the following quotation from his letter:

"His method of operating is always . . . strongly supported and desired by the British Resident."

This entire statement is deliberately false & does not contain one word of truth. It could emanate only from persons of the characters of Mr. Keay Mushtak Hossain and Maldi Hussun [Mehdi Hasan].[15]

Evident in Keay's correspondence were increasing references to Britain and Britishness, which Keay used as a means to further attack Plowden. He felt Plowden had besmirched what was "British" in his position as Resident. In Plowden's continued relationship with Server Jung, Keay wrote that it "resulted in a rank crop of the most sickening rumours, affecting the reputation both of Mr. Plowden himself and of some of his subordinates, whereby British honour and the British good name have now become a by-word in Hyderabad and elsewhere." Keay concluded with his most pointed suggestion yet: Plowden's actions were so egregious that the Government of India, "bound alike in honor and in conscience," had no choice but to remove him as Resident.[16]

Like Server Jung, Plowden was not a man to be abused and attacked without offering a stiff defense. To begin with, Keay had misunderstood the order of precedence at the Residency in terms of who would act as magistrate and who might serve in an appellate position.

Regardless, Plowden had preemptively addressed this potential conflict of interest by removing himself and Irwin from the judicial process. In his own defense, Plowden wrote to Durand. He explained, "in order to prevent either Mr. Irwin or myself being called upon to take part in any judicial proceedings in the Mehdi Hassan case, because its circumstances had come before us in other ways, I applied to the Government of India at the very outset of the proceedings to make the necessary arrangements for relieving us of this duty."[17]

In defending himself, Plowden addressed the charges made against him concerning Server Jung's poor reputation and their relationship. He began: "It is a mere truism to say that, speaking generally, no Political Officer ought to accept a man of known bad character as an intermediary between himself and the Chief of a State. But in the practical business of Indian political life, the application of this general principle is necessarily liable to some reservations."[18] He described Hyderabad's court and the damage done to many of its leading officials by rumor or innuendo. "It would be difficult to find any individual of rank or importance, whose reputation has not at one time or another been more or less seriously assailed, while unfortunately it is also true that some men in foremost positions have done things of which it is better not to speak here."[19] Plowden then pointed out that even Salar Jung had had his share of mud thrown on him, not to mention Mehdi or men like him. Plowden also stated, with notable relish, that Keay himself had been banned from the Residency by the three previous Residents. He went on to vigorously defend his meetings with Server Jung, repeatedly claiming that they were related to business matters and had nothing to do with the court case. He wrote, "I receive him and discuss confidential business with him, solely because the Nizam sends him to me for the purpose."[20] Plowden concluded his letter by questioning whether the Government of India and the Nizam's government should take Keay seriously.

I have been obliged to write at length, partly because the papers before me are voluminous and involved, and partly because I really do not know to what extent the Government of India take Mr. Keay seriously. To people here, Mr. Keay's position with reference to Hyderabad affairs generally, to the case of Mehdi Hassan, and to the recent changes in the administration, is well known. The Nizam has personally spoken to me of the annoyance which Mr. Keay's presence at Hyderabad and his intervention in Hyderabad affairs cause him, and I believe that His Highness is determined to sever permanently the connection which Mr. Keay has hitherto maintained with the State.[21]

Government of India officials reacted to Keay by showing judicious support of Plowden. For instance, Durand wrote Plowden, "I have shown them [your correspondence] to the Viceroy who agrees that you have disposed of them satisfactorily."[22] But the praise was brief, for there was a more pressing matter Durand wanted to raise with Plowden. Durand scolded Plowden for allowing anyone (especially Server Jung) to come between him and the Nizam. The Government of India depended on the political savvy of its Residents to maintain healthy relationships with the princes to whom they were assigned. Plowden's relationship with Server Jung alluded to a larger "problem" for the Government of India: how to encourage the Nizam to be more fully engaged with the administration of his state, rather than relying on underlings like Server Jung. Plowden had earlier defended his choice to have Server Jung as an occasional go-between, but Durand thought it was a poor decision.

When the viceroy, Lord Lansdowne, visited Hyderabad in 1892, he met with the Nizam and urged him to meet directly with the Resident. In a letter to Plowden, Durand recounted the meeting: "You will, however, remember that, when the Viceroy visited Hyderabad, His Excellency at the private interview with the Nizam strongly pressed upon His Highness the advantages which would follow if the latter adopted the plan of seeing you personally on important matters in preference to employing an intermediary for the transaction of business with Residency."[23] As the Nizam was somewhat reticent, the burden fell even more on Plowden to engage him on any important matters face to face rather than through an intermediary. Durand chided Plowden, "Now it would surely not be a matter of difficulty for you to hint to the Nizam that the constant use of Server Jung as an intermediary is not agreeable."[24] Durand described the Nizam as "naturally somewhat shy" and, in conclusion, recognized the general concern that Server Jung had been unfairly disparaged by not only Keay but previous Residents as well. "I gather from your memorandum that you consider that Server Jung has been painted blacker than he really is. This is quite likely, but at the same time he did not impress Sir Dennis Fitzpatrick very favourably, and if I am not mistaken, the result of the 'Pamphlet case' has not been to add to his reputation."[25]

Defending the Resident from Keay's attacks posed challenges for the Government of India. After the pamphlet case concluded, Steuart C. Bayley, secretary in the Political and Secret Department, sorted through Keay's vociferous attacks on Plowden. Having reports and correspondence in hand, the question Bayley now asked was what, if any, reply should be given to the charges made by Keay. Thus far, only a series of internal and confidential memos had circulated regarding what to do. Now, something of a conundrum arose. Plowden had written an official response to Keay's charges and, along with that correspondence, included Bosanquet's memo that provided the magistrate's view of Mehdi and the pamphlet case. If this part of the correspondence were released, it would largely demolish much of Keay's attack, but it would also make salacious details about Ellen even more widely known. Such information would prove embarrassing for the

British government because Ellen had been presented to Queen Victoria. Bayley wrote:

> The memorandum is written in reply to a question asked officially by the Government of India as to "the fitness of Mehdi Hasan for re-admission to a responsible position in the service of the British Government." It is very unsavoury reading, and shows that, in Mr. Bosanquet's opinion, the main facts in the libellous pamphlet were justified, and that, in addition, Mehdi Hasan has committed perjury, tampered with witnesses, and uttered if he did not forge a marriage certificate. This document, if published in a parliamentary blue book, though it demolishes Mr. Keay's client, will give a very unpleasant half hour to those who were responsible for the presentation of Mrs. Mehdi Hasan to the Queen, and her admission into London society. At the same time, if the papers are to be published, I do not see how this document can be withheld.[26]

Bayley went on to say that Keay had done everything he could to injure Plowden through the "ingeniously malignant form of his questions in Parliament."

Having summed up the charges, Bayley then expressed his own views on affairs at Hyderabad. He began by recognizing what seemed to be an understood practice in Hyderabad and other princely states: "the tradition of the Nizam's court since the beginning of the century has been for the Nizam himself to hold aloof from all public affairs, leaving the administration solely to his Minister, who was a delegate of power,—not an adviser."[27] Herein lies some explanation as to why Mahbub Ali Khan's own voice is so little heard in this story. Bayley noted that what little interference in the workings of his government and the pamphlet scandal the Nizam had attempted was not satisfactory.

"To speak frankly, I believe he has only done this by fits and starts, that he has no real business capacity, and his interference has led to much vexatious delay, and been productive of very little good." Asman Jah's performance as prime minister was also not in line with what Bayley expected from administrators. "Asman Jah is a good-natured man, who neither by natural ability nor by education is at all fitted for any official work, and still less for that of responsible Minister to a large Native State. He has been the puppet of his secretaries [Mehdi and Mushtak Hussain]."[28]

Bayley noted how politics aligned in Hyderabad during the case: Mehdi and Mushtak Hussain had Asman Jah's support and even the machinery of the state to help prosecute Mitra. On the other side, Server Jung—operating out of the palace—had the cover of the Nizam's good graces in his support of Mitra and opposition to Mehdi. Bayley seemed to agree with Plowden that Server Jung was largely free from guilt: "I think the Government of India sufficiently show that Surwur Jung was not a man of notoriously bad character . . . Then it is quite certain that Surwur Jung has not been 'practically admitted to be the author' of the libellous pamphlet, or responsible for its contents."[29] Bayley also summarized the *lakh* bribe scandal, recounting who gave what to whom, and who was innocent or guilty. At the end, Bayley wanted to know if the secretary of state agreed to a formal response, "without waiting for a renewal of the attack from Mr. Seymour Keay," and if he agreed generally with the action taken by the Government of India regarding Keay's attack against Plowden.

Kimberley's reply was categorical: "The conclusion which I have formed after a careful examination of all these papers, and after a full review of Mr. Plowden's proceedings, is that the character of your Resident at Hyderabad has been made the subject of attack on grounds which have been shown to be entirely untenable, and that charges have been made against him which have been altogether disproved upon enquiry."[30] Bayley's message to Keay was cold and clear: "Dear Keay,

Lord Kimberley has carefully considered your letter of 22nd February, and he requests me to say that the matter referred to in it has reached a stage in which he does not think it desirable to prolong the correspondence by sending you further papers."[31]

If Keay's attacks against Plowden were political in nature, his attacks against Server Jung were personal. Keay attacked Server Jung for two incidents that occurred before the pamphlet case had even begun. Server Jung had been under suspicion in the beating death of his groomsman. He was not convicted of any charge, but Keay felt this was due to "special influence." Keay also accused Server Jung of having authored a "scurrilous" pamphlet titled "Extracts from Mr. Valentine's Diary," which had defamed members of both the British and the Nizam's government. Furthermore, Keay launched a general accusation against Server Jung about his role within the state, charging him with representing the "united interests of the opponents of the present administration." According to Keay, Server Jung was constantly intriguing against the minister and his allies to bring about their downfall, all the while planting seeds of discontent in the Nizam's ear.[32] His machinations had brought about "a practical usurpation of all power in the State, the responsible Minister, Sir Asman Jah, being reduced to a mere cypher, who dares not inaugurate any measure knowing that it would be at once opposed and used against him by the Nawab Server Jung." Striking an ominous tone, he wrote, "there exists at this moment no government in Hyderabad." He added that Server Jung's influence in Hyderabad was a "reign of terror."[33] Specifically in relation to the pamphlet case, Keay wrote that Server Jung "is now plainly declared by the evidence to be the principal party [behind the pamphlet]."[34]

Attacking Server Jung seemed to be something of a hobby for Keay. Even three years after the trial concluded, Keay was still finding ways to pillory Server Jung. For instance, he wrote to Lord Elgin, the viceroy at the time, that Server Jung had used his position within the Nizam's government to find employment for his family members. He charged that Server Jung sought to "introduce into the service of the State a host of his own relations and creatures, while he has at the same time developed still further his course of conduct . . . the meting out of rewards and punishments to those who were with him, or against him, respectively, in the famous Pamphlet Case."[35] The response from Elgin's office was prompt. "His Excellency is of opinion that charge so made ought to be promptly substantiated or publicly withdrawn, and that in the meantime he is precluded from entering into any private correspondence with you on the subject."[36]

A Government of India memo reveals some doubt as to whether Server Jung was as bad as he was being made out to be. "[T]here is no evidence before us to show conclusively that the Nawab's character and antecedents are such as would justify the Resident in altogether declining to meet him, when sent by His Highness the Nizam, whose confidence the Nawab undoubtedly enjoys." The response continued, stating that there was no proof that Server Jung was the author of the pamphlet, "If it is to be understood that Server Jung has admitted himself to be the author, it is difficult to see why he has not been prosecuted instead of the man Mittra."[37] This position failed to understand that, for Mehdi to prosecute Server Jung, he would have needed the approval of the Nizam, which he never received.

Lansdowne was sympathetic to Server Jung and did not believe he was complicit in the pamphlet, which he described as "the vulgar and indecent manner and form in which the charges were first obtruded on the attention of the public."[38] He added that, based on the evidence, it appeared that Server Jung's comments concerning Ellen were all but true—the only exception, perhaps, being her "flight" to Kashmir when she supposedly left Mehdi in a dire financial state.

Keay attacked not only Plowden and Server Jung, but also Bosanquet for his handling of the trial. Keay was especially critical of the delay early on between witnesses deposed on the physical printing of the pamphlet and their later cross-examination; a similar critique came from the newspapers. Keay charged that this delay had allowed Server Jung and the defense to gather testimony about Ellen to support the claims made in the pamphlet, thus shifting attention away from the question of printing and publication to one of mud-slinging and character assassination. Keay wrote, "The only reasonable explanation appears to me to be that Mr. Bosanquet's mind had become so largely prejudiced by the attitude of the Resident, his superior, that he could not but feel that a finding that the plea of justification had failed would have amounted to an indirect but severe censure upon Mr. Plowden, who had so deeply committed himself as the supporter of the real defendant, the Nawab Server Jung."[39]

On 7 May 1894 in Parliament, Keay raised questions regarding the case. Members of Parliament could address the secretary of state for India during scheduled question and answer times. At this moment, the secretary of state for India was H. H. Fowler. Keay asked Fowler if he was aware that

> . . . the Court [in Hyderabad], by an error of procedure, allowed evidence to be led in support of the plea of justification, before deciding the preliminary question as to the publication of the pamphlet by the accused; and that the case was eventually dismissed, on the technical ground of non-proof of publication, without any finding as to the truth of the evidence in support of the plea of justification.[40]

This question painted a picture of misconduct in Bosanquet's court. Keay asked whether the secretary of state was "aware that Mehdi Hassan, who is a Civil servant of the Government of India lent to the Hyderabad State, has applied to be re-employed by the Indian Government under the ordinary Civil Service Rules, and that the Government of India have refused his application on account of the nature of the evidence given at the trial of the action in question." Knowing that Mehdi's career hung in the balance, Keay used the technical mistake he believed Bosanquet committed at the trial to undermine the Government of India's refusal to reinstate Mehdi into service, inquiring "whether there is any precedent for thus dismissing an Indian Civil servant on the ground of evidence which had been admitted in error by a Court of Law."[41] Keay wanted an investigation to ensure that no "injustice" had been committed.

Keay's attacks on Plowden, Server Jung, Bosanquet, and overall British policy in Hyderabad were at times acidic and always lengthy. At one point, a frustrated Lansdowne wrote, "I am often indignant at the inroads made upon our time by such heavy cases, as those which have been thrown upon us by the mischievous activity of men like Stansfeld, Paul, and Keay. All this extra work is a severe tax upon our Departments, and leads to the neglect of other and more important business."[42] For every ripple in Hyderabad's political waters, Keay made waves through his constant commenting and haranguing. While the pamphlet case revolved around a sex scandal, Keay's attacks make it clear that, like many such scandals, at its heart were issues of local, national, and in this case, imperial politics: the veracity of British justice in India's largest princely state. Keay remained a staunch ally of Mehdi and Ellen throughout, but, in the end, his efforts merely prolonged the inevitable. Plowden and Server Jung would continue their time in Hyderabad until their own departures from the princely state; Bosanquet left Hyderabad for other positions within the Government of India; and Mehdi and Ellen's fates were sealed. Keay succeeded in raising awareness about the couple's plight, but was ultimately powerless to provide them with tangible help.

A week after the pamphlet case verdict, on 25 April 1893, Mehdi—who had first been suspended—was now dismissed from the Nizam's service. His career in Hyderabad was over. Asman Jah, increasingly out of favor with the Nizam and Server Jung, seems to have been given the unpleasant task of getting Mehdi out of Hyderabad for good. Asman Jah wrote to Plowden, "I am commanded by His Highness to request you will be so kind as to arrange for the re-transfer of the Nawab Mehdi Hassan's services to the British Government. His Highness desires me to say that the Nawab Mehdi Hassan's stay in Hyderabad is no longer necessary, and that he should be sent back to the British service."[43] Over the next weeks and months Mehdi found himself rejected by both former masters—cast out of service in "yellow" princely state India and rejected from directly controlled "pink" British India.

Before leaving Hyderabad, however, Mehdi attempted a series of desperate efforts to reverse the court's decision. He wrote to Irwin, seeking to involve the local High Court rather than the Residency Bazaar Court, and have someone other than Plowden involved. Echoing concerns raised by Keay, Mehdi felt Plowden was too close to the court proceedings to be impartial. Mehdi continued to accuse Server Jung of being behind the pamphlet case. Writing to Irwin, "As the man who involves me in these difficulties is Nawab Server Jung, who has shielded himself behind the Nizam, my request, I hope, will be considered only just and reasonable."[44] As a way to strike back at him, he also tried unsuccessfully to sue Rafi-ud-din.[45] Additionally, he hoped his status as a onetime employee of the Government of India might curry some favor at the Residency and that his pay might be reinstated. The pamphlet case, however, had been so long, so unsavory, and had caused so much headache at the Residency that Mehdi's "just and reasonable" request was likely met with derision.[46]

In late April 1893, Mehdi and Ellen made their way through Hyderabad to Nampally Station, their life possessions packed in satchels and trunks. They might have had a servant or two who traveled with them to make the long, hot journey back to Lucknow more bearable.

In happier times, when they had left Hyderabad to go to Bombay and to London, they had taken their dog ("Petty") with them; now, too, he may have panted at their feet when they reached their railway carriage. As they began their journey "home," perhaps the past decade of their lives slowly passed through their minds: the recruitment by Salar Jung I and their arrival in Hyderabad; Mehdi's steady climb through the administrative ranks; Ellen's coming out from *purdah*; their visit to London and meeting Queen Victoria; their return to Hyderabad and the pamphlet's appearance; and the long, painful trial. We cannot know what the couple was thinking, but it was a poignant moment: while they would continue to redeem their name and seek justice, neither would ever come to Hyderabad again.

Mehdi and Ellen had left, but the aftermath of the trial continued to reverberate through Hyderabad. In a counterstrike to Mehdi's appeals, Bosanquet gave Rafi-ud-din, Server Jung's cousin and a key witness in the trial, permission to sue Mehdi for perjury. While the case never seems to have materialized, the bizarre turn of events, along with Bosanquet's judicial process, came under scathing attack by the *Pioneer*: "Seeing that the Magistrate carefully decided the case not on its merits but on the ground of want of proof of publication, his allowing a witness on either side to be indicted for false statements on questions of fact did certainly seem an extraordinary proceeding—we were going to say to the non-legal mind. This, however, might seem to imply that Mr. Bosanquet's intellect is of the legal order, which, after all that has passed, is perhaps rather an unjustifiable assumption."[47]

While Bosanquet endured the scorn of the newspapers and Plowden the wrath of Keay, the viceroy, Lansdowne, defended his men. "We further consider that Mr. Bosanquet was justified in declining to record an opinion on the propriety or impropriety of proceedings outside his Court, with which, assuming them to be improper, he had no judicial power to interfere." A similar line of support was extended to Plowden: "[I]t seems to us that Mr. Plowden has, in spite of the serious difficulties with which he has been confronted, succeeded, throughout the transactions to which this correspondence has reference, in doing his duty with ability and impartiality both to the Government which he serves and to the State whose interests are his immediate concern."[48]

In September, Mehdi made a last attempt to have the verdict appealed. He applied to the judicial commissioner, Assigned Districts. The judge, Henry Charles Anthony Szczepanski, reviewed the evidence and the manner in which Bosanquet conducted the trial. He found that on questions regarding publication of the pamphlet the prosecution witnesses "entirely broke down" when cross-examined. He also found that the defense was within its legal right to "reserve cross-examination" under the Criminal Procedure Code. Szczepanski recounted the two major questions Bosanquet addressed: did Mitra publish the pamphlet and was it defamatory? He suggested, "I think it would have been advisable to have restricted the trial to the first question before proceeding with the second," but did not see this as a reason to overturn Bosanquet's decision. Thus, he rejected Mehdi's appeal.[49]

After he arrived in Lucknow, Mehdi informed the officials of the North-Western Provinces that he was awaiting orders regarding his reinstatement, noting he had been without pay for two months. While Keay had publicly raised the pamphlet case in Parliament and argued for Mehdi's reinstatement in the Government of India's employ, so too did a second private correspondence begin within the Government of India—unbeknownst to Mehdi—calling into question his "fitness" for readmission into service. The debate covered two main points. First, was he to be readmitted at all? Was his conduct during the pamphlet case and the contents of the case itself enough to bar him from readmission to service? Second, if he were readmitted, at what rank should he be posted? While employed in Hyderabad, his rank and commensurate salary had dramatically increased, but would this necessarily entitle him to an equal type of position and salary in British India?

The Government of the North-Western Provinces thus found Mehdi on their doorstep, looking for and expecting a job. For many, this was unacceptable. James D. LaTouche, chief secretary to the government, wrote to the secretary of the Foreign Department, "as no vacancy is present available for him in these provinces, his services having been permanently transferred in 1884 to the Hyderabad State, this Government cannot hold itself responsible for the salary of Mehdi Hassan from the date of making over charge of his duties in Hyderabad."[50] Officials in the North-Western Provinces viewed Mehdi's salary, let alone his employment, as a liability they were not prepared to undertake. LaTouche raised questions about what had happened in Hyderabad that might affect Mehdi's placement back in British service. "Before re-appointing him this Government has a right to ask whether anything has transpired at Hyderabad which should be considered as affecting Shaikh Mehdi Hassan's character, and as disqualifying him from holding a responsible juridical appointment."[51] LaTouche was undoubtedly aware of the pamphlet scandal and trial and wanted to know how Mehdi had conducted himself. By raising the question of events in Hyderabad, he achieved at least two things: the Foreign Department (and thus the Hyderabad Residency) was forced to review the scandal and comment on Mehdi's "fitness" for re-employment, and the government officials bought themselves considerable time during which they could continue to hold off paying Mehdi or finding him a suitable position.

Inquiries from Calcutta now came down to Hyderabad. To answer them, Plowden needed to better understand the terms of Mehdi's suspension and dismissal. As such, he wrote to Asman Jah—himself days away from being permanently sacked—seeking details. Asman Jah reported that, after the pamphlet appeared, he asked the individuals named in the pamphlet to submit written explanations. The Nizam, having read them, asked Mehdi to do the same. "His Highness deemed it advisable to call upon Mehdi Hassan to submit his own explanation in the matter, so that, if possible, the disgrace of publicity might be avoided."[52] Yet, as we have seen, Mehdi did not submit an explanation. By the time he did, it was too late—his suspension was already underway. Asman Jah also recounted the position of the Nizam in the matter and revealed that, although the Nizam's own voice is little heard during this story, he appeared to have been paying close attention to Hyderabad affairs.

Another question remained as to who should cover the salary Mehdi believed he was due—the Nizam's government or the government of the North-Western Provinces—or whether it should be paid at all. As Asman Jah explained to Plowden, Mehdi had "disgraced himself" and "sullied the name of His Highness' Government." Mehdi's behavior was such that the Nizam's government would not pay anything toward his back salary.[53]

Government of India officials asked Plowden to comment on Mehdi's fitness to be reinstated into service. As we have seen, Mehdi was technically on leave from the Government of India to the Nizam's government, the latter paying his salary during this time. All sides seemed confused as to whether this was a permanent or temporary leave. Having now been dismissed from the Nizam's government, Mehdi wanted to return to employment under the Government of India. From Plowden's comments, we can glean his opinion of Mehdi, the veracity of the pamphlet, and ultimately his fitness to be reinstated. He agreed with Bosanquet's lengthy memo that Mehdi had perjured himself, and he believed that Mehdi was aware of Ellen's background when they were married and that subsequent changes made to the wedding document were an attempt to alter her age and thus render impossible the accusations of her immoral past. He concluded by casting doubt on the existence of the marriage document at all: "Personally, I am not satisfied that any marriage was performed. If the marriage deed had been in existence, surely something would have been heard of it in the course of the Minister's enquiry in 1889."[54]

The question of Mehdi's readmission to service in the Government of India now went to the Foreign Department office, where a series of internal communications took place. The secretary, for instance, noted Mehdi's "downfall" and Ellen's presentation to the Queen as an "outrage."[55] After communicating with the Home Department concerning Mehdi's employment, the secretary commented a few weeks later that Mehdi was likely to be reinstated, but at his old salary and his old position. In other words, his advancement in Hyderabad did not count when he returned to service in British India. However, this was not a choice looked upon favorably. A. W., secretary in the Foreign Department of the Government of India, wrote, "Our action would be taken as the mean between our impotence to prove anything against him and our desire to injure him."[56] As the different branches of the government requested further information regarding Mehdi and corresponded with each other, it became clear that the initial thought of reinstating him, even at the rate of pay that he had left on, was losing support. For instance, A. P. MacDonnell, a member of the viceroy's Executive Council, wrote,

I confess I am surprised at the difficulties which are raised by the Government of the North-Western Provinces in this matter. The question is not whether this man, Mehdi Hassan, should be prosecuted, but whether he should be admitted again to our service ... For my own part, I consider the course we are pursuing as an illustration of our extreme punctiliousness and adherence to form. It would, in my opinion, be a public scandal if this man were re-employed in the Government service; and I should, if the decision had rested with me, have directed him to resign, or failing his resignation, have dismissed him months ago.[57]

In Hyderabad during the summer and fall of 1893, the impact of the pamphlet scandal continued to ripple outward. Among the consequences was a mandatory six-month leave of absence of Asman Jah as prime minister, followed by his dismissal. Writing about Asman Jah in relation to the many north Indians employed in Hyderabad, Joseph Rock acidly noted that the Nizam "has at last driven out the whole brood of alien parasites."[58] In suspending Asman Jah, the Nizam wrote to the viceroy on 28 August 1893, "Public scandals have flourished. My Minister figured discreditably in the bribery case. His reputation, moreover, suffered in connection with the recent scandal known as the Hyderabad Pamphlet Case. His general inaptitude for business stands publicly self-confessed on the records of the Residency Magistrate."[59] In listing the problems experienced under Asman Jah's regime, the Nizam noted, "My Moen-ul-Mahams were sacrificed to the ambition of Secretaries, aliens for the most part, who gradually acquired all the real power of the State."[60] That the Nizam would refer to north Indians as "aliens" is indicative of the strong local sentiment that undergirded much of Hyderabad throughout the latter part of the nineteenth century. It also suggests something of a change of heart by the Nizam himself toward those from north India. Where once he and Mehdi had been somewhat close, with no sign of antagonism between them, now the Nizam had had enough.

The Nizam noted that Asman Jah had not supported his plans for administrative changes. "Sir Asman Jah, who at first outwardly accepted the scheme, has done all in his power to render it abortive."

Yet, while the Nizam was laying the groundwork for dismissing the most important member of his administration, there remained in him a deep sense of propriety that marked much of Hyderabad's political culture. He concluded his memorandum, "But, as I do not wish to disgrace him by a public dismissal, I have granted him leave of absence for six months, and have appointed Nawab Vikar-ul-Umra temporarily until I make a permanent arrangement."[61] Viqar-ul-Umra served as acting prime minister in 1893–94 and was then invested with full powers in the position, which he held until 1901.

The change in prime ministers was the subject of concerned correspondence between the viceroy of India, Lord Lansdowne, and secretary of state for India, Lord Kimberley. In September, Mahbub Ali Khan wrote to Lansdowne, stating his intention to replace his prime minister. Lansdowne was relieved, for he had never fully had faith in Asman Jah. He wrote to Kimberley, "I have always believed Sir Asman Jah to be a weak and thoroughly incompetent official. He has been notoriously idle and in the hands of his subordinates."[62] Lansdowne responded to the Nizam's letter a few weeks later. He acknowledged the "gravity" of the Nizam's proposal to remove Asman Jah. He reminded him, in a tone not dissimilar to a parent chiding a child, that he had previously removed high officials, with poor success. He added, "I desire, however, to point out to Your Highness that the step which you are about to take will throw upon Your Highness heavy additional responsibilities for the redress of the scandals and abuses which you have mentioned." Seeking to avoid creating yet another scandal in Hyderabad or embarrassing the prime minister more than necessary, Lansdowne concurred with the Nizam over the latter's plan for a gentle transition in power. He agreed that Asman Jah's removal "should be carried out with the utmost consideration, and that no effort should be spared to avoid humiliating him in the eyes of the public."[63]

Server Jung and other north Indian "aliens" formed a nonlocal contingent who were blamed in part for Asman Jah's downfall. Over time, schisms arose within this cohort; for instance both Mehdi and Server Jung were from north India, but that did little to save their friendship. They garnered increasing resentment from local Hyderabadis, whom they worked to remove from power. Rock described how Asman Jah suffered at their hands, writing that the prime minister was, "little more than a cypher in the hands of several astute and enterprising lieutenants, whose acts gave Hyderabad an unpleasant notoriety."[64] Server Jung, Mehdi, Mushtak Hussain, and Mehdi Ali were all part of this group, simultaneously allied and in conflict with each other as well as with their local hosts. Their shifting alliances reflected the unstable fault lines in the state's political ranks.

If the Nizam, Lansdowne, and Kimberley all felt that Asman Jah needed to go, Keay chastised the decision—pointing to Plowden and Server Jung as the real drivers behind the prime minister's downfall. Keay saw the suspension as the result of Plowden and Server Jung's unhealthy role in the politics of the state. In a letter to Kimberley, Keay argued that Plowden had carefully orchestrated the downfall of the prime minister. It was widely known that Plowden and Asman Jah were not close, and for some time, Plowden had wished to see a new man in power.[65] According to Keay, Plowden had continuously courted Server Jung, a known enemy of Asman Jah. Thus, Plowden reached a crossroads, where either he needed Asman Jah to go (in order to continue his alliance with Server Jung), or he himself needed to step aside (a possibility Plowden never raised). Keay summed up what he believed was Plowden's calculus: "therefore the only chance of his being continued by the Government of India as Resident lay in his getting rid of Sir Asman Jah from the office of Minister."[66]

Thus, as September dawned in Hyderabad, the state's political composition was changing in character. Many of the north Indians had been ousted, yet two of the most polarizing figures—Server Jung and Plowden—still clung to power and, perhaps to the consternation of men like Keay, to each other.

Earlier in the summer of 1893, a small advertisement began to appear in newspapers across north India. Just weeks after the trial's conclusion, the entire court proceedings became available in book form. The advertisement for the new book read, "The Sensational Scandal Case, Hyderabad.—Complete and detailed proceedings, Evidence of witnesses, Mr. Norton and Mr. Inverarity's full Speeches, Magistrate's Judgment and Exhibits, with Mrs. Gertrude Mehdi Hasan's Photo; over 600 pp. Price Rs. 3."[67] Newspapers had printed excerpts of the case while it was in process; now the entire proceedings were available in one volume. For the late nineteenth-century Victorian—Indian or British—who enjoyed a good scandal, they could read and reread the story of the scandal and trial. They could also ponder the single illustration: a photograph of Ellen, hand-pasted into the book, serving as a kind of frontispiece. By itself the much-discussed photograph of Ellen could have been considered provocative or even titillating, but the packaging of the book and photo together made its consumption more respectable.

The man responsible for the book was Babu Iswari Prasad Varma. He had the book printed not in Hyderabad but in Lucknow at the Ganga Prasad Varma Press. Ganga Prasad Varma was an early supporter of the Indian National Congress, having attended its first meeting in 1885. It is possible he knew of Mehdi's early disdain for the Congress, so the exposure and embarrassment the book brought Mehdi perhaps gave Varma some small satisfaction. The book catered to an audience that knew Mehdi and Ellen during their early years in Lucknow and then on their return to the city after the trial. No doubt its printing caused the couple a considerable degree of discomfort;

they likely had hoped to keep the entire affair behind them when they left Hyderabad. The book had two editions. The first printing was in 1893 in the immediate aftermath of the trial. The second printing came in 1909, five years after Mehdi's death and while Ellen was still living in Lucknow. In that year Keay died, and perhaps his death and connection to Mehdi generated renewed interest in the pamphlet case. Also in 1909 Britain's Parliament passed the Indian Councils Act, which allowed for greater participation by Indians in the governance of British India. In India, the act generated a good deal of discussion and reflection on Indian participation in their own government, and in that context, Mehdi Hasan's name came up again, which perhaps renewed interest in his life and the trial, contributing to the second printing.[68]

The political waters in Hyderabad remained far from calm after the trial. The scandal had engulfed several of the state's most prominent officials. The Nizam—embarrassed, frustrated, and fed up with the conduct of certain individuals—began to clean house. In July 1893, he had passed an order that Mehdi Ali, once Mehdi and Ellen's companion in London and common attendee at Nizam Club functions, tender his resignation. Adding weight to the order was the directive that Ali leave Hyderabad within ten days. Ali's time in the Nizam's government and in Hyderabad State was definitively over.

As a "foreigner" from north India working in Hyderabad, Ali had run afoul of Hyderabad locals. As the *Pioneer* reported, "Mehdi Ali's enemies are principally amongst the Hyderabadees. There has always been a dead set against the foreigners, as the officials whom Sir Salar Jung brought from the North-West are called."[69] The paper concluded, "The Hyderabadees have now got it their own way, and it remains to be seen what they will do to get themselves out of the very considerable mess in which they are now situated."[70]

Like the other recruits from north India, including Mehdi, Ali's career trajectory began in Lucknow, part of "pink" India, and paused in princely "yellow" India before returning north. Their careers serve as examples of the mobility that characterized late nineteenth-century India. The establishment of direct colonial rule in India after the uprising of 1857 allowed for a series of changes that fueled such mobility. The growth of the railways that crisscrossed India and increasingly bound it together allowed individuals to travel widely; the advent of new modes of communication like the telegraph and postal service allowed individuals to communicate and thus make contact far afield; and an increasingly large and bureaucratic colonial apparatus kept the various moving parts interacting smoothly. Yet not everyone was as sanguine about "foreigners" occupying valuable jobs and commanding increasingly large shares of political power. In Hyderabad, locals disliked seeing prominent government positions go to outsiders, depriving residents of both the experience that such positions brought and the power they bestowed, both of which had enabled locals to make a difference in their own community or family.

Ali departed the Deccan as instructed and made inquiries into working in the North-Western Provinces. Although Ali's abrupt dismissal would no doubt raise some questions in the eyes of potential employers, it seems that he put such concerns aside and turned his attention northward. The colonial machinery that bound India together allowed for word of Ali's misdeeds in Hyderabad to reach other corners of the empire. In August, Plowden wrote to Cunningham to suggest that officials in the North-Western Provinces be notified of Ali's background. "With regard to the Mehdi Ali case I think it would be right to communicate the papers to Sir Charles Crosthwaite. Mehdi Ali is sure to try and bring himself to the front in the N.W.P. [North-Western Provinces]. He is reported to have made a large fortune here (30 lakhs is the figure commonly stated) and there are men (like Donald Robertson) who believe in him. In my humble opinion he was about the very worst of the bad lot here."[71]

While a response from the administrators of the North-Western Provinces was pending, the newspapers assessed Ali's role in Hyderabad. Local papers might have viewed the loss of Ali as somewhat of a relief, but papers from north India saw it differently. For them, Hyderabad was a backwater that was admirably assisted by educated Indian elites from the north. Thus, it was not surprising when Allahabad's *Morning Post* stated, "This event, taking place close upon the banishment of Mushtak Hussain and the compulsory retirement of Mehdi Hassan, cannot but be looked upon as the last of the series intended to deal a deathblow to the aspirations of the intelligent and hardworking Hindustani element in the administration, not to say, to the native administration itself, by depriving the State of three of its most capable officials."[72] A different view came from the *Advocate of India* in a letter to its editor: "It, therefore, behooves the Government of India to inaugurate a policy of consolidating the power and prestige of this Minister for the reasons shown by the wholesale deportation of all the well known intriguers who promote trouble in this State at so much per cent." The author concluded with a jab at Plowden and Bosanquet: "Hyderabad has been the grave of the reputations for a long time and those of the Resident and the Magistrate, now famous for his April judgment, have not proved an exception to the general slaughter."[73]

At the same time, questions lingered over what to do with Mehdi. W. J. Cunningham was the officiating secretary to the Government of India's Foreign Department and corresponded accordingly with the chief secretary to the Government of the North-Western Provinces. Cunningham, having received Bosanquet's memorandum on the case as well as Plowden's letter, thought that Mehdi should be informed of the charges of perjury and bribery made against him by Bosanquet. He should have a chance to respond to those charges in a letter to the lieutenant-governor, who would then decide the matter.[74]

A few days later, the reply came from the lieutenant-governor. He felt that the suggested course would "constrain Mehdi Hassan to re-open the whole case." Mehdi would deny the charges and demand an inquiry. Further, it was pointed out that Bosanquet's memorandum was "not signed or authenticated by any one," and bringing it into the public record (by giving a copy to Mehdi) would "probably lead to further complications."[75] The final decision came from the governor-general, whose position was unequivocal. Having considered the evidence from the trial and Mehdi's dismissal from the Nizam's ser-vice, he stated, "as matters stand Sheikh Mehdi Hassan cannot be permitted to resume any place in the public service in India. Sheikh Mehdi Hassan is, therefore, allowed two months within which to submit his resignation, failing which suitable orders will be passed."[76]

Interest in Mehdi and the pamphlet case continued to circulate in the newspapers. He was the subject of several articles that liberally mixed fact, rumor, and opinion. Among them was a false report that he had gone to England. In fact, around 1894 he had gone on pilgrimage to Karbala and Mecca. The report included references to Mehdi's sup-porters in the British government and among members of Parliament, likely a reference to Keay. "The rumour is that he will try to create public opinion against the pamphlet party now in power in Hyderabad. It is an open secret here that some of the M P's are identifying them-selves with Nawab Mehdi Hassan's cause and you should not at all be surprised if the Nawab succeeds in getting back into the Nizam's service and pay off his antagonists in their own coin."[77] The same report, like other newspaper coverage, alluded to Server Jung's role in the pamphlet case, suggesting that he had obtained information from Lucknow while the trial was taking place in Hyderabad. "Many in Lucknow know what steps were adopted to procure evidence by Sarvar Jung's brother. The Babu was of course the cat's paw."[78]

In the year after the trial verdict, Mehdi and Ellen all but fled Hyderabad and returned to Lucknow. They undoubtedly held out hope that their reputations could be salvaged. In London, Keay continued to ask questions about their treatment. Meanwhile, in Hyderabad the Nizam was cleaning house of officials close to the scandal. From Lucknow, Mehdi made efforts to be reinstated in a government job in the North-Western Provinces, where he had begun his career. With no salary or pension from Hyderabad or the Government of India, the couple's finances were likely straitened. Mehdi would return to practicing law, so perhaps he took a few cases to help pay their bills. Ellen had no living family in India: her father and eldest sister Lucy were dead, and her other sister, Esther, and niece Isabelle were in Europe. The couple likely visited with Mehdi's relation Fakrudeen and reunited with old friends in Lucknow while fancifully dreaming that their fortunes would stabilize or rise again one day.

9

TURNED ADRIFT

APRIL 1894 BROUGHT Ellen's voice to the Government of India's attention. No record of her appears after her final statements at the close of the pamphlet trial. On 15 April 1894, Ellen (writing as she always did as Mrs. Mehdi Hasan) wrote to the viceroy, Lansdowne. She began with apologies for "troubling" the viceroy and her "ignorance of all official communications." She asked that the decision for Mehdi to submit his resignation from British service might be revoked. She wrote, "Such an order means absolute ruination" for her and her husband. Her husband was not, she argued, formally charged or maligned by the verdict of the pamphlet case. She asked, "why is that made the ground of Mehdi Hassan's practical dismissal from the British service?" She denied all the charges made in the pamphlet. If they had been true, she added, she would not have told Mehdi, so she wondered why he was being blamed. She praised Mehdi's career in the Government of India and the Nizam's government, correctly noting that he was never sanctioned or found deficient in his job performance. Ellen questioned the wisdom of accepting Mehdi's resignation, which would mean that the Government of India was confirming that everything in the pamphlet was true. Using the third person voice, she wrote that "if Mehdi Hassan had got some appointment it would have compensated in some measure for all they had suffered and lost, and their enemies would not have had the satisfaction of thinking that they had conquered in every thing." Ellen concluded by asking why the government kept Mehdi in "hope and suspense" for a year's time.[1]

A few days later Ellen again penned a letter, this time to J. D. LaTouche, chief secretary in the Government of India. She explained that Mehdi was not in Lucknow or India at the time, as his doctors had advised him to go on leave, so he had gone to Mecca, Baghdad, and Karbala.[2] Ellen requested that the two months time given to Mehdi to resign be counted from the date of his return on or about 5 May rather than the date of the government's letter, 1 April.[3]

Mehdi returned to Lucknow shortly thereafter and immediately wrote to the North-Western Provinces government. As Ellen had done, he first asked for an extension to submit his resignation. The extension was not an effort to necessarily delay his departure, he noted, "as I have fully made up my mind to resign in any case."[4] Rather, Mehdi wanted time to write and clear his name before he formally resigned. He pleaded, "Having regard to the fact that after I have spent the best years of my life in the service of Government without any fault ever having been found with me, I am now virtually being turned adrift, without a pension, with reproach and even opprobrium attaching to my name, which is very painful and serious for me, and certain to mar my whole future career."[5] Mehdi's tone had changed; he wanted to salvage his name, recognizing that the damage to his career was complete and his future prospects were increasingly bleak. The Foreign Department acceded, granting him more time in which to deliver his resignation.[6]

By now, Mehdi had also distanced himself from his one-time parliamentary ally, Seymour Keay. After Keay had raised Mehdi's name again in Parliament, Mehdi wrote to the North-Western Provinces government, separating himself from what Keay had said in London. Perhaps he sensed that pursuing the matter further in Parliament would not be useful. Mehdi wrote, "I altogether disclaim all knowledge of this proceeding; it has been taken without any reference to me, and Mr. Keay has in his hands now a letter of mine asking him to take no action in my case." He concluded, "I feel extremely upset at the step Mr. Keay has taken in this matter, thereby making my resignation a public topic."[7]

At the same time as Keay's barrage of questions about the treatment of Mehdi unfolded in Parliament, Hyderabad continued to be subjected to new pamphlets and potential scandals. Yet Mehdi and Ellen's case served as a benchmark against which all other "scandalous" pamphlets were compared. One newspaper described a new pamphlet's author as an "anonymous scoundrel" and lamented that, although the work might not have raised any attention in London, in Hyderabad "many people will devour it with the avidity begotten of an appetite for such immoral filth since the Mehdi Hasan case."[8] It bemoaned the damage done to the city's reputation:

> Not many years ago Hyderabad was a model for all the virtues imperative to good government in a Native State. Now it is rapidly becoming an Alsatia for the scoundrelism of India—a place where the anonymous libeler is sure of a warm welcome and a pocketful of rupees; a refuge for black-mailers and loafers, whose career is played out elsewhere. What is to be the end of it all? Can nothing be done to check the moral disintegration which is going on?[9]

With a new scandal on the horizon, the *Hyderabadee* looked back to Mehdi and Ellen's pamphlet scandal. "The author or authors of the Scandal Pamphlet were, if scoundrels, no ordinary ones. They experimented for a new method of the old difficulty—of having to rid of enemies or those who block the way ahead by their very substantiality, so to say."[10] The success of the pamphlet case was a "devil's seed bound to sink into the ground" and produce a crop of "foul libelers."[11]

Over time, the pamphlet scandal continued to be invoked as a measure for other scandals. Reporting on a subsequent "case" in Hyderabad, the *Deccan Budget* wrote, "If but half of what one hears on all sides is true, the *Evening Mail* Defamation Case promises to surpass in sensational interest the Scandal Pamphlet Case."[12] While this other sensation came to naught, the pamphlet scandal continued to catch the public's interest and serve as a benchmark.

Mehdi himself underwent a reappraisal by the newspapers. Nearly a full year after the pamphlet case concluded, he still made for interesting reading, or at least some newspapers assumed he would. As time passed, Mehdi's chroniclers began to reshape the nature of his career in Hyderabad. In June 1894, a story ran in the *Hyderabadee* that seemed to recast him from an unlovable official to a victim. It began, "Mehdi Hassan was never a very loveable official. And his public acts, such as many of them were, could have, by themselves, been enough to bring his career to an abrupt termination anywhere." Nonetheless, his fate was undeserved:

> But the way in which he was saved from the penalty of his wrong-doing, and handed over to the malevolence of his enemies, must ever sink his sins into oblivion and represent him as a most pathetic charter in recent Hyderabad History. If he had deserved nothing but censure for his official conduct before his enemies found him, now that he has fallen a prey to them he deserves nothing but our sympathy. Retribution may have come to him, if some may be believed, in a round about way; but woe to those who have helped him over to his fate![13]

On Saturday, 30 June 1894, Mehdi wrote his letter of resignation. But with the letter, in an attempt to further delay his departure from service and clear his name, he included a petition addressed to the secretary of state for India, Henry Fowler. He asked that no decision be made concerning his resignation until the secretary had considered his petition.[14] On the following Monday, Mehdi wrote to the private secretary to the viceroy. He explained that he had sent a petition to Fowler, but also wanted to bring to the attention of Lansdowne facts he had not wanted to raise until this point.

Mehdi framed his newest missive in broader terms of British justice and impartiality than those in which the pamphlet case had hitherto been considered. He recognized that the case had larger implications and that the decision of the Government of India with regard to his employment would be the final chapter in how the public perceived the case. "The case is one unparalleled in the history of the British administration in India, and involves a question of far more importance than that of my personal humble interest only, *i.e.*, the question of public confidence in British justice and impartiality."[15] Although the pamphlet had targeted Ellen and her sexual history, Mehdi understood the larger political motives behind the pamphlet and the repercussions of its adjudication.

Mehdi was unclear about the specific charges made against him that resulted in his loss of pension and the Government of India's inability to employ him again. He turned "with great reluctance" to a laundry list of offenses committed against him and Ellen. He argued "that our ruination was pre-arranged seems obvious from all the proceedings of the Residency, from the time of my suspension."[16] Mehdi recounted how an order had circulated forbidding members of the Nizam's government from communicating with Mehdi. The Nizam, probably with Server Jung's nudge, had passed such an order, thus depriving Mehdi of the ability to gather witnesses for his case. As Mehdi describes it, "The result was that I was shunned by everybody, and regularly boycotted, none of my own witnesses (in His Highness's service) daring to see me, and there was a general belief that the Nizam was espousing the cause of Mitra."[17] As evidence of tampering, Mehdi provided an anecdote about the court proceedings not evident in the court transcript itself. It seems that he had asked for a photograph of Server Jung's family, in particular his wife, to be produced for the court. The reason was to show the ways in which "native ladies" dressed, countering some of the testimony that suggested Ellen was not dressed like a "lady" but like a prostitute. According to Mehdi, Rafi-ud-din smashed the glass plate negative, apparently concerned about his own wife appearing in the photograph. But, Mehdi wrote, it was proven that Rafi-ud-din's wife was not in that photograph, and thus a key piece of evidence was openly destroyed. When brought to Bosanquet's attention, he ignored it and excused Server Jung from appearing in court to explain what had happened.

Near the end of his letter, for the first time Mehdi invoked race as part of his defense. How long had he felt a sense of racial discrimination? Did he feel doubly persecuted both as an Indian and as the husband of a woman of European descent? From his early days in public office, through his letters to the newspapers, in his travel diary, and his professed loyalty to the British, he had never hinted that being an Indian was in any way a disadvantage in his life; rather, he seemed to feel that he had benefited from British rule. Now he changed his tune. If he once thought his marriage and service to the Government of India had helped him professionally, now it seemed like a curse. Nevertheless, Mehdi defended Ellen to the end, never hinting at anything less than deep loyalty, if not love. His frustration now rang out, "there is little doubt that *had I been an Englishman* the British Resident would never have permitted my being treated as I was,—a way which showed an utter want of feeling, consideration, and even humanity."[18] He stated that he was "morally forced" to prosecute Mitra, even though he knew that Server Jung was the true culprit behind the pamphlet. Mehdi thus seems to have pursued the case because he had to *do* something; to let the charges made against him and Ellen rest would be too much. His moral sense of right and wrong compelled him to act.

A few days after Mehdi's letter was posted, on 10 July 1894, the *Morning Post* reported that the Government of India had dismissed him from service.[19] This was, in fact, not entirely correct: Mehdi had submitted his resignation conditional upon a response to the petition he sent with it. By September 1894, having received no reply for months from Fowler or Lansdowne, an obviously embittered Mehdi sent one more letter to officials in the North-Western Provinces. In it, he withdrew an earlier offer to let the whole matter drop if he were allowed an honorable resignation and commensurate pension. Shifting from a once loyal servant of the British Raj to a disgruntled and unemployed ex-servant, Mehdi now made more strident demands, the least of which was 500,000 rupees in compensation.[20]

Mehdi's correspondence required government attention. The private secretary to the governor-general took up the task and in an internal memo responded carefully. The response summed up Mehdi's wishes in the following points: to have comments against him by the Government of India withdrawn; to be reassigned to the government so that he might be able to resign; to receive a pension upon resigning; to receive some back salary due to him; and to be compensated 500,000 rupees for damages.[21] In nearly six typeset pages, the private secretary dispassionately replied to each of Mehdi's points, paragraph by paragraph. When Mehdi attacked Bosanquet, the private secretary coldly noted, "In paragraph 6, Mehdi Hassan impugns the action of Mr. Bosanquet on the following imbecile ground."[22]

October 1894 brought Mehdi's pursuit of recompense one step closer. At the beginning of the month, the new viceroy of India, Lord Elgin, addressed a letter to Fowler. Elgin defended the steps the Government of India had taken in evaluating Mehdi's fitness for re-employment. He recounted the ways in which the government needed to best understand the conditions under which Mehdi had been suspended and then dismissed from employment in Hyderabad. This led to an examination of the charges against him, the court case, and Bosanquet's memo, along with Plowden's notes. What these men had suggested was that Mehdi likely had married Ellen knowing of her questionable background. The lies and other unsavory details elicited at the trial were bad enough; presenting a former prostitute to the queen of England was an absolute outrage. Elgin found that he could not ignore Mehdi's "misconduct" and thus justified the Government of India's request for his resignation. He wrote, "We believe that he took to England a woman whom he knew to have been of the most degraded antecedents, and who possibly was not even his wife, and allowed her to be presented to Her Majesty."[23] Elgin ignored the failure of the British Government officials responsible for vetting people presented to Queen Victoria. But he gave force to the accusations made by Mehdi's enemies, both during the trial and afterward, including witness bribing and perjury: "We cannot permit an officer, who has to admit having tampered with witnesses in a Court of Justice, to continue in the employment of the Government in a judicial capacity."[24] Elgin coldly concluded, "We have no recommendation to make in behalf of Mehdi Hassan, and we suggest that his memorial [i.e. petition] be rejected by Her Majesty's Government."[25]

In early 1895, both Mehdi and Mehdi Ali continued to apply for Government of India positions in the North-Western Provinces. Ali sought employment there immediately after his dismissal, and Mehdi appears to have also followed suit. From Hyderabad, Plowden sent a warning to his colleagues in Calcutta. What seems to have driven his comments was concern over the government's inconsistent practice in the ways in which it recognized certain individuals. Plowden wrote to William Cuningham, foreign secretary to the Government of India:

I mentioned to you the other day the conversation I had with
La Touche at Allahabad about the proceedings of Mehdi Ali
Muslah [sic, illegible] & Mehdi Hassain and the live [sic] they
took up in the N.W.P. He said it was advisable that the N.W.P.
Government should be informed of the real positions of these
men so that they may know how to receive them and so forth.
It makes us look ridiculous if local Governments accord "izzat"
to people who have disgraced themselves like Mehdi Ali and
Mehdi Hussain have done. But local Governments cannot act
unless they are informed of the facts. I suggest that a copy of
my No. 91C of the 2nd August 93 be sent officially to the N.W.P.
Government for their confidential information. This will have
a very wholesome effect and will show these offenders that they
cannot purge themselves of their sin merely by changing their
climate.[26]

Fowler now had Mehdi's petition and Elgin's opinion in hand. He
began his response by summarizing Mehdi's current demands: first,
he requested that he be compensated with five *lakhs* of rupees compensation for the "injuries done him in Hyderabad"; the withdrawal
of the accusations against him, and the reinstatement by the Government of India of his pension. He also outlined what he believed was
his poor treatment at the hands of Hyderabad officialdom, especially
Plowden. Finally, Mehdi argued—as Fowler summarized—that "the
facts brought to light at the trial do not justify the censure implied in
the letter of the 31st March 1894, and he [Mehdi] claims his pension
from the Government of India as though he were retiring in the ordinary course, and not compulsorily in order to avoid dismissal."[27]
    Fowler then proceeded to give his own opinion on the merits of
Mehdi's claim to compensation. On Bosanquet's conduct in the trial,
Fowler wrote, "I am of opinion that the Memorialist had a full opportunity at the trial of disproving the statements in respect of which

the action for libel was brought, and the facts to which he calls attention in no way prejudiced the discovery of the truth." Fowler portrayed Mehdi's actions as unworthy of reinstatement and certainly not a pension. His judgment was blunt and harsh: "the conduct of the memorialist himself in the prosecution of the case is inexcusable. It is evident that he made statements on oath which he knew to be untrue; that he altered, or allowed to be altered, the document which he tendered in proof of his marriage; and that he attempted to suborn evidence." From Fowler's position as Secretary of State for India, it was Mehdi's conduct during the case that justified his removal from service, and therefore, he agreed with the opinion of the Government of India (through the viceroy's office) that Mehdi should not be granted any compensation or pension. Fowler concluded his letter: "Shaikh Mehdi Hassan has thus by his misconduct forfeited his position in the public service and all claim to pension . . . I shall be glad if Your Excellency will consider the question whether it would be right to grant him, as an act of grace, any gratuity."[28] A gratuity would have been a one-time payment, which Fowler raised because, during Mehdi's employment at Hyderabad, he had contributed toward his government pension.

As spring dawned across north India in 1895, no sense of hope or renewal seems to have lifted Mehdi's mood. In April, he wrote to the private secretary of the viceroy. A tone of desperation and despair had crept into his once confident writing. He began by reminding the private secretary that he had written to him before and was without any salary or pension to sustain himself and Ellen. Mehdi had also written to the Nizam's government asking unsuccessfully for his *wazeefa*. Mehdi appealed to the private secretary, "I hope you will pardon me if I say that I cannot help thinking my position could scarcely be worse had I been convicted by a court of law of sedition and treason, whereas I have been a most loyal servant of the Government for the last 22 years." The tone is one of newfound humility. Mehdi no longer restated his request for compensation. He simply wanted to hear some news, *any* news, concerning his original petitions. "The only favour I now ask is to be informed of even the worst. Having exhausted every source of writing officially, I now take the liberty of writing to you, and shall indeed feel extremely obliged if you can let me know when I should expect a final answer to my memorial."[29] Thus while he had resigned months earlier, Mehdi's petition and its response by the Government of India delayed him having any final news of his fate.

Ellen now picked up her pen. At forty-one years old, she had seen the last of her days of banquets and balls, of bejeweled finery and visits to the queen. The arc of her life, from humble origins to imperial socialite, was now on a descent whose pitch seemed to grow steeper with each passing week. She wrote Elgin in a letter dated 16 April 1895:

> I beg and entreat, if any reply has been received from the Secretary of State to my husband's memorial, it may be announced at once. This suspense and anxiety are killing us, especially as now we have reached the end of our resources, and I am ashamed to have to say that for the last few months we have been barely able to manage with the sale of some articles of value which I still had. It is sometimes almost enough to make us inclined to end our existence rather than live on in this way. Utterly ruined through the machinations of our enemies, in position, and honour, through enemies who would not have dared to persecute and ill-treat us as they did had they not have been passively encouraged to do so by Mr. Plowden, is it not enough that we have suffered all this, but are we now to be reduced to absolute want?[30]

Ellen, like Mehdi, desperately wanted some news from the Government of India concerning the last requests sent in his petition. The urgency of the request was matched by the growing financial desperation that had settled over them, making ends meet by selling jewelry and other valuables.[31] Yet her plea was not without its barbs, directed at enemies in Hyderabad and singularly aimed at Plowden and Bosanquet. Unlike Mehdi's letter, which made no mention of his personal state of mind, Ellen painted a much more intimate portrait of his condition. "My husband has been so completely broken down with this long and hopeless waiting that his energy seems all gone. I, being a woman, and without money, can do nothing, or I would take our case up to the highest tribunal in the land. It is allowed by every one that we were shamefully treated in Hyderabad: such a case as ours was unparalleled there, as elsewhere, and especially for the partiality and injustice with which it was conducted." Ellen continued to balance a sympathy-inducing narrative with both direct and veiled attacks. Referencing the pension from the Government of India, and the life pension granted by the Nizam, she wrote,

> This is little to ask from him [the Nizam] through whom *indirectly* we suffered so cruelly, for had he allowed my husband to prosecute the *real* culprit in our case, "Survur Jung," it is almost impossible that we could have lost it, as we did. I now *beseech* Your Excellency to announce the decision of the Secretary of State, as soon as it arrives, and I beg that I may be pardoned if in this letter there is anything apparently wanting in proper respect. I am copying it out now fairly. Whilst writing the original, I wept so bitterly that it was not fit to send. I wept through grief and vexation at our utter impotence to do anything. I can do nothing but curse the people who brought us to this pass.

She concluded with an apology: "I again beg to be pardoned for all errors in this letter and for all want of etiquette. It is due to ignorance. I do not write to Your Excellency as only to the Viceroy, but as to a gentleman and a human being, and I trust you will find it in your heart to pity us in our fallen state, and to make allowance for all the mistakes of any sort in this letter, and in addressing one in so exalted a position as Your Excellency."[32]

Ellen wrote again the next day, this time to Steuart C. Bayley, now a member of the India Council in London and once a Resident at Hyderabad. She began the letter with humility and referred to the couple's dire circumstances. "I will first ask you to pardon my troubling you solely on our own account, and I beseech you not to throw this letter aside, but kindly read it through, and if possible please help us; it is not very much I have to ask now." She noted the diminishing expectations she had for her and Mehdi's future. "I have written to every one who I thought might find it in their hearts to pity us now in our fallen state, and to help us."[33] Recounting how the couple had asked for help in his reinstatement and compensation, Ellen now requested only a speedy response to Mehdi's petition. She acknowledged that "then I asked for a great deal, still having some hope in the Government; then my husband hoped to be reinstated and much more. Now I would only beg you, if you can in any way help towards this end, to try and have the decision of the Secretary of State on my husband's appeal to him announced soon." Ellen recounted their mistreatment in Hyderabad, much as she had done in her letter to Elgin. However, in writing to Bayley, she added a vignette to clear up the confusion surrounding Mehdi's employment status.

When he had submitted his resignation to the Government of India, Mehdi had asked that it not be accepted until the decision from the secretary of state was known. Following this, Mehdi's name appeared on two successive quarterly civil lists, but his name was erased from the subsequent lists. When he inquired why his name had been removed, the secretary informed him it was because he had resigned. Ellen asked, "Now if the Government has accepted his resignation, ignoring his request for delay pending the answer of the Secretary of State to his memorial, why was he not informed of it?" She continued, "I cannot imagine what heinous crime my husband committed to be treated so shamefully and so unjustly by the Government; he has always been a loyal and faithful servant to it." Ellen appealed to Bayley's first-hand knowledge of Hyderabad, where he had been Resident from 1881 to 1882, and to his generosity: "you have a kind heart and a sense of justice . . . and especially as you know Hyderabad well." At the end of her letter, as she had done in the letter to Elgin, she seemed to be at pains to point out her own unfamiliarity with this type of correspondence and begged for forgiveness for any mistakes she might have committed. "I really would not trouble any one, and do so very backwardly, especially as I have never written official letters, and I fear so much that the want of proper etiquette and forms, etc., in addressing exalted personages may give offence or be misconstrued, though it is due to ignorance only." Given her background, these epistolary pleas for forgiveness were likely not just examples of rhetoric of the time, but rather genuine concern over a kind of correspondence she had no experience producing. "Our position is well nigh desperate now," she concluded, "we are in deep distress and affliction, and in great monetary difficulties. So please forgive all errors in this letter."[34]

What remains unclear from Ellen's letters is the extent to which Mehdi was involved in their composition. Did she sit at her writing desk and pen these letters in secret while her husband lay prone with worry? Or did Mehdi in some way encourage his wife to write them, perhaps hoping that an appeal from a woman—whose prose could, in the Victorian spirit—be more personal and impassioned? No clear answer suggests itself from the letters themselves, but both were collected in a Government of India file, and so, although they were addressed to two men in very different locales, they came to rest side by side in the archival record.

One option that never appears in the record was any suggestion that Mehdi and Ellen relocate to Britain. Although many Britons came out to India and then went home to Britain, for Ellen, India was home. She had been born and raised in India, and her trip to London and Europe had been her only time out of India. Her parents were both buried in India, as was her oldest sister, Lucy. Her second sister, Esther, lived in France for a while, but was not in a position to look after Mehdi and Ellen. Being a subject of the British Empire granted Mehdi some rights in Britain, and he seemed to have enjoyed his time in London very much, yet he was an Indian-born Muslim, his roots firmly in Indian soil. Furthermore, he and Ellen were in financial straits; they likely did not have the funds to leave India, and Mehdi had little or no hope of employment should they have reached London again. Leaving was not an option.

In June 1895, Mehdi wrote again to the viceroy's private secretary. He began with a chronology of his difficulties: suspension from the Nizam's government; his loss of any income; and the refusal to allow him back into Government of India service. He noted that one aspect of his private life had not come under scrutiny during the pamphlet case—his finances. Mehdi implied that he had not profited from his position. "The judicial proceeding in my case at Hyderabad (in which all my private accounts were allowed to be carefully examined) must have shown clearly to His Excellency that I never took any advantage of my position or that of the loose system of administration of that State to enrich myself; and therefore my pecuniary circumstances at present are worse than His Excellency can imagine."[35] Mehdi concluded by asking to be informed of the decision of the Nizam's government regarding his petition. He also asked that the

Government of India intervene and have his *wazeefa* reinstated. "I *earnestly appeal* to His Excellency's personal sense of justice, and ask his favour to relieve me from this suspense, which I have borne with as much patience and loyalty as any other man in similar circumstance could scarcely have shown."[36]

On 25 June 1895, three weeks after Mehdi's last letter, Elgin addressed a formal response to Fowler. It would be the last word from the Government of India regarding Mehdi Hasan. Elgin's letter notified Fowler that Mehdi had been informed of the final decision to accept his resignation, thus closing the door on any re-employment, and also refusing his requests for access to his pension. Fowler had left open the question of a gratuity. Elgin responded to Fowler's question of a one-time gratuity that granting such "would be inadvisable for the reason that an acceptance of the principle that an officer in Foreign service who contributes for pension has, if he subsequently forfeits his pension, any claim to a refund of those contributions, would amount to an admission, in this and future cases, of a right that is expressly barred by the provisions of Article 834 of the Civil Service Regulations."[37] Elgin outlined the bizarre possibility that if anyone should receive compensation, it might be the Nizam's government.

> Moreover in the present case the salary sanctioned for Sheikh Mehdi Hassan on his transfer to Foreign service in Hyderabad was expressly fixed at a gross salary calculated to leave him a net monthly pay of Rs. 800 *hali sicca* rupees exclusive of his contributions for pension. If, therefore, any one had a claim to refund of contributions in this case it would be the Nizam's Government and not Sheikh Mehdi Hassan.[38]

Elgin wrote, "We also see no sufficient reason for granting any compassionate allowance to Sheikh Mehdi Hassan, and we deprecate such a grant as it would establish a very undesirable and inconvenient precedent." The letter concluded with signatures from not only Elgin but also many of the men who worked for the viceroy, helping him adjudicate Mehdi's different requests. Among the signatories was O. V. Bosanquet.

In July 1895, three years after the pamphlet scandal case had concluded, a story appeared in the *Morning Post* providing new information about the pamphlet. It suggested that an original version of the pamphlet had been found, and it pointed a finger at Vasudeva Rao (here spelled as "Roa").

> The original manuscript of the Mehdi Hassan pamphlet, containing internal testimony of its genuineness, has been found. It is in the handwriting of Vasudeva Roa, B.A., late of the Raja Murli Monohur's service, now assistant to Mr. Dunlop. Vasudeva Roa admits his guilt, but says that he wrote under Syed Ali Bilgrami's dictation, which he can prove. Vasudeva Roa's complicity in the production of that filthy pamphlet was all along suspected. Before the pamphlet case judgment was delivered the "Deccan Budget" challenged Vasudeva to deny his finger in the pamphlet pie. Vasudeva kept quiet. Immediately after the pamphlet case ended Vasudeva Roa was appointed Assistant Census Commissioner on Rs. 300 a month.[39]

If Vasudeva Rao was indeed involved in the pamphlet, it is unclear what his motive may have been. Perhaps as a *mulki* he was weary of Mehdi and men like him who had come from north India and assumed a large degree of power within Hyderabad. Perhaps it was personal enmity from some encounter or interaction. Or perhaps it was a ploy to curry favor with those who would benefit from Mehdi's downfall. Regardless of possible motive, no definitive proof of the pamphlet's authorship ever surfaced, and when this story broke, no communication from Mehdi or Ellen appears to have occurred concerning the revelation. Exhausted, under increasing financial stress, and perhaps hoping to put the event behind them, they remained silent.

Mehdi and the pamphlet case continued to appear in newspapers. A year after the connection to Vasudeva Rao was made, the *Deccan Post* reported that it was "generally believed" Mehdi had been "hard up" for some time. This would be in line with Ellen and Mehdi's representation of themselves as being in dire financial straits. Yet perhaps things were not all that bad. The paper also reported that Mehdi "promised" a one-thousand-rupee donation to Aligarh College. The short article concluded, "Certainly, in only three years a Hyderabad Secretary ought not to be 'hard up.'"[40] Mehdi had not attended Aligarh, but owed something to Syed Ahmed Khan, who had initially supported his recruitment to Hyderabad.

In 1901, officials at Hyderabad heard from Mehdi. Perhaps pressed for money, he formally petitioned the Nizam's government to redeem some bonds related to the railway. His original petition is lost, but the subsequent correspondence indicates that no such bonds could be found in any of the possible government offices.[41] We can assume that Mehdi was denied whatever compensation such bonds might have offered him.

By the end of 1896, Plowden's tenure as Resident at Hyderabad began to look increasingly tenuous. Newspapers openly attacked him. The *Deccan Mail* two days after Christmas reported: "the Nizam is entangled in numberless and inexpressible difficulties and intricacies from that inauspicious day when Mr. Plowden became the Resident at Hyderabad. His highhandedness and arbitrary procedure and acts are effecting that harm and injury to Hyderabad which they had failed to achieve in Cashmere."[42] The story also suggests that the once-close relationship between Plowden and Server Jung had spoiled—the very relationship Keay had rallied against and doggedly criticized for years: "Let us take the case of the very Sarawar [*sic*] Jung who is not liked by this self same Resident who is now biting his teeth as to why he allowed him to occupy such exalted position." The article concluded, "The people are thoroughly dissatisfied with Mr. Plowden. Whenever they hear even a false rumour regarding his departure from Hyderabad they light lamps in their homes fed by ghee."[43]

Between Plowden and Server Jung, it was, in fact, the latter who was first to go. In early 1897, Server Jung left Hyderabad for good. He had been there for twenty-four years and had played a central role in the pamphlet case. The exact reasons for his departure are not clear: perhaps the Nizam was ready to part ways with his old tutor; perhaps enemies had finally engineered his departure; or perhaps Server Jung—sensing his time was over in Hyderabad and that his life had entered its twilight—decided to leave of his own volition. In his autobiography, published later that same year and carefully crafted to make his departure as grandiose as possible (while at the same time taking swipes at his enemies), he described leaving the city. "After the morning prayers, belted and turbanned, I entered the Government carriage and pair, with the 'chobdar seated on the coach-box, and left direct for the station."[44] Once at the station, he sent a message to Plowden, a couplet that prophesied the latter's downfall. "Lo, I leave the presence of my beloved, / But thou too, O rival, shalt not long remain!"[45]

Commentators were quick to note that Server Jung's departure marked a turning point in the life of Hyderabad politics. Joseph Rock wrote, "With the downfall of Survar Jung a disastrous epoch has closed at Hyderabad, and relieved from the mischievous counter-influence of a Mayor of the Palace, the present Minister, Sir Vikar-ul-Umra, will be able to commence practically a new era."[46] Rock wrote that, during Server Jung's time in Hyderabad, after many of the north Indians, including Mehdi, were out of office and banished from Hyderabad, "there still remained a supreme and sinister influence in the palace itself not amenable to any ordinary check, answerable, indeed, to the pleasure of the Nizam alone, and by some strange accident enjoying the favour of the British Resident as well as of the titular Prince."[47] He described Server Jung in this way: "His influence was supreme, but it was never exerted in a good cause or for any cause but his own aggrandisement."[48]

Server Jung's departure was featured in the *Times of India* as the "sensation of the hour." As his position under the Nizam was never well defined, according to the paper, he "exercised an almost unbounded autocracy in Hyderabad."[49] Six days later, the *Times of India* again ran a lengthy story on Server Jung. "The man who was nearest to the Nizam was the man whom many people rightly or wrongly regarded as the most powerful personage in the State next to the ruler himself. His Highness is not the man to allow even the most trusted of confidants to exercise undue influence over him, and the public possibly formed an exaggerated estimate of the power of the functionary who was supposed out of doors to 'shape the whisper of the Throne.' But the estimate was formed all the same, and it did harm."[50]

Plowden remained in Hyderabad as Resident for three years, then, in the late summer of 1900, he notified the Indian Political Office that he wished to retire. He had been in Hyderabad for nine years. His time in the largest princely state was not hailed as successful. Hearing of his retirement, the newspapers bitterly weighed in on his tenure. The *Bombay Gazette* chortled, "It would be idle to pretend even in the mellow moments of farewell that his long term of office, which has extended to just nine years, can be considered a success." It continued, "The first six years of his time at the Residency were the most troublous period that the Hyderabad of this generation remembers."[51] What, according to the popular press, was Plowden's weakness? He had an "unfortunate way of dealing with Orientals" that was neither a "velvet glove" or "wrist of steel" but instead wielded a "prickly grip" that drove people he encountered into a "passive and sulky obstruction." Adding to this unflattering description, the article concluded that Plowden was no less than "the round man in the square hole" and that "his reputation has suffered accordingly."[52]

Plowden had not always been so disliked. Four years earlier, a rumor had circulated that Plowden was going on leave to Britain, but when this turned out to be untrue, the *Deccan Mail* gushed, "We are assured that Mr. Plowden's attachment to Hyderabad is too great to induce him to leave it for his native country on any account. If he can only help it he would only be glad to spend the whole of the remaining official life in Hyderabad."[53] A few days later the same paper ran another story, this one concerning Plowden's "strained relation" with the Nizam. The article insinuated that Plowden was passed over for a position as lieutenant-governor of Punjab. The post went to William Mackworth Young, who had been Resident at Mysore, a smaller state than Hyderabad. The *Deccan Mail* described the "long talked of rumour" that Plowden might get the post. Further, his leave to Britain was also nothing more than a "hoax." The writer lamented that a "mightier pen than ours" must come forward and investigate the true nature of Plowden's position and relationship with the Nizam. Such an exposé would "rescue it [Hyderabad] from the hands of greedy persons that have found their way into Hyderabad officialdom."[54]

With Plowden and Server Jung both gone Hyderabad seemed to be entering a new era, and it would not be until 1904 that the pamphlet scandal case would again be in the news. This time it was to announce that its hero-villain had permanently left the stage. On 20 January 1904 Mehdi Hasan died in Lucknow. He was fifty-two years old. In his final years, he seems to have returned to practicing law to help make ends meet. Obituaries for Mehdi appeared in multiple papers, including the *Indian People* as well as in the *Pioneer*. The *Indian People* lamented, "It is with very great regret that we have learnt of the death of Mr. Mehdi Hassan, Bar-at-law of Lucknow, better known to fame in the political world of Hyderabad as Nawab Fateh Nawaz Jung." The obituary recounted Mehdi's work in Hyderabad and his visit to Britain, a visit made memorable by Mehdi's "contributing some letters to the *Times* in support of Sir Syed's then pretty active anti-Congress propaganda." It highlighted a widespread sentiment that working in Hyderabad was particularly perilous. "Shortly after his return he had to suffer the 'inevitable concomitant' of Hyderabad service—enforced retirement due to machinations and intrigues of the rival party." The obituary concluded by highlighting Mehdi's "veering round in favour of the Congress." In 1899 he had hosted a banquet for then Congress President R. C. Dutt at the Prince of Wales Hotel in Lucknow during the annual meeting.[55] The obituary concluded by noting how Mehdi was "extremely sociable, full of geniality and urbanity."[56] The *Pioneer*'s obituary, reprinted in the *Indian People*, stated that Mehdi had suffered for three weeks from "blood poisoning"—a condition whereby bacteria enter the bloodstream, which if not properly treated can result in death. The *Pioneer* summarized local politics during Mehdi's tenure in Hyderabad rather than providing further details about his last days. It stated that Mehdi returned to "private life in his native country" and that he "occasionally ventilated his opinions" in different English magazines.[57]

The obituary recast Mehdi as a congressman at his death, or at least one who was not antithetical to the Congress. By the turn of the century the Congress had become a major political force. Mehdi's earlier opposition to the Congress had put him at odds with Norton and many others. Yet, it was increasingly clear that the Congress was a serious political party and mass movement and that it was not the "loose dynamite" Mehdi once so vocally claimed. As Congress demands of the British government grew more strident and more common, so too did its clashes. Further, tension within Congress was growing, with moderates seeking quiet political means to an end, and more radical members arguing for public agitations against their British masters. Not every recollection of Mehdi was flattering. For instance, an angry letter in the *Leader* a few years after Mehdi's death linked Sir Syed Ahmed Khan and the "Anglo-Muslim alliance" of the 1880s directly to Mehdi and his outspoken writings in the *Times*.[58] Mehdi's opinion of the Congress seems to have softened over time, and after his death, when the Congress had gained ascendancy in India's growing nationalist movement, Mehdi was fitted in with Congress politics and his earlier affiliation scorned. None of the obituaries mentioned Ellen.

We know even less about Ellen's last days. She had a piano and pet dogs, and had entrusted her final arrangements to other poor Britons who lived near her in Lucknow. She was in touch with her sister Esther, whom in her later years had moved from Paris to Chicago and back. Regardless of her daily affairs, Ellen's financial condition worsened over time and prompted her to act.

Around the time of Mehdi's death, Ellen had been in touch with Faridoonji in Hyderabad, political secretary in the Nizam's government. With her husband's illness and death, she found herself in strained financial circumstances and continued selling some of her jewelry and other assets—a practice she followed when Mehdi was still alive and their finances became perilous. Ellen could have easily sold her jewelry in a local Lucknow market, but she took the time to write to an old friend in Hyderabad. Perhaps she felt that because she had been poorly treated there, her friend might be more sympathetic to her plight. Or it may be that she did not want the shame of being seen hawking her possessions in Lucknow. She requested an estimate for a diamond-encrusted buckle she wished to sell. The Nizam's government made her an offer of 1,500 rupees, which she accepted.[59]

At the same time, she also asked Faridoonji to pursue the possibility of a compassionate allowance for her.[60] After a career working for the Nizam's government, an official who retired would be entitled to a form of pension. If a career ended early for some reason, the Nizam often granted a form of compassionate allowance. After Mehdi's death in January, Ellen wrote to Faridoonji, asking for some consideration on this front. When she did not receive any reply, she wrote again, this time directly to the Nizam himself.

Her letter of April 1904 recounts the mysterious ending of Mehdi's small 300-rupee pension in 1893, and places Mehdi's service to the Nizam in comparison with Hormusji, Mushtak Hussain, and Mehdi Ali, all of whom received 400 more rupees in their pension than Mehdi did. Ellen's letter, written on the same style of stationery Queen Victoria herself used—cream-colored with a thick black border—is worth quoting at length.

> Your Highness
>
> I beg to be pardoned for troubling & appealing direct, but my position is so serious and I have no other hope from any one, that, I must write direct. The sad & painful illness, & death of my late husband, Mehdi Hasan, Fateh Nawaz Jung, Your Highness' most faithful servant, has left me almost destitute, except for a few thousand rupees, the bulk of which will go to pay his debts. My husband served Your Highness for 10 years, & and of the years he served the Govt. of India be added, as is usual when an official's services are transferred, then 20 years. Your

Highness was pleased to grant my husband a munsub or mauzifa of 300 Rs a month, which he drew for some years, but it was stopped in 1893, though he never heard of any order to this effect . . .

[And] now he is dead, & I can only entreat & beseech Your Highness to consider my helpless position . . . I know that your Highness will feel for me, when I say that I have no means of livelihood, & also have some relatives of my husband, helpless women with me, & we all appeal to your Highness' mercy. Your obedient servant, Mrs. Mehdi Hasan.[61]

She sent an identical letter in Urdu along with the English version. Ellen's letter suggests she was well aware of what other members of the Nizam's government commanded for their pension. Further, she implies that Mehdi's death was not easy, but rather a "painful illness." And Ellen alludes to some of Mehdi's relatives as staying with her—"helpless women"—but it remains a mystery as to who this might have been. Mehdi's mother was dead, and he had no sisters, so perhaps it was a more distant relation. Nonetheless, it suggests that Ellen's home was not exclusively British or European, but rather welcomed local Indian guests and family members under its humble roof. Ellen thus practiced none of the increasing racial separation that was occurring across the British Raj in India. She demonstrated a mix of British straightforwardness by writing to the Nizam directly combined with a clear knowledge of Indian cultural norms and practices by sending a copy in Urdu, as well as taking her husband's relations into her home.

In early May 1904, Ellen again took up her pen. It had been a month since she wrote to the Nizam, and not having heard anything, now she turned to Ahmed Hussain. At the time, Hussain was serving the Nizam as peshi secretary; a kind of personal assistant. Ellen began by admitting that she did not directly remember Hussain from her time in Hyderabad: "I do not remember your name quite clearly, but I <u>must</u> have seen you often . . ." In fact, Hussain arrived in Hyderabad as Mehdi and Ellen were leaving, so they may have never met. Ellen recounted that she had sent a petition earlier to the Nizam, but had not yet heard back. She writes, "my poor husband is dead & I am left quite destitute, except for a little money which will be left from some insurance money, to be paid away towards his debts." She reiterated the same point in her letter to the Nizam about other nobles like Mushtak Hussain and Mehdi Ali, who received larger and continuous pensions while her husband received none. She also repeated from her earlier letter that some of Mehdi's female relations were staying with her, "unable to work for themselves, they all look to me." When an "Afath" (*afat*; adversity) came upon the couple, she writes, "everyone turned against us, & no doubt [everyone] prejudiced H. H. mind against us in every way."[62] The record falls silent on whether Ellen received any replies to her letters.

Ellen's voice is lost in the record for two years, but in 1906, we hear something again. A file from the Nizam's government records for that year shows payment to Ellen for the purchase of a pair of gold bangles with inlaid pearls.[63] That Ellen repeatedly offered to sell jewelry to the Nizam's government suggests she faced ongoing financial difficulty. And it appears that members of the Nizam's government had begun to look again (and more kindly) on Mrs. Mehdi Hasan.

In the late summer of 1906, Ellen sent Nizam Mahbub Ali Khan a petition for some sort of financial allowance. The petition began, "That Your Highness' humble petitioner is now in a most deplorable position . . ." What money she had, she explained, she used to cover her husband's debts. She wrote, "That Your Highness was always a kind and considerate master until Mehdi Hasan was so unfortunate as to incur Your Highness' displeasure by committing some fault which was considered unpardonable." She also noted that Mehdi had left her "totally unprovided for." She reminded the Nizam, "That Your

Highness' humble petitioner most humbly and respectfully prays Your Highness to forgive and forget her husband's fault and offences and to remember only that he was once a favoured and a faithful servant of Your Highness." Of the Nizam's anger toward Mehdi, Ellen wrote, "your humble petitioner beseeches Your Highness on her bended knees not to continue it against her who is quite helpless." At the end of the petition, she asked for reinstatement of the 300-rupee *mansab* that had been granted to Mehdi but stripped after the trial's conclusion, or any other compassionate allowance the Nizam might offer.[64]

There was no immediate response to Ellen's request. Perhaps the Nizam and prime minister deliberated over what to do and how much, if anything, might be sanctioned. Yet help for Ellen was soon forthcoming. In May 1907, then prime minister of Hyderabad, Maharaja Sir Kishen Pershad, sanctioned 1,000 British government rupees to Ellen for the purpose of travel to Paris to see her sister, Esther, and niece Isabelle.[65] In a letter, Ellen suggested that she wished to bring Esther back to India. Ellen, however, never left Indian soil again.

In 1910, now several years after Mehdi's death, Faridoonji Jung submitted a *guzaarish* to the Nizam. The document is evidence of the long afterlife of the scandal, and resolves some mysteries as to who had been advocating for Ellen in her old age and difficult circumstances. The document seems to have been prompted by Faridoonji's conversation with then Resident of Hyderabad, Sir Charles Stuart Bayley.[66] Bayley had not been in Hyderabad during the time of the scandal. In conversation, not only did Bayley evince concern over Ellen's well-being, but he also revealed that both LaTouche and David Barr had taken an interest in her situation. Barr, who had been the Resident at Hyderabad preceding Bayley, would have likely seen documentation regarding Ellen's plight and been made aware of the scandal. In his request, Faridoonji recounts how Barr communicated to Bayley that Mehdi and Ellen had "been rather badly treated" and that "the case ought not to have been tried in the manner it was, as it was washing one's dirty linen in public."[67] The sentiment, whether from Barr, Bayley, or Faridoonji, acknowledged the transgression of Mehdi and Ellen's private lives being brought into the public world of the Raj. It demonstrates that years after the trial's conclusion, the scandal continued to live on—literally for Ellen as its last living victim—but also for members of both the Hyderabad and British governments in India.

Faridoonji reminded Bayley that Plowden was in part responsible for what happened. It must have been a difficult moment in the conversation for Faridoonji, perhaps the two men sharing tea, to calmly remind Bayley that it had been one of his predecessors who had in a sense encouraged Mehdi to go to court and thus bring a calamity down upon him. Faridoonji told Bayley that Plowden, "had emphatically suggested that Fatteh Nawaz Jung Bahadur should clear himself of the aspersions cast on him, by bringing an action for defamation against Mr. S. M. Mitra." At this moment, Bayley revealed to Faridoonji that "this [the court case encouraged by Plowden] had been a mistake, and that he felt very sorry for Mrs. Mehdi Hassan, who, he was reliably informed, was left in destitute circumstances and was actually starving." Clearly, in the years since Ellen petitioned the Nizam and Ahmed Hussain, her situation had steadily worsened.

One mystery, however, was now about to be resolved. Ellen *had* periodically received some financial assistance, and she often made inquiries about the identity of her benefactor. It was Charles Bayley. He sent her money through a friend on the condition that his name not be revealed. Why Bayley intervened is unclear. Had he crossed paths with the couple years before and felt sorry for them? Had he followed their case in the newspapers or in the halls of the Raj and recognized a tragedy? Could he not stomach a woman of British heritage living so poorly in Britain's crown jewel of India?

Bayley suggested to Faridoonji that perhaps the Nizam could offer Ellen some financial assistance. Faridoonji explained that the Nizam's government *had* made grants of 1,000 rupees to Ellen so that she might go to Britain. However, Ellen never made this trip and instead explained that she used the money to pay her debts. Perhaps unspoken by Ellen was that she had no family in Britain, had only visited the country once in her life, and that India was her true home.

Bayley now suggested that if the Nizam agreed, Faridoonji himself could write to Ellen and ask for an accounting of what she owed, and try to find funds to cover those debts as well as passage to Britain. The Nizam would assume the expense, but only Faridoonji's name would be attached to the matter, thus maintaining the Nizam and Bayley's confidentiality. Faridoonji, however, made a different suggestion to the Nizam. Rather than paying Ellen's debts and sending her to Britain, he suggested that the Nizam grant Ellen a small monthly allowance (40 or 50 rupees) "so that she may end the remaining days of her life in peace and happiness." Faridoonji made explicit Ellen's life circumstances, arguing that India, not Britain, should be her final resting place:

> I do not personally think that Mrs. Mehdi Hassan has any relations in England who could support her, and England is so expensive that she could not afford to live there on any small pittance she may get. I believe she has a niece in England who is married, but this niece is not so well off as to support her. Mrs. Mehdi Hassan has been born and bred in India, and I think she will find it very difficult to live in England. I respectfully trust I may be pardoned for having made this suggestion; I have done so simply because I know for a fact that the poor woman is leading a most miserable existence in Lucknow and is absolutely destitute. Since her husband's death, she has been deserted by all, and has been leading a precarious existence, some times not knowing how to obtain a meal.[68]

Although Faridoonji referred to Ellen's niece, Isabelle (who had been living in Paris), Ellen's sister Esther was the best hope for a familial home in Britain. But Esther, as we shall see, was starting a new chapter in her life and could be of no help to her Lucknow sister.

A few months later in October 1910, grateful for the support she received, Ellen wrote to Faridoonji, wondering who in Hyderabad had championed her cause. Humbled and reflective, she noted how the hardships she had faced had irrevocably changed the person she was:

> You never told me who spoke on my behalf, whoever it was must have forbidden it. What I would have done or how lived these last months had it not been for dear Mr. or rather Sir Syed Hosain, I do not know, but had I not had all these terrible troubles and trials, I would have still been the same frivolous, careless person you knew, now I am quite different, but adieu dear kind friend, you friendship also I can never repay.[69]

In another letter—the top corner of the stationery torn off and thus missing a date—Ellen again asked who interceded on her behalf. "Now tell me who it was whom you managed to interest in my deplorable circumstances, as I wish to remember the name in my prayers."[70]

Finally, Ellen's request for some form of regular compassionate allowance was granted. Officials in Hyderabad required certain personal information from her in order to send the money safely, foremost her age. This, of course, had been highly contested during the trial—was she fifteen at the time of marriage, as she claimed, or was she nineteen as her opponents claimed and her baptismal record recorded? In a letter, she agreed to provide the information requested, but noted, "I am not absolutely certain about my age."[71] In the same letter, she again asked Faridoonji to share with her who had intervened on her part to get the compassionate allowance. "I beg you to tell me

<u>who</u> it was who spoke on my behalf, do please let me know, unless you have promised not to." She concluded her letter, despondently, "ah, my friend, what does it matter where I live or how, I am only filling up my time till the hour strikes to release me from this prison of the flesh, you have saved me from want, God bless you dear Faridoon. Your old friend, E. Hasan."[72] In an internal memo, Faridoonji expressed both frustration and sympathy concerning Ellen's allowance. She had received her allowance in April but not in May, so he wrote to the office that dispensed her gratuity: "How is this? In future please arrange so that the poor woman gets her allowance regularly every month. She is in great poverty."[73]

During her twilight years in Lucknow, Ellen had a small network of friends who supported her. First among these were Mr. and Mrs. Pigott. Second was Mr. H. Gardener, who claimed to have known the Donnelly family since Ellen's childhood. Ellen made Gardener and the Pigotts executors of her will. These three seem to have worked together to assist in finalizing last details. In addition, Ellen's relation on Mehdi's side, Fakhrudeen, then living in Indore, about 430 miles from Lucknow, was in touch with Ellen and became involved with her affairs after her death.[74] Finally, Ellen's sister Esther also was in touch—herself having undergone a change in position—and she too became involved in Ellen's final affairs. In June 1910 Ellen wrote a letter to Mrs. Pigott that was something of a last will and testament.

> As life is very uncertain, and I may die at any moment, I give you below the name of the man in Hyderabad, to whom you should write for money, as after all there is only yourself and dear Mr. Gardener to do all for me. I would not know what to do, I will try and arrange to have my body buried, even in the primitive way, provided it was done effectually, but if impossible,

then of course have my place made near dear Lucy's, as I was with her longer than with others in life, maybe, I will be with or near her dead also, please don't think dearie that I feel in the least bit gloomy or lugubrious about this, nor am I despondent nor ill in mind, and I look upon it quite indifferently the day of the body's death and the release of the spirit from the prison of flesh is an occasion to rejoice upon, rather than to be sad about, and the keys which open any boxes are on a bunch with a silver chain, in the almirah there is another bunch in case you can't find a key, send all my dresses to Esther, and take any thing you like yourself, and give F what he might like, and if you could keep my dogs, I mean ask Sita Ram to keep them, I am sure Furdoon would send the money for their food every month, it will not be for long, as not one of them, would live long without me, and give poor Sita Ram something for his trouble monthly.

I make you and your husband and Mr. Gardener Executors to all I possess. The piano sell and send the money to poor Esther, and for the rest do whatever you think best I trust you and your husband implicitly. With Love, Yours affectionately, Sd. E. M. Hasan.

Though I may live some time yet, but it is waste to try and prepare for all contingencies. For 2 or 3 days I have been feeling impelled to write all this to you.[75]

In fact, Ellen did not "die at any moment" but lived two more years. In 1912, she and Faridoonji exchanged another series of letters. Her allowance was late, and she wrote expressing concern over the delay. Faridoonji responded, apologetically, that the delay was due to the Eid holiday when the treasury was closed, but that the allowance would be sent immediately and regularly from that time forth. On 19 February, Ellen wrote to Faridoonji, acknowledging the arrival of her January allowance. She said, "I cannot tell you dear friend how thankful

I am to whomsoever got me this sum, pittance[?], as it is, it serves to keep me from utter destitution, what should I have done having no money and nothing coming in, to you too dear Faridoon I owe a great debt." She reflected on her and Mehdi's time in Hyderabad. "I can never thank you all enough and H. H. also, for after all dear Mehdi offended <u>him</u> most of all, but the whole thing was a plot of course, and we were ruined. I can never cease thinking of it all, now if only the Gt. of India would give me a refund of that pension money which we subscribed for nearly 9 years and which was forfeited for only 3 months nonsubscription. I would be able to go and see my sister in Paris and bring her back here to live with me."[76] Ellen must have known Esther's life had been difficult. By this point, Esther seems to have been living again in Paris, possibly with her daughter Isabelle, whom, in happier times, Mehdi and Ellen had visited. However, the two sisters would never see each other again.

On 9 April 1912 Ellen wrote to Ahmed Hussain. The letter accompanied a petition to the new Nizam, Mir Osman Ali Khan. His father, Mahbub Ali Khan, had died in August 1911. In her letter, Ellen alludes to a change in her relationship with one of the key figures of the pamphlet scandal, Server Jung. After having a falling out with Plowden and reaching the end of the goodwill extended by Mahbub Ali Khan, Server Jung had left Hyderabad for retirement in Simla. He had once been a friend and champion of Mehdi, and knew Ellen both from their shared time in Lucknow and also in Hyderabad. But Server Jung had lined up squarely in opposition to Mehdi in the trial.

Yet in her letter, Ellen suggests that—perhaps—the two had reconciled. She writes, "I was told by Nawab Surour [sic] Jung who once was an enemy that you [Ahmed Hussain] were beyond everything, a perfectly <u>just</u> man."[77] Did Ellen and Server Jung correspond in the years after each had left Hyderabad? Did he meet her in Lucknow while visiting? No clear answer is possible, but Ellen's phrase "once was an enemy" suggests that they may have reconciled.

In Ellen's petition to the young new Nizam (dated the same as her letter to Ahmed Hussain), she requests an increase in the compassionate allowance she had been receiving. At the time, she received 33 rupees per month, but laments, "the amount is so small that with all my efforts at economy I cannot manage to keep my expenses within that sum."[78] Ellen reminds the Nizam that during Mehdi's service in Hyderabad, Mahbub Ali Khan had granted him a *mansab* of 300 rupees per month, which was stopped without any formal order when the couple left the city. Ellen asks for half of that original amount as her new level of allowance. She explained that she was unable to pay her house rent, and was indebted to a "friend's kindness," one on whom she has no claim, "therefore I implore Your Highness to grant me a compassionate allowance of 150 Rs. a month to enable me to <u>live</u> without contracting debts or burdening kind friends unnecessarily."

Ellen then reveals where she felt the true blame for her and Mehdi's troubles lay: "His late Highness was very angry with my dear husband, but still H. H. would never have stopped his munsub, had it not been for Mr. Plowden, who insisted on it."[79] Unlike his relationship with Server Jung, Mehdi never seemed to have any rapport with Plowden, and indeed, Plowden seems to have strategically helped Mehdi fail. Now, years later, Ellen blamed Plowden for her and Mehdi's troubles, suggesting that he interfered in their *mansab*. No direct evidence bears this out, but given Plowden's relationship with Mehdi and Ellen, or lack thereof, her suggestion seems more likely true than not. Ellen signed her petition, "Your Highness' most obedient servant, Mrs. Mehdi Hasan, widow of Nawab Fatteh Nawaz Jung once Home Secretary of Hyderabad." These are the last known words from Ellen Hasan.

Exactly two weeks later, on the evening of 23 April 1912, Ellen died. Two days afterward, a letter began its journey from Lucknow to Hyderabad, bearing the bad news. It was from Fakhrudeen, Mehdi's relation. Years earlier, he had been the one to escort Ellen to Bombay, where she met up with Mehdi to begin their journey to Europe. He had also very briefly testified in the trial. He wrote to Faridoonji, "I am sorry to inform you that Mrs. Mehdi Hassan wife of my brother N. Mehdi Hassan died on Tuesday last. Unfortunately I was not here when she died I was at Indore. I hope H. H. the Nizam may be please to show his usual generosity in her care too. Yours faithfully, Fakhrudeen Hassan, Bar-at-Law."[80]

At the same time, we hear a voice that has been until now all but silent in the record: Esther Donnelly, the second eldest Donnelly sister. Esther had escaped the trauma that Lucy and Ellen had faced in Lucknow. She married and became Esther Bigex. It is unclear what happened to her husband, but the next record of her comes far from either Hyderabad or Lucknow, in Chicago, Illinois. A marriage certificate from Cook County, Illinois, dated 26 June 1897, indicates that Esther Bigex married one Egisto Amedeo Benvenuti.[81] The marriage record shows her name as "Esther or Ester Bigex," and subsequent correspondence from Esther Benvenuti to officials at Hyderabad confirms that this was indeed Ellen's sister. Yet how Esther came to Chicago and who Egisto Amedeo Benvenuti was remain a mystery. Adding to the mystery is why her letters addressed to Hyderabad are stamped "Paris." Why and when she went back to Paris is unknown. It may be that her daughter, Isabelle, was still living there. While the date of the marriage is certain, both Esther and Egisto seem to have altered personal details for the purpose of the marriage record, which shows both as twenty-eight years old and thus both born in the same year, 1869. However, Esther's baptismal records show that she was in fact born in 1850. Recording a false age may have been an attempt to recreate herself, to erase her first nineteen years spent in India and her early marriage at sixteen. Whatever the reason, we know that she kept in touch with Ellen, and now Esther vigorously attempted to help ensure that Ellen received a proper burial and to settle accounts

after her death. Her letter is dated 23 May 1912, and is addressed to
Faridoonji:

> I write to you in behalf of my sister who died in great poverty,
> and there was not a penny in the house to pay the funeral ex-
> penses and burial, nor medical attendance.
>
> My dear sister often mentioned your name to me in her let-
> ters, and spoke of you as a friend. As she had a small pension
> from the bounty of H. H. the Nizam, could you use your influ-
> ence now in that quarter to obtain at least 300 Rs. British to
> enable us to settle Mrs. Hassan's affairs definitely. I have asked
> a friend of mine in Lucknow to see to her affairs. I am a very
> poor woman working for my maintenance daily, and find I am
> powerless to send any sum beyond a pound, which is quite in-
> sufficient in such a case. This is the last demand that will be
> made in behalf of the poor woman now gone to her last home.
> Will you please send the Nizam's gift or a contribution to Mr. H.
> Gardener, c/o Mr. Pigott, 2 Neil Road, Lucknow, Oudh, N.W.P.
> I thank you before hand, as I know you are a just man and good,
> I remain Sir, Yours gratefully Esther Benvenuti.[82]

On 16 June, Mr. Pigott also wrote to Faridoonji. "I should have written
earlier, but you will excuse an octogenarian in indifferent health, in
this trying <u>hot</u> weather, for the delay." Pigott explained that Ellen's
relation, Fakhrudeen, was at Indore at the time of her death, but
rushed back to Lucknow upon hearing the news. "He has frequently
been with us since, helping in her affairs. She certainly had great pecuniary difficulties to contend with but never complained, though she
came to us often." Pigott then recounted how the Nizam's government
had granted Ellen a compassionate allowance but suggested she never
received it. This is not entirely accurate, as we know from Ellen's own

letters that she received payments before her death. Pigott believed a small sum of about 150 rupees might be collected from the money sent to help offset the cost of her funeral expenses and other debts. That expense, Pigott explained, would be used to place a tombstone over her grave. He continued, "The late Mrs. Mehdi Hassan was most anxious to provide for the keep of her dogs. We are glad to say we found homes for them immediately after her demise."[83] While the dogs were looked after, no mention is made of the Hasan women Ellen had once given shelter.

The next day, 17 June, Gardener wrote to Faridoonji in looping cursive. Begging to be forgiven for being a "perfect stranger" writing on behalf of Mrs. Mehdi Hasan, Gardener stated that he had been made executor of Ellen's will. In fact he shared this role with the Pigotts. Gardener wrote, "on my taking an inventory of her property etc. I find she has scarcely enough to pay her funeral expenses, doctor's fees etc . . ." In asking for financial support, he noted how Ellen had always spoken fondly of Faridoonji and Syed Husain.

Despite her social fall, Ellen found support from a circle of friends and family as well as from sympathetic members of the Nizam's government. Thus, officials in Hyderabad received correspondence from no less than four different members of Mehdi and Ellen's circle: Esther and Fakhrudeen representing the family, and the Pigotts and Gardener, elderly British friends residing in Lucknow.

With these pleas in hand, the Nizam's government and Government of India machinery sputtered into gear. On 27 June, Reginald Glancy, finance minister in Hyderabad State, wrote to Faridoonji. His typed letter came on thick cream stationery, embossed with the Finance Office seal in one corner and the office name in the other. "I beg to state that in my opinion His Highness' Government have behaved with the greatest generosity. The writer of this last letter is in no way bound to pay any debts left by Mrs. Mehdi Hasan nor is it usual in such cases amongst Europeans for sisters to attempt to do so."[84] He concluded by stating that enough had been done already, but that if the Nizam's government wanted to do more, it should make inquiries in Lucknow as to the legitimacy of the claim that Ellen had debts to be paid.

At the beginning of July, Faridoonji wrote to Arthur C. Hankin, inspector general of Hyderabad's police, asking him to contact the Lucknow police via secret means to ascertain some facts surrounding Ellen's death. Had she died in debt? If so, how much was owed and to whom? And if funds were paid to Gardener, "is it likely to be properly used?"[85] Meanwhile, a few weeks later, Mrs. Pigott wrote to Faridoonji asking for help. She noted that a month had gone by since she had received an acknowledgment of her letter and noted that in Lucknow "creditors are making frequent enquiries and cause needless trouble."[86]

By August, inquiries raised by the Nizam's government with the police in Lucknow bore fruit. A confidential report from Inspector Syed Vikar Husain Rezvi of the Lucknow police arrived in Hyderabad. The report stated that Ellen was in debt 200 rupees on her death, and that she had left her property in her will to Mrs. Pigott. Mrs. Pigott had told Rezvi that she sold all Ellen's furniture to help cover the costs of the funeral. The report continues, "Only one piano remains about which Mrs. Mehdi Hussain mentioned in her will that the cost of it, after selling it, should be sent to her sister in France." Rezvi notes that the piano would easily fetch three hundred to four hundred rupees, which would cover any last debt.[87]

In early September, J. H. Devlin, assistant secretary of the Nizam's Financial Department, wrote to Faridoonji. He noted that, following the confidential report by the Lucknow police on Ellen's state of affairs, no further pecuniary assistance was needed to cover her debts. They would be erased by the sale of her piano, the last object of value she seemed to have owned.[88] On 11 September, Faridoonji wrote to

Pigott that, given the pending sale of the piano, no further aid would come from Hyderabad.[89]

The sale of the piano was the last chord struck in the lives of Mehdi and Ellen Hasan. The couple had no children, so no subsequent generation would ponder their rise and fall. No further word came from Fakhrudeen or Esther. The latter never returned to India, and the former presumably receded back into his law practice at Indore. Almost all of the Donnelly family rested in India—Michael Donnelly, the family patriarch, was buried at Ambala; Mrs. Donnelly was buried at Kanpur; Lucy was buried at Ambala; and now Ellen was laid to rest at Lucknow.

The Hyderabad pamphlet case was typically scandalous. Scandals flourish in their ability to make private matters into public spectacles. This depends heavily on forms of media. While the scandal circulated through the printed pamphlet itself and through newspapers, today a similar story would travel instantaneously through electronic mediums, especially if sex was involved. Charges of prostitution, incest, adultery, and trading sexual favors were then, as they are now, titillating and potentially shocking. The scandal worked, in part, because the subject matter—sex—normally a private matter, was made public through the trial and then spread through newspapers, telegrams, and at "scandal points." Numerous Government of India and British government investigators all helped propel Mehdi and Ellen's story far afield.

The pamphlet scandal shocked because Mehdi and Ellen crossed an increasingly wide racial chasm that existed between Indians and Britons in the late nineteenth century. Ellen, born in India, fluent in Urdu, comfortable moving between Indian and European sartorial norms (even between Christianity and Islam) disconcerted British officials. She behaved more like her eighteenth-century predecessors than a late nineteenth-century Englishwoman. At that time of "white Mughals," such cultural hybridity or "crossing over" between things Indian and European was more common and better tolerated. But in the late nineteenth century, her marriage to an Indian Muslim man went against the increasingly conservative social practices of the day: members of the ruling class were not supposed to marry the ruled.

Mehdi came of age and rose to power during the height of the British Raj. He believed in British rule and demonstrated his loyalty to the Raj when he visited London and met Queen Victoria (with tears in his eyes). His marriage to Ellen only further cemented his embrace of the empire. Mehdi believed that under British rule, relationships such as his and Ellen's were supported by the rule of law and good for the empire. Only at the end of his life did he begin to see race as a possible underlying cause of the pamphlet and his downfall. This was evident when he suggested that his treatment by Plowden might have been different if he had been an Englishman, which he had come to understand was synonymous with whiteness. Near the end of his life, Mehdi seems to have become more attuned to the changing nature of the Raj at the turn of the century. The Indian National Congress had gained momentum and was making increasingly strident claims on the British government in India, some even calling for agitation in the streets against the British. In this environment, Mehdi's loyalty to British rule in India was fast becoming a relic of a previous era, his arguments in favor of warm Indo-British relations replaced by nationalist calls for Indian independence.

The scandal raised questions about Ellen's private life before her marriage, what Mehdi knew and when, and the nature of their marriage—if they had been married at all. Were she and her sister Lucy prostitutes in Lucknow? Like scandals of more recent times, in part the answer depends on the definition of prostitute. Perhaps the sisters did share their beds with different men. Perhaps money was exchanged, either in a purely transactional way, or as some of Ellen's lovers described it, as a "gift" given out of affection. It seems less likely that Ellen and Lucy worked openly in a bazaar—their background would have made them easily visible and open to police attention and registration, none of which is evident in the historical record. Was Ellen kept by several men who formed a "joint stock company" to help satisfy their carnal needs? It is certainly possible. If Ellen chose to share sexual favors with multiple partners, pooling resources would be one way for her lovers to fund this venture.

When Mehdi courted and married Ellen, did he know something or everything about her past? He most likely did. Mehdi, like Server Jung and other young nobles from Lucknow at this time, shared stories about sexual conquests, and it seems difficult to believe he never heard anything about Ellen's background. What happened on the day of their supposed marriage? The marriage document, the subject of so much of the pamphlet case, seems unlikely to have been created as the trial began. This would have required a complicated forgery and equally complicated lies to sustain it. More likely, there was some genuine confusion about the role of the document at the time of Mehdi and Ellen's marriage. Perhaps Mehdi had it written up after the ceremony, or had one version and later revised it.

Did the couple actually marry? In some ways, this seems irrelevant, as throughout their lives they behaved as a married couple. For Mehdi and Ellen, it appears to have been love or at least loyalty from the beginning. It may have been a mutually beneficial union between an aspiring Indian nobleman and a poor British girl who saw in each other the possibility of improving their lives, trading on the status that accrued to class and race, but this would not explain the length of their marriage. When the pamphlet scandal erupted, Mehdi felt bound to defend his wife's reputation. The question of their marriage took on greater weight because they had presented themselves to Queen Victoria. If they had misrepresented themselves, they would have been dishonest, and they would have disgraced those who vetted guests for the Queen's levée. Throughout the onerous trial and into their twilight years, Mehdi and Ellen remained together. He could have divorced her according to Muslim custom; she could have left him and joined her father or sisters elsewhere, but neither availed themselves of these options. To her last days, she signed her name as Mrs. Mehdi Hasan, never abandoning her husband, her marriage, or this identity despite difficult times. Thus, loyalty and love are the best possible explanations for what bound the couple together. Then, as today, it remains an ideal in any relationship.

Who wrote the pamphlet? In all probability it was a multi-authored work. Server Jung and Syed Ali Bilgrami, who knew Mehdi and Ellen from their north Indian Lucknow days, could have provided some details of the couple's past, while local Hyderabadis such as Vasudeva Rao—fed up with Mehdi's success—might have added the fuel of jealousy to the fire. The pamphlet charged that Ellen had become being Salar Jung II's lover, the suggestion being that this helped advance Mehdi's career. As Salar Jung II was dead by the time of the trial, only Ellen remained to deny the charge. The accusation seems driven less by a desire to hurt Ellen's reputation, although it certainly did this, than an aim to destroy Mehdi's success. His career had flourished in Hyderabad, and linking Mehdi's success to "pimping" his wife to a powerful noble may have served as one way to undermine him.

Loyalty bound Mehdi and Ellen together, and sex made the scandal particularly appealing to the late–nineteenth-century reader, but in the end, it was the powers of a princely state and the British Raj that raised the couple up and then brought them tumbling down. Mehdi was an ambitious man, and he no doubt enjoyed his rise through the ranks of the Nizam's government. He and his allies were widely reported to have all but controlled the government of the state. Yet this rise to power exacerbated multiple tensions. His sometimes pushy attitude rubbed the increasingly snobbish British Residents and their staff the wrong way, and his success undoubtedly caused local Hyderabadis to be jealous, if not outright hostile, to this north Indian interloper who had found so much success in the south. Ellen was a beautiful young woman in Lucknow who may have shared her bed with one or more lovers. Mehdi's marriage proposal, her conversion to Islam, and an early married life in relative seclusion boded well for their nuptial happiness. But once in Hyderabad, her emergence as a respectable English woman was too much for their enemies to take. Mehdi and Ellen were thus forced to serve as an object lesson in the power of scandal at the height of empire. The events that drove them to disgrace and destitution only underscored the many anxieties played out in a princely state and the British Raj.

NOTES

GLOSSARY

BIBLIOGRAPHY

ACKNOWLEDGMENTS

CREDITS

INDEX

NOTES

During the time I was conducting research for this book, the archive in Hyderabad went from being part of the Andhra Pradesh State Archive to also being part of the Telangana State Archive. I have indicated the Telangana and Andhra Pradesh State Archive as T/APSA. Files from this archive are from departments and subdepartments within the Nizam's government. Not every file was housed in a subdepartment, but where they exist I have named them in the note. All files use a three-part numbering system, with separate numbers for the installment, list, and file. I have denoted this as three numbers separated by slashes; for instance, 11/1/345 refers to Installment 11, List 1, and File 345. The Chowmahalla Palace Archive (CMP) is organized chronologically, thus I have provided the date and document name in the notes.

Prologue

1. Zareena Parveen, "Contribution of Non-Mulkis for the Development of Administration and Literature in Hyderabad State (1853–1911)" (Osmania University, 2000). *Fateh* can mean "conqueror"; *Nawaz* "prince," "loving," or "cherisher"; and *Jung* was usually a separate honorary title meaning "war" or "righteous." His title might be (very) roughly translated as "cherished conqueror; righteous in war."
2. R. Venkata Subba Rau, *The Hyderabad Pamphlet Scandal Case* (Lucknow: G. P. Varma Press, 1893).

1. New Beginnings in Hyderabad

1. For an overview of the history of the princely states, see Barbara Ramusack, *The Indian Princes and Their States* (Cambridge: Cambridge University Press, 2004).

2. In 1891, Hyderabad State included 5,031,069 Telugu speakers; 1,198,382 Urdu speakers; 3,493,858 Marathi speakers; 1,451,046 Kannada speakers; and 362,685 speakers of other languages. *Imperial Gazetteer of India, Hyderabad State* (Calcutta: Superintendent of Government Printing, 1909), 23.

3. Karen Leonard, "Hyderabad: The Mulki-Non-Mulki Conflict," in *People, Princes and Paramount Power: Society and Politics in the Indian Princely States,* ed. Robin Jeffrey (Delhi: Oxford University Press, 1978).

4. Histories of the East India Company abound. For instance, see Phillip Lawson, *The East India Company: A History* (London: Longman, 1993); Nick Robins, *The Corporation That Changed the World: How the East India Company Shaped the Modern Multinational* (London: Pluto Press, 2006).

5. These men who participated freely in Indian cultures and lived an often lavish form of hybrid Indo-European lives were dubbed "white Mughals." On this community, and the story of Kirkpatrick, see William Dalrymple, *White Mughals: Love and Betrayal in Eighteenth-Century India* (London: HarperCollinsPublishers, 2002).

6. R. Venkata Subba Rau, *The Hyderabad Pamphlet Scandal Case* (Lucknow: G. P. Varma Press, 1893), 10 (hereafter cited as Rau).

7. Rau, 10, 446.

8. Michael Donnelly had two brothers. The first, Thomas, worked for the Oudh-Rohilcund Railway, largely centered at Lucknow and linking that city to others in the greater Indo-Gangetic Plain. The other brother, John, served as deputy surgeon-general in the Indian Medical Service in the Madras Presidency. Rau, 439.

9. Ellen verified this in her testimony. Rau, 448.

10. Rau, 448.

11. Rau, 447.

12. Rau, 20.

13. Rau, 250.

14. She appears in the record at the time of her own marriage on May 11, 1891, to Charles George Russell. This wedding took place in either Karachi or Bombay—the record lists both. Rau, 12.

15. Rau, 450.

16. *The Beauties of Lucknow Consisting of Twenty-Four Selected Photographed Portraits, Cabinet Size, of the Most Celebrated and Popular Living Histrionic Singers, Dancing Girls and Actresses of the Oudh Court and of Lucknow* (Calcutta: Calcutta Central Press, 1874).

17. Henry Yule and A. C. Burnell, *Hobson-Jobson: The Anglo-Indian Dictionary* (London: John Murray, 1886; Ware, Hertfordshire: Wordsworth Reference, 1996), 344.

18. Yule and Burnell, *Hobson-Jobson*, 344.

19. In 1919, then Second Assistant Political Resident at Hyderabad, H. R. Lynch-Blosse, recounted the tumultuous decades of the 1880s and 1890s. He described Ellen as "a lady of Eurasian extraction who was received in the highest society in Hyderabad and had even been presented to the Queen." L/PS/20/F137/1, OIOC. H. R. Lynch-Blosse, *Hyderabad Political Notebook* (1919), 84. Hyderabad Residency Press.

20. Mehdi Hasan, *Extracts from the Diary of Nawab Mehdi Hasan Khan Fathah Nawaz Jung* (London: Talbot Bros., 1890), 51.

21. In the court case, his father is listed as Fasli Hasan. Hasan, *Extracts*, 10.

22. Rau, 264.

23. Rau, 441.

24. Hasan, *Extracts*, 20. Another "relative" of Mehdi Hasan, Bashirudden, finds mention in the newspapers because he received a promotion to the rank of police superintendent at the grade of 300 rupees from his former position at the grade of 200 rupees, "in supercession of many old and deserving Superintendent of higher grades." Hyderabad Correspondent, *Hyderabad in 1890 and 1891* (Bangalore: Caxton Press, 1892), 81.

25. "Personal Intelligence," *Indian Magazine and Review*, April 1888, 224.

26. Omar Khalidi, introduction to *An Indian Passage to Europe: The Travels of Fath Nawaz Jang,* by Fathah Nawaz Jang (New Delhi: Oxford University Press, 2006), xiii.

27. Server-ul-Mulk, *My Life: Being the Autobiography of Nawab Server-Ul-Mulk Bahadur,* trans. Jiwan Yar Jung (London: Arthur H. Stockwell, 1932), 252.

28. Omar Khalidi, "The Amazing Abid of Hyderabad and Devon," *Devon & Cornwall Notes & Queries* 38, no. 6 (Autumn 1999): 161–168.

29. The Residency at Hyderabad remains an impressive architectural testament to British power in the Deccan. On its history, see Omar Khalid, *The British Residency in Hyderabad: An Outpost of the Raj 1779–1948* (London: British Association for Cemeteries in South Asia, 2005).

30. M. Soobaraya Moodellear, *Hyderabad Almanac and Directory for 1875* (Madras: Foster Press, 1874), 178.

31. M. A. Nayeem, *The Royal Palaces of the Nizams* (Hyderabad: Hyderabad Publisher, 2009), 74–99.

32. John F. Hurst, "Hyderabad and Golconda," *Harpers,* vol. 76, Dec. 1987–May 1988, pp. 440–449 (New York: Harper Brothers, 1888), 444. Such points existed in many cities and towns across India and were usually public intersections where locals—Indian, British, or both—could gather and gossip about the latest scandal. During her year in an Indian fort, one Mrs. Guthrie noted that even in a small town like Belgaum (located near Goa) people gathered together at a "scandal point." While the hill-station town of Simla has, perhaps, the most famous "scandal point," Guthrie notes that, "there is a scandal-point at every station." Mrs. Guthrie, *My Year in an Indian Fort,* 2 vols. (London: Hurst and Blackett, 1877), 1:279.

33. For an overview of Hyderabad and its political participants, see Karen Leonard, "The Hyderabad Political System and Its Participants," *Journal of Asian Studies* 30, no. 3 (1971): 569–582.

34. Vasant Kumar Bawa, *Hyderabad under Salar Jung I* (New Delhi: S. Chand & Company Ltd., 1996).

35. Joseph Rock, "The New Era at Hyderabad," *The Fortnightly Review* 61, no. 366 (June 1897): 911–922.

36. Allen Andrews, *The Splendid Pauper* (Philadelphia: J. B. Lippincott, 1968), 118.

37. Server Jung belonged to the distinguished Berlass clan of Chaghathai Mughals.

38. Abbas Beg is a familiar name in the history of north India during the mid-nineteenth century. He served with Sir Henry Lawrence in the Punjab wars, and, when the latter shifted to Oudh, Abbas Beg went with him. Lawrence lost his life in Lucknow during the siege of the Residency, but Abbas Beg survived him, and the Company in turn recognized him for his service. Lord Canning made him a *taluqdar* in Oudh, and he received the confiscated state of Baday Gaon in the district of Sitapur as his reward. Sitapur is about fifty-five miles north of Lucknow. Abbas Beg's lands remained in the family after his death, providing Server Jung and his brothers a permanent source of income and prestige (Server-ul-Mulk, *My Life*, viii).

39. William Dalrymple, *The Last Mughal: The Fall of a Dynasty, Delhi, 1857* (New Delhi: Penguin, 2006).

40. Server-ul-Mulk, *My Life*, 29.

41. Server-ul-Mulk, *My Life*, 85–86.

42. Server-ul-Mulk, *My Life*, 86.

43. An English tutor was also deemed necessary for the young Nizam. At first, the Resident, Charles B. Saunders (who served in that position from 1868 to 1875), intimated that the Government of India would appoint a person. Salar Jung and the Amir-i-Kabir rejected the idea of a person unknown to them being appointed for such an intimate and important post. They in turn called on Captain John Clerk. Coming from Queen Victoria's household Clerk had sterling credentials. Upon arrival in Hyderabad, he was granted the title of Superintendent of Education. Clerk and Server Jung met with the young Nizam, and thus began a daily routine of tutoring. Server Jung describes these early happy times. "In three or four days we became free, and he [the Nizam] as much at home with us as if we had known one another all our lives" (Server-ul-Mulk, *My Life*, 132).

2. A Grand Tour to the Heart of Europe

1. Syed Hossain [Husain] Bilgrami, *A Memoir of Sir Salar Jung, G.C.S.I.* (Bombay: The Times of India Steam Press, 1883), 127.

2. A. Claude Campbell, *Glimpses of the Nizam's Dominions* (Philadelphia: Historical Publishing Co., 1898), 43. This account nearly quotes Bilgrami's account, published earlier.

3. Mehdi remained in contact with Syed Ahmed Khan, writing articles for Khan's journal, *Tahzib al-Akhlaq*.

4. Assistant Financial Secretary, His Highness' Government, to Private Secretary to His Highness' Minister, 27 June 1893, R/1/1/142, OIOC. A photograph shows Mehdi, likely during his time as chief justice, centered and seated among a group of other judges and legal officials. He is, unfortunately, not identified as such. See M. A. Nayeem, *The Splendour of Hyderabad: Last Phase of an Oriental Culture (1591–1948 AD)* (Bombay: Jaico Publishing House, 1987), 164, image no. 89.

5. Joseph Rock, "The New Era at Hyderabad," *The Fortnightly Review* 61, no. 366 (June 1897): 911–922, 912.

6. Allen Andrews, *The Splendid Pauper* (Philadelphia: J. B. Lippincott Company, 1968), 104.

7. Rock, "New Era at Hyderabad," 913.

8. Server-ul-Mulk, *My Life: Being the Autobiography of Nawab Server-Ul-Mulk Bahadur*, trans. Jiwan Yar Jung (London: Arthur H. Stockwell, 1932), 252.

9. A rollicking account of Frewen's life, including his brief stint in Hyderabad, can be found in Andrews, *The Splendid Pauper*.

10. During his career, he collected an array of titles befitting his positions: Intezar Jung, Waqar-ul-Mulk, and Nawab. He died at the age of 76 in 1917.

11. Hyderabad Correspondent, *Hyderabad in 1890 and 1891* (Bangalore: Caxton Press, 1892), 31.

12. Server-ul-Mulk, *My Life*, 252.

13. Mehdi Hasan, *Extracts from the Diary of Nawab Mehdi Hasan Khan Fathah Nawaz Jung* (London: Talbot Bros., 1890), 105.

14. Server-ul-Mulk, *My Life*, 200.

15. Server-ul-Mulk, *My Life*, 252.

16. *The Pioneer*, 28 November 1877.

17. On India's clubland and the role of the secretary and president, see Benjamin B. Cohen, *In the Club: Associational Life in Colonial South Asia*, Studies in Imperialism (Manchester: Manchester University Press, 2015), 100–105.

18. This English newspaper began in Allahabad in 1865. Two months after Mehdi's letter, it hired a young assistant editor whose name would come to far outshine Mehdi's—Rudyard Kipling.

19. *The Pioneer*, 20 September 1887.

20. *The Pioneer*, 20 September 1887.

21. "Will of Mrs. Mehdi Hasan in favor of Nawab Mehdi Hasan, dated 27th October 1887," in R. Venkata Subba Rau, *The Hyderabad Pamphlet Scandal Case* (Lucknow: G. P. Varma Press, 1893), v (hereafter cited as Rau).

22. He returned to Hyderabad in January of 1889, and Ellen made her way back the following November.

23. For an example of this, see the diary of Amar Singh, in Susanne Hoeber Rudolph, Lloyd I. Rudolph, and Mohan Singh Kanota, eds., *Reversing the Gaze* (Cambridge, MA: Westview Press, 2002).

24. Arguably, Mehdi participated in a form of broader Muslim cosmopolitanism. See Eric Lewis Beverley, *Hyderabad, British India, and the World: Muslim Networks and Minor Sovereignty, c.1850–1950* (Cambridge: Cambridge University Press, 2015), 49–53.

25. Hasan, *Extracts*, 41.

26. Hasan, *Extracts*, 50.

27. Hasan, *Extracts*, 51. At different times and in different places, both Mehdi and Ellen made different sartorial choices. On this strategic type of practice, see Beth Fowkes Tobin, *Picturing Imperial Power* (Durham, NC: Duke University Press, 1999).

28. Mehdi Hasan was one of many Indians who visited Britain and Europe. For an account of the early Indian visitors, see Michael Fisher, *Counterflows to Colonialism: Indian Travellers and Settlers in Britain 1600–1857* (Delhi: Permanent Black, 2004).

29. Hasan, *Extracts*, 54.

30. Hasan, *Extracts*, 57.

31. This interview ran in several papers: *Birmingham Daily Post*, 29 March 1888; *The Leeds Mercury*, 31 March 1888; and *Liverpool Mercury*, 2 April 1888.

32. Mehdi Hassan, "Mr. Hume's 'Loose Dynamite' in India," *The Times*, 3 September 1892.

33. Hasan's anti-Congress leanings were picked up in other corners of the British Empire. News of his letter to the *Times* was, for instance, covered in the *Singapore Free Press and Mercantile Advertiser*, 13 September 1892.

34. Hasan, *Extracts*, 64.

35. Hasan, *Extracts*, 76.

36. Coralie Younger, *Wicked Women of the Raj* (New Delhi: HarperCollins, 2003).

37. Scholars have begun to recover the roles of women and children, both Indian and British, in the Raj and British Empire. Some occupied class positions similar to Ellen's. See, for example, Elizabeth Buettner, *Empire Families* (Oxford: Oxford University Press, 2004); Durba Ghosh, *Sex and the Family in Colonial India: The Making of Empire* (Cambridge: Cambridge University Press, 2006).

38. *Indian Daily News*, 27 March 1889.

39. *Indian Daily News*, 27 March 1889.

40. Godley to Colquhoun, 15 May 1888, Foreign Department, Secret-I., Pros. NAI.

41. Technically, David Ochterlony Dyce Sombre was the first Indian elected to Parliament, but he was Anglo-Indian, and lost power due to corruption.

42. Hasan, *Extracts*, 82.

43. A later mention comes when Mehdi and Ellen attended an "At Home" hosted by the Earl of Northbrook. Hasan, *Extracts*, 106.

44. Hasan, *Extracts*, 89.

45. Hasan, *Extracts*, 98.

46. Hasan, *Extracts*, 98.

47. Hasan, *Extracts*, 103.

48. Hasan, *Extracts*, 103.

49. Hasan, *Extracts*, 104.

50. *Madras Mail*, 2 June 1888.

51. Durand to Minister, 25 July 1889, in Rau, 192.

52. Hasan to Wallace, 18 May 1888, Foreign Department, Secret-I., Pros., NAI.

53. Hasan to Wallace, 18 May 1888.

54. Hasan to Wallace, 18 May 1888.

55. Hasan to Wallace, 18 May 1888.

56. Hasan to Wallace, 18 May 1888.

57. Dufferin to Howell, 25 May 1888, Foreign Department, Secret-I., Pros., NAI.

58. Howell to Dufferin, 26 May 1888, Foreign Department, Secret-I., Pros., NAI. Sir Edward Bradford was an old India hand; at the time of Mehdi's visit to London, he was serving as secretary of the Political and Secret Department of the India Office.

59. *The Tribune*, 14 July 1888.

60. *Indian Spectator*, 8 July 1888.

61. *Deccan Times*, in *Madras Mail*, 21 June 1888.

62. *Madras Mail*, 14 July 1888.

63. Robertson to Edmund Neel, 30 September 1888, Foreign Department, Secret-I., Pros., NAI.

64. This is likely one Major Robertson with whom Mehdi met during his time in London. Hasan, *Extracts*, 119.

65. Robertson to Neel, 30 September 1888, Foreign Department, Secret-I., Pros., NAI.

66. Server-ul-Mulk, *My Life*, 257.

67. Hasan, *Extracts*, 144.

68. Hasan, *Extracts*, 152.

69. Hasan, *Extracts*, 152.

70. "Edict," 16 October 1888, Foreign Department, Secret-I., Pros., NAI.

71. Foreign Secretary to Secretary, Political and Secret Department, 1 November 1888, Foreign Department, Secret-I., Pros., NAI.

72. Dufferin to Secretary of State for India, 5 November 1888, Foreign Department, Secret-I., Pros., NAI.

73. *Deccan Times*, 19 January 1889. Moulvi Syed Mahdi Ali, ed., *Hyderabad Affairs*, vol. 10 (London: Talbot Brothers, 1889).

74. *Deccan Times*, 21 January 1889.

75. News of the deal being signed in Hyderabad was carried by, among others, the *Glasgow Herald*, 27 March 1889.

76. *Birmingham Daily Post*, 6 January 1890.

3. The Pinnacle of Power

1. *Madras Mail*, 9 December 1889.

2. *Pioneer*, 13 December 1889.

3. *Pioneer*, 13 December 1889.

4. *Pioneer*, 13 December 1889.

5. Fitzpatrick was born in Dublin in 1837 and later attended Trinity College, Dublin. Like Mehdi, he was called to the bar at Inner Temple. A member of the Indian Civil Service, he began his time in India in 1858 and posted to Delhi, where he served as an assistant magistrate. During his early decades in India he served in the legislative department as judge of the Chief Court of the Punjab, chief commissioner of the Central Provinces, Resident in Mysore, chief commissioner of Coorg and in Assam, all before finally coming to Hyderabad. Fitzpatrick and his wife's time in India could not have been easy. The couple lost three daughters to illness, and the last and youngest died of typhoid in Hyderabad in early March 1891. After leaving the princely state, Fitzpatrick went on to become lieutenant governor of Punjab before retiring in 1897. From then until 1907 he served on the Council of India. His honors included GCSI (Knights Grand Commander of the Order of the Star of India). He died in 1920 in London at the age of 83. Fitzpatrick was also involved in an earlier nineteenth-century domestic legal case. The Begum Samru of Sardhana was the ex-wife of David Ochterlony Dyce Sombre (himself of Anglo-Indian heritage, one-time Resident at Delhi, and the first person of Indian descent to be elected to Britain's Parliament). He had divorced her, and upon his death, she sued to overturn his will. A grand court case, a strong woman, and high politics highlight the themes this case shares with that of the pamphlet scandal. For a full exploration of Dyce Sombre, see Michael H. Fisher, *The Inordinately Strange Life of Dyce Sombre: Victorian Anglo-Indian MP and Chancery "Lunatic"* (New York: Columbia University Press, 2010).

6. Keay to Ardagh, 31 December 1889, Foreign Department, Secret-I., Pros., NAI.

7. Keay to Ardagh, 31 December 1889.

8. Keay to Ardagh, 31 December 1889.

9. Keay to Ardagh, 31 December 1889.

10. Fitzpatrick to Ardagh, 11 January 1890, Foreign Department, Secret-I., Pros., NAI.

11. Fitzpatrick to Ardagh, 11 January 1890.

12. The nomination was opposed by the acting Resident, Howell. Some coverage of this can be found in Moulvi Syed Mahdi Ali, ed., *Hyderabad Affairs*, vol. 10 (London: Talbot Brothers, 1889), 441–450.

13. Fitzpatrick to Ardagh, 11 January 1890, Foreign Department, Secret-I., Pros., NAI.

14. Fitzpatrick to Ardagh, 11 January 1890.

15. Fitzpatrick to Ardagh, 11 January 1890.

16. Fitzpatrick to Ardagh, 11 January 1890.

17. Fitzpatrick to Ardagh, 11 January 1890.

18. Hyderabad Correspondent, *Hyderabad in 1890 and 1891* (Bangalore: Caxton Press, 1892), 8.

19. Hyderabad Correspondent, *Hyderabad*, 15.

20. Hyderabad Correspondent, *Hyderabad*, 33.

21. Hyderabad Correspondent, *Hyderabad*, 37–38.

22. Hyderabad Correspondent, *Hyderabad*, 110.

23. Hyderabad Correspondent, *Hyderabad*, 110.

24. Hyderabad Correspondent, *Hyderabad*, 113–114. J. M. Macpherson, *British Enactments in Force in Native States; Compiled by J. M. Macpherson, of the Inner Temple, Barrister-at-Law, and Secretary to the Government of India, Legislative Department*, 2nd ed., Southern India (Hyderabad) (Calcutta: Superintendent of Government Printing, 1900). See page 706 concerning an 1891 law about newspapers.

25. Mehdi Ali to Durand, 21 October 1891, Foreign Department, Secret-I., Pros., NAI. Mehdi Ali sent a similar but shorter version of this same letter to then Resident at Hyderabad, Sir Arthur Cunningham Lothian.

26. Hyderabad Correspondent, *Hyderabad*, 160–161.

27. Hyderabad Correspondent, *Hyderabad*, 154.

28. Hyderabad Correspondent, *Hyderabad*, 155.

29. Hyderabad Correspondent, *Hyderabad*, 154–156.

30. Mahbub Ali Khan to Viceroy, 30 January 1892, Foreign Department, Secret-I., Pros., NAI.

31. Walter F. C. Chicheley Plowden, *Records of the Chicheley Plowdens* (London: Heath, Cranton & Ouseley Ltd., 1914), 191.

32. Chicheley Plowden, *Records*, 186.

4. The Scandal Unleashed

1. Mirza Bakir Hussain, *A Shocking Social Scandal. An Appeal to the Ladies of Hyderabad* (Lucknow, 1892), 2.

2. I will simply refer to the "author" of the pamphlet, not Mirza Bakir Hussain.

3. M. A. Khan, *The History of Urdu Press* (New Delhi: Classical Publishing Company, 1995), 27.

4. The pamphlet scandal was about sex, but, as with all scandals, it only became such because so much more was at stake and because the private details of the couple were made so very public. Hyderabad was awash in scandals at this time, yet they have not received adequate attention from scholars. However, a robust literature exists on specific scandals and on the value of studying them. On theories of scandal and some Victorian era case studies, see Ari Adut, *On Scandal: Moral Distrubances in Society, Politics, and Art* (Cambridge: Cambridge University Press, 2008); William A. Cohen, *Sex Scandal: The Private Parts of Victorian Fiction* (Durham, NC: Duke University Press, 1996); Tanika Sarkar, "Scandal in High Places: Discourses on the Chaste Hindu Woman in Late Nineteenth Century Bengal," in *Embodiment: Essays on Gender and Identity*, ed. Meenakshi Thapan (Delhi: Oxford University Press, 1997); Anna Clark, *Scandal: The Sexual Politics of the British Constitution* (Princeton: Princeton University Press, 2004); Benjamin B. Cohen, "The Utility of Scandal: Examples across Disciplines from Europe and India," *History Compass* 14, no. 7 (2016): 304–313. On the ways in which scandals constitute significant historical events—needing no justification for their "importance"—see William H. Sewell, *Logics of History: Social Theory and Social Transformation* (Chicago: University of Chicago Press, 2005).

5. Hussain, *Shocking Social Scandal*, 1.

6. For examples of dancers in colonial south India, see Davesh Soneji, *Unfinished Gestures: Devadāsīs, Memory, and Modernity in South India* (Chicago: University of Chicago Press, 2012). On the ways in which princely state rulers were patrons of music specifically, see Janaki Bakhle, *Two Men and Music: Nationalism in the Making of an Indian Classical Tradition* (Oxford: Oxford University Press, 2005).

7. Mehdi at least attended such dance performances if he did not host them himself. He is visible as either host or esteemed guest in a photo of a nineteenth century dance recital "at the residence of a Nawab." He is not identified in the photo. See Zahid Ali Khan, ed., *Images of Hyderabad* (Hyderabad: Siasat, 1994), 74.

8. Specific to nineteenth century Lucknow, see the novel about that city's most famous courtesan, Umrao Jan. See Mirza Mohammad Hadi Ruswa, *Umrao Jan Ada*, trans. Kushwant Singh and M. A. Husaini, (1961; New Delhi: HarperCollins, 2003).

9. Hussain, *Shocking Social Scandal*, 2. Caesar's wife Pompeia had once held a women-only party. A man disguised as a woman sneaked into the event with the aim of seducing Pompeia. He was caught, but, nonetheless, Caesar divorced Pompeia on suspicion. This led to the expression, "Caesar's wife must be above suspicion."

10. On the role of race, colonialism, and prostitution, see Philippa Levine, *Prostitution, Race and Politics: Policing Venereal Disease in the British Empire* (New York: Routledge, 2003).

11. Server-ul-Mulk, *My Life: Being the Autobiography of Nawab Server-Ul-Mulk Bahadur*, trans. Jiwan Yar Jung (London: Arthur H. Stockwell, 1932), 200.

12. Hussain, *Shocking Social Scandal*, 5.

13. Hussain, *Shocking Social Scandal*, 5.

14. Server-ul-Mulk, *My Life*, 201.

15. Hussain, *Shocking Social Scandal*, 6.

16. On the ways in which Queen Victoria was increasingly shaped by international and colonial forces, see Arianne Chernock, "Queen Victoria and the 'Bloody Mary of Madagascar,'" *Victorian Studies* 55, no. 3 (2013): 425–449.

17. Hussain, *Shocking Social Scandal*, 7: "oh the times, oh the manners!" (Cicero).

18. Hussain, *Shocking Social Scandal*, 8.
19. Yusuf-uz-Zaman to Mehdi Hasan, 15 April 1892, in R. Venkata Subba Rau, *The Hyderabad Pamphlet Scandal Case* (Lucknow: G. P. Varma Press, 1893), 183 (hereafter cited as Rau).
20. Mehdi Hasan to Yusuf-uz-Zaman, 23 April 1892, in Rau, 183.
21. Yusuf-uz-Zaman to Mehdi Hasan, 10 May 1892, in Rau, 184–185.
22. Mehdi Hasan to Yusuf-uz-Zaman, 16 May 1892, and Yusuf-uz-Zaman to Mehdi Hasan, 20 May 1892, both in Rau, 185–186.
23. Rau, viii–ix.
24. Yusuf-uz-Zaman to Server Jung, 2 May 1892, in Rau, viii–ix.
25. Server Jung to Raja Shaban Ali Khan, 18 May 1892, in Rau, xii.
26. Server Jung to Asghar Jan, 6 July 1892, in Rau, xviii–xix.
27. Asghar Jan to Server Jung, 11 August 1892, in Rau, xv–xvi.
28. Rafi-ud-din to Mehdi Hasan, 16 April 1892, in Rau, ix.
29. Rafi-ud-din to Mehdi Hasan, 1 May 1892, in Rau, ix.
30. Rafi-ud-din to Server Jung, 10 May 1892, in R/1/1/130, OIOC.
31. Syed Husain Bilgrami to Mehdi Hasan, 7 April 1892, in Rau, x.
32. Hasan to Asman Jah, 11 May 1892, in Rau, i.
33. Hasan to Asman Jah, 25 May 1892, Political and Private Secretary's Office, Judicial, 22/8/19, T/APSA.
34. Hasan to Asman Jah, 25 May 1892, Political and Private Secretary's Office, Judicial, 22/8/19, T/APSA.
35. Hasan to Asman Jah, 31 May 1892, Political and Private Secretary's Office, Judicial, 22/8/19, T/APSA.
36. *Indian Daily News*, 30 April 1892, Political and Private Secretary's Office, Judicial, 22/8/19, T/APSA.
37. *Indian Daily News*, 6 May 1892, Political and Private Secretary's Office, Judicial, 22/8/19, T/APSA.
38. *Indian Daily News*, 19 May 1892, Political and Private Secretary's Office, Judicial, 22/8/19, T/APSA.
39. *Evening Mail*, 21 May 1892, Political and Private Secretary's Office, Judicial, 22/8/19, T/APSA.
40. *Indian Daily News*, 23 May 1892, Political and Private Secretary's Office, Judicial, 22/8/19, T/APSA.
41. Hasan to Asman Jah, 7 June 1892, in Rau, iv.
42. Hasan to Asman Jah, 7 July 1892, in Rau, iv. Emphasis added.

43. Plowden to Asman Jah, 23 June 1892, Political and Private Secretary's Office, Judicial, 22/8/19, T/APSA.
44. Hasan to Asman Jah, 7 July 1892, in Rau, iv.
45. Plowden to Durand, 10 April 1892, R/1/1/148, OIOC.
46. 2 June 1892, R/1/1/148, OIOC. At the time (1892), A. S. Lethbridge was Superintendent for Suppression of Thagi and Dacoiti, and then became a named member of the Imperial Legislative Council (1895–1897).
47. 2 June 1892, R/1/1/148, OIOC. Although I was unable to find this original correspondence, the evidence is clear that the Government of India had in fact investigated Mehdi and Ellen's marriage at the time of their visit to London.
48. 7 June 1892, R/1/1/148, OIOC.
49. 27 July 1892, R/1/1/148, OIOC.

5. The Prosecution Charge

1. Before the pamphlet case, Bosanquet's name briefly appeared in conjunction with his decisions in other cases; for instance, in that of Mr. W. D. Edwards, who was charged by his deranged wife with murdering their ten-year-old son but later found not guilty based on medical testimony proving the boy had died of chronic dysentery. Bosanquet also presided over what was known as the "City Murder Case" in 1891, and in the same year, delivered the verdict in yet another case, one between Gallagher and Gribble. Hyderabad Correspondent, *Hyderabad in 1890 and 1891* (Bangalore: Caxton Press, 1892), 30. Edwards, associated with the *Hyderabad Telegraph,* was at the center of another scandalous case, the "Hyderabad Libel Case" of 1885. He was convicted, by his own admission, of libel. *Bombay Gazette,* 28 July 1885; Hyderabad Correspondent, *Hyderabad,* 92.
2. Bosanquet was born in 1866. He retired in 1920 and penned one book, *British Enactments in Force in Indian States* (1930). He died in 1933.
3. R. Venkata Subba Rau, *The Hyderabad Pamphlet Scandal Case* (Lucknow: G. P. Varma Press, 1893), 533 (hereafter cited as Rau). References to the unnamed court scribe happened during Inverarity's closing address.
4. Unfortunately, we know only John Duncan Inverarity and A. C. Rudra by name.

5. Inverarity was born in Bombay in 1847 and died there in 1923. He married Margaret Ewerette Grant, and the couple had two children.

6. *New York Times*, 29 December 1889.

7. Hyderabad Correspondent, *Hyderabad*, 61.

8. Hyderabad Correspondent, *Hyderabad*, 62–64.

9. Hyderabad Correspondent, *Hyderabad*, 86.

10. Rau, 1.

11. Rau, 2.

12. Rau, 3.

13. Rau, 4.

14. Rau, 7.

15. Rau, 10.

16. Rau, 13.

17. Mehdi Hasan, *Extracts from the Diary of Nawab Mehdi Hasan Khan Fathah Nawaz Jung* (London: Talbot Bros., 1890), 57.

18. Rau, 16.

19. Rau, 17.

20. Quoted in David Gilmour, *The Ruling Caste: Imperial Lives in the Victorian Raj* (New York: Farrar, Straus and Giroux, 2005), 194.

21. Plowden to Durand, 15 September 1892, R/1/1/148, OIOC.

22. Durand to Plowden, 26 September 1892, R/1/1/148, OIOC.

23. Rau, 18.

24. Rau, 18.

25. Rau, 20.

26. Rau, 20. The princely state of Kapurthala was in Punjab and spread across about 216 square miles of territory.

27. Rau, 27.

28. Rau, 28.

29. Rau, 34.

30. Rau, 37.

31. Rau, 42.

32. Norton to Durand, 2 September 1892, R/1/1/148, OIOC.

33. 3 September 1892, R/1/1/148, OIOC.

34. Rau, 44.

35. Rau, 48.

36. Rau, 51. Pratapghar is a small town southeast of Lucknow where Mehdi briefly worked.

37. "Memorandum on the Mehdi Hasan Case," 9 August 1893, R/1/1/130, OIOC.

38. Barabanki is nineteen miles east of Lucknow, about halfway to the Ghanghara River. It was an important district town in the Lucknow region. Nearby, north of Barabanki and about the same distance from Lucknow, is Fatehpur, natal home of Mehdi.

39. Rau, 52.

40. Rau, 57–59.

41. Wajid Ali to Munshi Sajjad Husain, 25 August 1892, in Rau, xvii.

42. Rau, 63.

43. Rau, 63.

44. Rau, 67.

45. Rau, 71.

46. Rau, 72.

47. Rau, 80.

48. Rau, 88.

49. Rau, 90.

50. Rau, 93.

51. Rau, 94.

52. Rau, 94.

53. Rau, 94.

54. "Declaration of D. C. Braganca [sic], dated 12th October 1892," in Rau, xiv.

55. "Declaration of D. C. Braganca."

56. For overviews of this community, see C. J. Hawes, *Poor Relations: The Making of a Eurasian Community in British India 1773–1833* (Surrey, UK: Curzon, 1996). Harald Fischer-Tine, *Low and Licentious Europeans: Race, Class and 'White Subalternity' in Colonial India* (Hyderabad: Orient Blackswan, 2009).

57. Copies of the *Deccan Budget* are no longer extant but were at the time reprinted in other newspapers. *Deccan Budget* in the *Madras Mail*, 3 November 1892.

58. Rau, 101.

59. Rau, 103.
60. "Declaration of G. D. Archer, dated 22nd October 1892," in Rau, xiv.
61. Rau, 104, 107.
62. Ram Pal Singh to Yusuf-uz-Zaman, 29 September 1892, in Rau, xxiii.
63. Ram Pal Singh to Yusuf-uz-Zaman, 17 October 1892, in Rau, xxiii–xxiv.
64. Yusuf-uz-Zaman to Ram Pal Singh, 19 October 1892, in Rau, xxii–xxiii.
65. Rau, 112.
66. Singh's testimony included one other surprise. Although the trial transcript in book form provides a clear line of question and answers, in Singh's case, he seemed to blurt out, "There is no foundation for the suggestion that I have had improper intercourse with boys. Nor is there any truth in the suggestion that I helped Mr. Brodley to get boys." This reference to pedophilia comes without a printed question before it, thus the context of such accusations remains lost. The response was immediately followed by other testimony and never mentioned again.
67. Rau, 114.
68. "Proceedings of the 14th November," 14 November 1892, R/1/1/170, OIOC.
69. "Proceedings of the 15th November," 15 November 1892, R/1/1/170, OIOC.
70. Rau, 120.
71. Rau, 121.
72. The Court of Wards was an administrative branch of the Nizam's government charged with raising young heirs to different estates around Hyderabad State. While the child heirs were educated by the Court of Wards and groomed for future leadership of their estates, the head of the Court of Wards and his staff administered those estates—often handling large sums of cash. Benjamin B. Cohen, "The Court of Wards in a Princely State: Bank Robber or Babysitter?" *Modern Asian Studies* 41, no. 2 (2007): 395–420.
73. Rau, 128–129.
74. Rau, 132.

6. I Have Seen This Lady Before

1. Norton argued other cases before the Hyderabad court and, in that way, may have known Mehdi Hasan personally before opposing him in the pamphlet case. Hyderabad Correspondent, *Hyderabad in 1890 and 1891* (Bangalore: Caxton Press, 1892), 59.

2. Hyderabad Correspondent, *Hyderabad*, 145.

3. R. Venkata Subba Rau, *The Hyderabad Pamphlet Scandal Case* (Lucknow: G. P. Varma Press, 1893), 145 (hereafter cited as Rau).

4. Rau, 146.

5. Rau, 146–148.

6. Rau, 150.

7. Rau, 195.

8. Rau, 151.

9. Rau, 153.

10. Rau, 155.

11. Rau, 155.

12. Rau, 160–161.

13. Rau, 164–165.

14. Rau, 168.

15. Rau, 169.

16. Rau, 171.

17. Rau, 173.

18. Rau, 175.

19. Rau, 174.

20. Rau, 180.

21. Rau, 182.

22. Rau, 193.

23. Rau, 196.

24. Rau, 207.

25. Rau, 211.

26. Rau, 217.

27. Lauchlin was born at Dinapur, a small town adjoining Patna in north India. He was fifty-four years old at the time of the trial.

28. Rau, 233.

29. Rau, 225.

30. Rau, 244.

31. Rau, 226.

32. Rau, 226.

33. Rau, 239.

34. Rau, 227.

35. Rau, 230.

36. Rau, 246.

37. Rau, 260–261.

38. Rau, 251–252.

39. Likely from the Urdu / Hindustani *rāṇḍi*, meaning prostitute or courtesan, and *baz*, a player or frequenter.

40. Rau, 256.

41. Like others who testified, Zaman was engaged with the court proceedings and depositions through the newspapers. "I did not know that the inquiry was a confidential one. I was not informed so, but I learned it from reading the proceedings of this Court." As his testimony continued, he added, "I have been reading the newspaper-reports of this case regularly, and since my arrival here, I had heard of the proceedings in this Court." Rau, 258–259, 263.

42. Rau, 280.

43. Rau, 274.

44. Rau, 282.

45. 8 November 1892, Lansdowne to Kimberley, MSS EUR D/558/5, OIOC.

46. 30 November 1892, Kimberley to Lansdowne, MSS EUR D/558/5, OIOC.

47. 28 December 1892, Lansdowne to Kimberley, MSS EUR D/558/5, OIOC.

48. "Telegram from Colonel Ludlow, Inspector General of Police, to the District Superintendent Police Lucknow, dated 9th April 1892," in Rau, xxv.

49. Rau, 283.

50. Rau, 285.

51. "Certificate of Rafi-ud-din by the Principal of Canning College, dated 13th November 1872," in Rau, xiv–xv.

52. Rau, 289.
53. Rau, 288.
54. Rau, 291.
55. Rau, 292.
56. Rau, 298.
57. Rau, 300.
58. Rau, 298.
59. Rau, 288.
60. Rau, 309.
61. Rau, 312.
62. Rau, 316.
63. Rau, 319.
64. Rau, 321.
65. Rau, 329.
66. Rau, 333.
67. Rau, 335.
68. Rau, 341.
69. Rau, 349.
70. Rau, 345.
71. It is unclear what the Stanley Company was. It might have been a traveling circus.
72. Rau, 349.
73. This was also attested to by Mustafa Ali. Rau, 362.
74. Rau, 353.
75. Rau, 353–354.
76. Asman Jah to Durand, 28 January 1893, R/1/1/148, OIOC.
77. 31 January 1893, R/1/1/148, OIOC. The document bears the initials A. W.
78. Durand to Asman Jah, 8 February 1893, Political and Private Secretary's Office, Judicial, 22/8/19, T/APSA.
79. Rau, 357.
80. Rau, 363.
81. Rau, 366.
82. Rau, 361.
83. The archived copy is an enclosure in a letter addressed to first assistant Resident George Irwin.

84. Mehdi Hasan to Irwin, 21 January 1893, R/1/1/142, OIOC.

85. Mehdi Hasan to Irwin, 21 January 1893.

86. Mehdi Hasan to Irwin, 21 January 1893.

87. Mehdi Hasan to Irwin, 21 January 1893.

88. Mehdi Hasan to Irwin, 21 January 1893.

89. Rau, 374.

90. Rau, 389.

91. Rau, 393.

92. The request came from the Residency, assuring Asman Jah that Plowden would arrange the deposition, to be supervised by Bosanquet. Irwin to Asman Jah, 9 January 1893, Political and Private Secretary's Office, Judicial, 22/8/19, T/APSA.

93. Rau, 400.

94. Rau, 403.

95. Rau, 404.

96. Rau, 405.

97. Rau, 406.

98. Rau, 407–408.

99. Rau, 408.

100. On the ways in which rumors served as important sources of information, see C. A. Bayly, *Empire and Information* (Cambridge: Cambridge University Press, 1996), 18–19 and 199–201.

101. Rau, 412.

102. Rau, 415–416.

103. Rau, 418.

104. Rau, 418.

105. Rau, 421.

106. In an undated affidavit, he made much the same statement. See "Affadavit [sic] of Mr. E. H. Quiross [sic] filled in the Court of the City Magistrate of Lucknow." Rau, xxiv.

107. Rau, 425.

108. Politicians worried about the health of their armed forces enacted the 1864 Contagious Diseases Acts in Britain and later in India. The acts allowed police to arrest women suspected of being prostitutes. Prostitutes themselves were required to register with the police and were subjected to regular health inspections to prevent the spread of venereal disease.

7. Star Witnesses and a Verdict

1. R. Venkata Subba Rau, *The Hyderabad Pamphlet Scandal Case* (Lucknow: G. P. Varma Press, 1893), 434 (hereafter cited as Rau).

2. Rau, 434.

3. Rau, 435.

4. Rau, 437.

5. Rau, 440.

6. Rau, 450.

7. Rau, 440–441.

8. Rau, 462.

9. Rau, 452.

10. Rau, 453.

11. Rau, 453.

12. Rau, 456.

13. Rau, 442.

14. Rau, 455.

15. Rau, 451.

16. Rau, 442.

17. Rau, 442.

18. Rau, 443.

19. Rau, 460.

20. Rau, 464.

21. Mehdi Hasan, *Extracts from the Diary of Nawab Mehdi Hasan Khan Fathah Nawaz Jung* (London: Talbot Bros., 1890), 58. (Here Mehdi refers to a "W. Fitzgerald," who might in fact have been G. Fitzgerald; Hasan, 109, 110.)

22. Rau, 464.

23. Mehdi Hasan to Irwin, 9 March 1893, R/1/1/1220, OIOC.

24. The known facts are that Asman Jah handed over the money—through a middleman—to Server Jung, who promptly handed it over to the Nizam. Whether the money was a gift, a bribe, or for some other purpose is not clear. All sides of the pamphlet case weighed in on the *lakh* scandal: Mehdi and Keay saw it as an example of further corruption and meddling by Server Jung; Server Jung believed that having handed the money over to the Nizam, he avoided any conflict of interest; and in the end both Mehdi Ali and Asman Jah found themselves dismissed

from service, partly over their involvement with this scandal. For Asman Jah's perspective, see Asman Jah to Mahbub Ali Khan, 28 March 1893, R/1/1/1220, OIOC. For Keay's perspective, see Keay to Kimberley, 24 October 1893, R/1/1/130, OIOC. For Plowden's perspective, see Plowden to Durand, 1 May 1893, R/1/1/1220, OIOC. For the Nizam's perspective, see Server Jung to Mahbub Ali Khan, 22 April 1893, R/1/1/1220, OIOC; and Mahbub Ali Khan to the Minister, 9 July 1893, R/1/1/1220, OIOC. Also see *The Pioneer*, 18 July 1893; and *The Lakh Bribery Case, of Hyderabad, Deccan: A Compilation of a Series of Articles Published in Several Issues of the Bangalore "Evening Mail"* (Bangalore: Caxton Press, 1895).

25. Mehdi Hasan to Irwin, 12 March 1893, R/1/1/1220, OIOC.

26. Plowden to Asman Jah, 14 March 1893, R/1/1/1220, OIOC.

27. Rau, 467.

28. Rau, 470.

29. Rau, 470.

30. Rau, 473.

31. Inverarity's reply is ninety-eight pages long in the transcript. I have arranged his closing remarks in chronological order.

32. Rau, 474.

33. Rau, 477.

34. Rau, 478.

35. Kurshed Jah's ancestor, Mulla Jalal-ud-din, had originally served the Mughal emperor Akbar, and a subsequent descendant had come with Nawab Asaf Jah to the Deccan, where he settled. In 1800, Muhammad Fakhr-ud-din married one of the Nizam's daughters, thus cementing the family position as valuable nobles within the state. Kurshed Jah's brother was Sir Vikar-ul-Umra, and both were related to Sir Asman Jah. Of the three Paigah nobles at the time, Kurshed Jah held the largest number of villages (468), which were spread over 1,512 square miles. *Imperial Gazetteer of India, Hyderabad State* (Calcutta: Superintendent of Government Printing, 1909), 293–294.

36. Rau, 511–512.

37. This plan is spelled out by Inverarity. Rau, 519.

38. Rau, 520.

39. Rau, 513.
40. Rau, 527.
41. Rau, 528–530.
42. Rau, 523.
43. Rau, 535.
44. Rau, 543.
45. Rau, 555.
46. Rau, 525.
47. Rau, 530.
48. Rau, 531.
49. Rau, 551.
50. Rau, 555.
51. Rau, 539.
52. Rau, 550.
53. Rau, 558–559.
54. Rau, 559.
55. Rau, 499.
56. Rau, 506–507.
57. Rau, 225.
58. Rau, 502.
59. Rau, 504a.
60. Rau, 500.
61. Rau, 504b.
62. Rau, 504b.
63. Rau, 510.
64. Rau, 485.
65. Mirza Bakir Hussain, *A Shocking Social Scandal. An Appeal to the Ladies of Hyderabad* (Lucknow, 1892), 5.
66. Rau, 486.
67. Rau, 487.
68. Rau, 575.
69. This section of the Criminal Procedure Code asks for the accused to present evidence and have it cross-examined. Hasan and his lawyers chose not to cross-examine first, but to proceed to trial. *The Code of Criminal Procedure, 1882 as Modified up to December 1888* (Calcutta: Superintendent of Government Printing, 1888), 129.

70. Section 256 of the Criminal Procedure Code deals with acquittal. *The Code of Criminal Procedure, 1882 as Modified up to December 1888* (Calcutta: Superintendent of Government Printing, 1888), 130.

71. Rau, 579.

72. "Memorandum on the Mehdi Hasan Case," 9 August 1893, R/1/1/130, OIOC.

73. "Memorandum on the Mehdi Hasan Case."

74. "Memorandum on the Mehdi Hasan Case."

75. "Memorandum on the Mehdi Hasan Case."

76. "Memorandum on the Mehdi Hasan Case."

77. "Memorandum on the Mehdi Hasan Case."

78. "Memorandum on the Mehdi Hasan Case."

79. "Memorandum on the Mehdi Hasan Case."

80. "Memorandum on the Mehdi Hasan Case."

81. Faridoonji to Gough, 5 May 1892, in "Memorandum on the Mehdi Hasan Case," 9 August 1893, R/1/1/130, OIOC.

82. "Memorandum on the Mehdi Hasan Case."

8. Pink and Yellow Accusations

1. Hasan to Irwin, 25 April 1893, R/1/1/170, OIOC.

2. Coverage occurred, for instance, in faraway Birmingham. See *Birmingham Daily Post*, 21 April 1893.

3. *Madras Weekly Mail*, 27 April 1893.

4. "An April-Fool Judgment," *The Indian Jurist* (1893), 212.

5. "An April-Fool Judgment," *The Indian Jurist* (1893), 213.

6. "An April-Fool Judgment," *The Indian Jurist* (1893), 213.

7. He was born on 30 March 1839 at Bathgate, Linlithgowshire, West of Edinburgh. Perhaps prescient of his long connection to India, Keay attended the Madras College in St Andrews.

8. Mary Cumpston, "Some Early Indian Nationalists and Their Allies in the British Parliament, 1851–1906," *English Historical Review* 76, no. 299 (1961), 290n2.

9. "Mr. Seymour Keay, M.P.," *Vanity Fair*, 8 October 1892. Keay returned to Britain in 1882, where he launched a career in government. His first

attempt to enter politics in 1885 was unsuccessful, but he was later elected as an advanced Liberal on 8 October 1889 in a by-election for Elginshire, in the north of Scotland. He was re-elected in 1892, but lost re-election bids in 1895 and 1906. In Britain, Keay continued to raise questions about British policy in India and in Hyderabad, as well as show support for the Indian National Congress, of which he was a British committee member. See Charles Welch, "Keay, John Seymour," in *Oxford Dictionary of National Biography* (Oxford: Oxford University Press, 2004).

10. R. S. W___ [illegible] to Sutherland, 10 August 1876, MSS EUR B/397, OIOC.

11. Keay to Durand, 2 November 1892, Foreign Department, NAI.

12. Keay to Durand, 2 November 1892.

13. Keay to Durand, 2 November 1892.

14. Keay to Durand, 2 November 1892.

15. Server Jung to Durand, 7 November 1892, R/1/1/1211, OIOC.

16. Keay to Fowler, 26 May 1894, R/1/1/170, OIOC.

17. Plowden to Durand, 28 February 1893, Foreign Department, NAI.

18. Plowden to Durand, 28 February 1893.

19. Plowden to Durand, 28 February 1893.

20. Plowden to Durand, 28 February 1893.

21. Plowden to Durand, 28 February 1893.

22. Durand to Plowden, 29 March 1893, Foreign Department, NAI.

23. Durand to Plowden, 29 March 1893.

24. Durand to Plowden, 29 March 1893.

25. Durand to Plowden, 29 March 1893.

26. "Note by Sir S. C. Bayley in regard to Mr. Seymour Keay's charges against the British Resident at Hyderabad," 27 November 1893, L/P&S /18/D/107, OIOC.

27. "Note by Sir S. C. Bayley," 27 November 1893.

28. "Note by Sir S. C. Bayley," 27 November 1893.

29. "Note by Sir S. C. Bayley," 27 November 1893.

30. Kimberley to Lansdowne, 15 December 1893, R/1/1/130, OIOC.

31. Russell to Keay, 3 March 1894, R/1/1/130, OIOC.

32. Keay to Durand, 2 November 1892, Foreign Department, NAI.

33. Keay to Durand, 11 January 1893, Foreign Department, NAI. To this end, some newspaper coverage—after the trial's conclusion—suggested that Server Jung was in fact keeping officials on a sort of payroll for their cooperation; one Mr. Munden was pointed out as receiving money in this regard. *Evening Mail*, 21 April 1894, in "Newspaper Cuttings 1894–1896," T/APSA.

34. Keay to Durand, 11 January 1893, Foreign Department, NAI.

35. Keay to Elgin, 11 January 1895, R/1/1/170, OIOC.

36. Bayley to Keay, 22 January 1895, R/1/1/170, OIOC.

37. GOI to Kimberley, 13 June 1893, Foreign Department, NAI.

38. Lansdowne to Kimberley, 1 November 1893, R/1/1/130, OIOC.

39. Keay to Kimberley, 31 July 1893, R/1/1/130, OIOC.

40. *The Parliamentary Debates*, vol. XXIV (London: Eyre and Spottiswoode, 1894), 458.

41. *The Parliamentary Debates*, 24:458.

42. Lansdowne to Kimberley, 1 November 1893, MSS EUR D558/6, OIOC.

43. Asman Jah to Plowden, 26 April 1893, R/1/1/142, OIOC.

44. Hasan to Irwin, 27 April 1893, R/2/66/10, OIOC.

45. *Madras Mail*, 11 May 1893. Nothing seems to have come of this suit.

46. After the judgment, Mehdi also tried to have the verdict overturned by a different court. In the *Index to the Proceedings of the Foreign Department for the Year 1893* in the National Archive of India, under "Hyderabad" is listed "Mehdi Hassan (Nawab)." For the entry, the following is given: "Transfer to the Berar Courts of the application for revision of the judgment in the 'pamphlet case.' Request that the case should be transferred to a chartered High Court." Eight days later, Mehdi informed the Residency of his appeal. He wrote to Irwin that he had instructed his counsel to "move the local High Court against the finding." These attempts all failed. *Index to Proceedings of the Foreign Department for the Year 1893* (Calcutta: Office of the Superintendent of Government Printing, 1895), 213. In researching this aspect of the scandal, I visited the National Archive of India (NAI) in New Delhi. Upon my request for this record, the NAI responded by returning the request with the note "Brittle" and did not deliver the document.

However, from the index entry itself, we know that Mehdi tried to get the judgment changed and the court moved.

47. *Pioneer,* 3 May 1893.

48. Lansdowne to Kimberley, 1 November 1893, R/1/1/130, OIOC.

49. "In the Court of the Judicial Commissioner, Hyderabad Assigned Districts. Criminal Side. Revision Case No. 58 of 1893," 20 September 1893, R/1/1/142, OIOC.

50. J. D. LaTouche to Secretary to the Government of India, Foreign Department, 22 May 1893, R/1/1/142, OIOC.

51. LaTouche to Secretary to GOI, 22 May 1893, (51). From this point on, Hasan is at times referred to as Shaikh Mehdi Hasan. In some cases, this honorific title is appended to men's names when they reach forty years of age. At other times, it can refer to one who has completed a level in Islamic schooling.

52. Asman Jah to Plowden, 7 August 1893, R/1/1/142, OIOC.

53. Asman Jah to Plowden, 7 August 1893.

54. Plowden to the Secretary to the Government of India, Foreign Department, 19 August 1893, R/1/1/142, OIOC.

55. A. W. [Arthur Wilson?], Secretary, Foreign Department, 28 August 1893, R/1/1/142, OIOC.

56. A. W., Secretary, Foreign Department, 23 September 1893, R/1/1/142, OIOC.

57. A. P. MacDonnell, Member, Viceroy's Executive Council, 7 February 1894, R/1/1/142, OIOC.

58. Joseph Rock, "The New Era at Hyderabad," *Fortnightly Review* 61, no. 366 (June 1897): 911–922, 921.

59. Mahbub Ali Khan to Lansdowne, 28 August 1893, R/2/66/13, OIOC.

60. "Memorandum by His Highness Mir Mahboob Ali Khan, Nizam of Hyderabad, dated Hyderabad, Deccan, the 28th August 1893," R/1/1/130, OIOC.

61. "Memorandum by His Highness Mir Mahboob Ali Khan."

62. Lansdowne to Kimberley, 12 September 1893, MSS EUR D558/6, OIOC.

63. Lansdowne to the Mahbub Ali Khan, 12 September 1893, R/1/1/130, OIOC.

64. Rock, "New Era at Hyderabad," 913.

65. In his letter described below, Keay included a clipping from the *Pioneer* that openly discussed Plowden's antipathy toward the prime minister. *Pioneer*, 18 November 1893.

66. Keay to Kimberley, 14 December 1893, R/1/1/130, OIOC. Keay continued by narrating what he called a "crafty substitution" in the *jarida* announcing Asman Jah's leave. In this substitution, the word "during" was replaced with "after." He explained, "By this device the announcement had been made to read that the Minister would be relieved of his duties after instead of merely during his six months' leave." Keay believed that Server Jung had orchestrated the substitution. He felt that such a betrayal could have been possible only with Plowden's involvement. Keay to Kimberley, 14 December 1893.

67. *Pioneer*, 1 June 1893. Prasad also ran a local paper, the *Advocate*. See testimony in R. Venkata Subba Rau, *The Hyderabad Pamphlet Scandal Case* (Lucknow: G. P. Varma Press, 1893), 336, 339. This particular advertisement recognized Ellen's marriage by referring to her as "Mrs.," but like the defense in the trial, and the pamphlet itself, it used her middle name, Gertrude.

68. See, for instance, a letter to the editor at this moment invoking Mehdi Hasan's name. *Leader*, 2 December 1909.

69. *Pioneer*, 18 July 1893.

70. *Pioneer*, 18 July 1893.

71. Plowden to Cunningham, 25 August 1893, R/1/1/1233, OIOC.

72. *Morning Post*, 15 July 1893, R/1/1/130, OIOC.

73. *Advocate of India*, 5 July 1893, R/1/1/130, OIOC.

74. W. J. Cunningham to Chief Secretary to the Government of the North-Western Provinces and Oudh, 16 January 1894, R/1/1/142, OIOC.

75. Chief Secretary to the Government of the North-Western Provinces and Oudh to W. J. Cunningham, 25 January 1894, R/1/1/142, OIOC.

76. W. J. Cunningham to Chief Secretary to the Government of the North-Western Provinces and Oudh, 21 March 1894, R/1/1/142, OIOC.

77. *Evening Mail*, 19 April 1894, in "Newspaper Cuttings 1894–1896," T/APSA.

78. *Evening Mail*, 19 April 1894.

9. Turned Adrift

1. All quotations in this paragraph from Mrs. Mehdi Hassan to Lansdowne, 15 April 1894, R/1/1/142, OIOC.

2. Individuals who visit these holy lands acquire the title of sheikh or sometimes maulvi.

3. Mrs. Mehdi Hassan to J. D. LaTouche, 28 April 1894, R/1/1/142, OIOC.

4. Mehdi Hasan to Chief Secretary to the Government of the North-Western Provinces, 7 May 1894, R/1/1/142, OIOC.

5. Mehdi Hasan to Chief Secretary to the Government of the North-Western Provinces, 7 May 1894.

6. A. Williams, Under-Secretary to the Government of India, Foreign Department, to the Chief Secretary to the Government of the North-Western Provinces, 23 May 1894, R/1/1/142, OIOC.

7. Mehdi Hasan to Chief Secretary to the Government of the North-Western Provinces, 23 May 1894, R/1/1/142, OIOC.

8. This new pamphlet was about Mehdi Ali. *Deccan Budget*, 25 May 1894, in "Newspaper Cuttings 1894–1896," T/APSA.

9. *Deccan Budget*, 25 May 1894.

10. *Hyderabadee*, 4 June 1894, in "Newspaper Cuttings 1894–1896," T/APSA.

11. *Hyderabadee*, 4 June 1894.

12. *Deccan Budget*, 6 July 1894, in "Newspaper Cuttings 1894–1896," T/APSA.

13. *Hyderabadee*, 4 June 1894.

14. Sheikh Mehdi Hasan to Chief Secretary to the Government of the North-Western Provinces, 30 June 1894, R/1/1/142, OIOC.

15. Sheikh Mehdi Hasan to Private Secretary to His Excellency the Viceroy, 2 July 1894, R/1/1/142, OIOC.

16. Sheikh Mehdi Hasan to Private Secretary to His Excellency the Viceroy, 2 July 1894.

17. Sheikh Mehdi Hasan to Private Secretary to His Excellency the Viceroy, 2 July 1894.

18. Italics in the original. Sheikh Mehdi Hasan to Private Secretary to His Excellency the Viceroy, 2 July 1894.

19. *Morning Post,* 10 July 1894, in "Newspaper Cuttings 1894–1896," T/ APSA.

20. Mehdi Hasan to the Chief Secretary to the Government of the North-Western Provinces, 19 September 1894, R/1/1/142, OIOC.

21. Private Secretary to the Governor-General, 6 August 1894, R/1/1/142, OIOC.

22. Private Secretary to the Governor-General, 6 August 1894.

23. Elgin to Fowler, 3 October 1894, R/1/1/142, OIOC.

24. Elgin to Fowler, 3 October 1894.

25. Elgin to Fowler, 3 October 1894.

26. Plowden to W. Cuningham, 9 January 1895, R/1/1/1233, OIOC.

27. Fowler to Government of India, 8 February 1895, R/1/1/152, OIOC.

28. Fowler to Government of India, 8 February 1895.

29. Hasan to Private Secretary, 5 April 1895, R/1/1/152, OIOC.

30. Mrs. Mehdi Hasan to Elgin, 16 April 1895, R/1/1/152, OIOC.

31. The same newspaper report that announced Mehdi's dismissal from the Government of India also mentioned that "Mrs. Mehdi Hasan gets Rs. 300 pension," but since no other mention of this is evident, it is possible that the report was wrong. *Morning Post,* 10 July 1894, in "Newspaper Cuttings 1894–1896," T/APSA.

32. Mrs. Mehdi Hasan to Elgin, 16 April 1895, R/1/1/152, OIOC.

33. Mrs. Mehdi Hasan to Bayley, 17 April 1895, R/1/1/152, OIOC.

34. Mrs. Mehdi Hasan to Bayley, 17 April 1895.

35. Hasan to Private Secretary, 1 June 1895, R/1/1/152, OIOC.

36. Hasan to Private Secretary, 1 June 1895.

37. Elgin to Fowler, 25 June 1895, R/1/1/152, OIOC.

38. Elgin to Fowler, 25 June 1895.

39. *Morning Post,* 29 July 1895, in "Newspaper Cuttings 1894–1896," T/ APSA. Both of these men continued to have successful careers in Hyderabad. See, for instance, the thanks that A. J. Dunlop lavished on them. A. J. Dunlop, *Report on the Relief Operations, His Highness the Nizam's Dominions During 1306 Fasli (1896–97)* (Hyderabad: H. H. The Nizam's Printers Press, 1898), 55.

40. *Deccan Post,* 24 April 1896.

41. Lawder to Faridoonji, 7 November 1901, Political and Private Secretary's Office, Public Works, 34/3/805, T/APSA.

42. *Deccan Mail*, 27 December 1896, in "Newspaper Cuttings 1896–1901," T/APSA.

43. Elgin to Fowler, 25 June 1895.

44. Server-ul-Mulk, *My Life: Being the Autobiography of Nawab Server-Ul-Mulk Bahadur*, trans. Jiwan Yar Jung (London: Arthur H. Stockwell, 1932), 305–306.

45. Server-ul-Mulk, *My Life*, 306.

46. The early medieval title and position, "Mayor of the Palace," refers to one who holds power behind the scenes. Joseph Rock, "The New Era at Hyderabad," *Fortnightly Review* 61, no. 366 (June 1897): 911–922, 911.

47. Rock, "The New Era at Hyderabad," 919.

48. Rock, "The New Era at Hyderabad," 920.

49. *Times of India*, 5 February 1897, in "Newspaper Cuttings 1896–1901," T/APSA.

50. *Times of India*, 11 February 1897, in "Newspaper Cuttings 1896–1901," T/APSA.

51. *Bombay Gazette*, 13 October 1900, in "Newspaper Cuttings 1896–1901," T/APSA.

52. Ibid.

53. *Deccan Mail*, 18 November 1896, in "Newspaper Cuttings 1896–1901," T/APSA.

54. *Deccan Mail*, 6 December 1896, in "Newspaper Cuttings 1896–1901," T/APSA.

55. Hasan had been a speaker at an anti-Congress demonstration at the same time. J. N. Gupta, *Life and Work of Romesh Chunder Dutt* (London: J. M. Dent, 1911), 276.

56. *Indian People*, 20 January 1904.

57. *Pioneer*, "The Late Nawab Mehdi Hasan," in *Indian People*, 20 January 1904.

58. *Leader*, 2 December 1909.

59. Ellen to Faridoonji, 21 January 1904, Political and Private Secretary's Office, Miscellaneous, 30/3/117, T/APSA.

60. Faridoonji to Secretary Financial Department, 21 January 1904, Political and Private Secretary's Office, Miscellaneous, 30/3/124, T/APSA.

61. Ellen to Mahbub Ali Khan, 13 April 1904, CMP.

62. Ellen to Ahmed Hussain, 2 May [1904], CMP. This letter has no year next to the date, but references Ellen's letter sent to the Nizam "about a month ago" which corresponds perfectly with her letter of 4 April 1904.

63. Faridoonji to Imad Nawaz Jung, 27 September 1906, Political and Private Secretary's Office, 41/15/94, T/APSA.

64. Ellen to Mahbub Ali Khan, 17 August 1906, Political and Private Secretary's Office, Public Charities, 11/1/376, T/APSA. This amount tallies with earlier newspaper reports that she received some form of pension from the Nizam's Government. Those reports mistakenly assign the pension to Ellen, when in fact it seems to have been given to Mehdi, until it was stopped at the trial's end.

65. Assistant Secretary to the Minister to the Political and Private Secretary, 13 May 1907, Political and Private Secretary's Office, Public Charities, 11/1/376, T/APSA.

66. Charles Stuart Bayley (1854–1935) was Resident at Hyderabad from 1905 to 1908. He is not to be confused with Steuart Colvin Bayley (1836–1925), who served as Resident at Hyderabad in 1881–1882.

67. Guzaarish, 23 June 1910, CMP.

68. Guzaarish, 23 June 1910.

69. Ellen to Faridoonji, [illegible] October 1910, Political and Private Secretary's Office, Public Charities, 11/1/376, T/APSA.

70. Ellen to Faridoonji, [probably mid-1910], Political and Private Secretary's Office, Public Charities, 11/1/376, T/APSA.

71. Ellen to Faridoonji, 22 November 1910, Political and Private Secretary's Office, Public Charities, 11/1/376, T/APSA.

72. Ellen to Faridoonji, 22 November 1910.

73. Faridoonji, 4 June 1911, Political and Private Secretary's Office, Public Charities, 11/1/376, T/APSA.

74. At one point, it seems that Fakhrudeen and the Pigotts had some altercation surrounding Ellen's final financial affairs. Fakhrudeen filed a complaint against the couple in the local Lucknow police station, Hazarat Ganj, but nothing seems to have come of this action. "Copy of a Confidential Report," Syed Vikar Husain Rezvi, 25 August 1912, Political and Private Secretary's Office, Public Charities, 11/1/376, T/APSA.

75. "Copy of letter from Mrs. E. Mehdi Hasan of 1st June—to Mrs. Pigott," Political and Private Secretary's Office, Public Charities, 11/1/376, T/APSA.

76. Ellen to Faridoonji, 19 February 1912, Political and Private Secretary's Office, Public Charities, 11/1/376, T/APSA.

77. Ellen to Ahmed Hussain, 9 April 1912, CMP.

78. Ellen to Osman Ali Khan, 9 April 1912, CMP.

79. Ellen to Osman Ali Khan, 9 April 1912.

80. Fakhrudeen Hassan to Faridoonji, 25 April 1912, Political and Private Secretary's Office, Public Charities, 11/1/376, T/APSA.

81. Egisto Amedeo Benvenuti and Esther or Ester Bigex, 26 June 1897, "Illinois, Cook County Marriages, 1871–1920," index, FamilySearch, https://familysearch.org/pal:/MM9.1.1/N7WZ-65Q, accessed 5 July 2013.

82. Esther Benvenuti to Faridoonji, 23 May 1912, Political and Private Secretary's Office, Public Charities, 11/1/376, T/APSA.

83. Pigott to Faridoonji, 16 June 1912, Political and Private Secretary's Office, Public Charities, 11/1/376, T/APSA.

84. Glancy to Faridoonji, 27 June 1912, Political and Private Secretary's Office, Public Charities, 11/1/376, T/APSA.

85. Faridoonji to Hankin, 1 July 1912, Political and Private Secretary's Office, Public Charities, 11/1/376, T/APSA.

86. Pigott to Faridoonji, 24 July 1912, Political and Private Secretary's Office, Public Charities, 11/1/376, T/APSA.

87. "Copy of a Confidential Report," Political and Private Secretary's Office, Public Charities, 11/1/376, T/APSA.

88. Devlin to Faridoonji, 6 September 1912, Political and Private Secretary's Office, Public Charities, 11/1/376, T/APSA.

89. Faridoonji to Pigott, 11 September 1912, Political and Private Secretary's Office, Public Charities, 11/1/376, T/APSA.

GLOSSARY

ayah	a maid
bhadwa	a pimp
chunnam	plaster made from egg whites and mother of pearl
dacoit	a robber belonging to a gang
dupatta	a length of cloth worn as a scarf or head covering by women
durbar	a court or levee
gosha	in *purdah*; secluded
guzaarish	request; petition
hakim	a judge
Hali Sicca	coins struck in Hyderabad
imambara	a place to perform ceremonies, especially those related to Muharram
izzat	respect
jaali	stone screen
jarida	official notice
jung	a common surname meaning battle or war; also a hereditary and honorific title
kayasth	member of the scribe caste; keeper of public records
khanji wink	social blackballing
khansamah	manservant
kharita	official order
koti	[lit., fort] home, palace, or residence

lakh	100,000
mansab	office; a military title and rank
mela	a fair; an assembly
memsahib	a respectable woman
moffusil	countryside
mulki	a native; countryman
munsif	low-ranking civil servant judge
nawab	a nobleman or person of high status
nazr	gift, tribute, or payment
purdah	[lit., a curtain] observing a form of seclusion
raat ki rani	[lit., queen of the night] jasmine
rendibaz	one who frequents prostitutes; from *randi* (prostitute; courtesan) and *baz* (player; frequenter)
sahib	an honorific title used to address men; "Sir"
samasthan	a small Hindu feudatory
sepoy	foot soldier
server	a man's name or title, meaning chief or leader
sherwani	men's knee-length coat buttoned at the neck
tahsildar	revenue collector
taluqdar	holder of a *taluq*, district, or subdistrict
wazeefa	amount; a form of pension or compensation
zamindar	land holder
zenana	women's private quarters

Sources: H. H. Wilson, *A Glossary of Judicial and Revenue Terms*, 2nd ed. (Delhi: Munshiram Manoharlal, 1968); Henry Yule and A. C. Burnell, *Hobson-Jobson: The Anglo-Indian Dictionary* (London: John Murray, 1886; rpt. Ware, Hertfordshire: Wordsworth Reference, 1996).

BIBLIOGRAPHY

Hyderabad State, the Deccan, and the princely states have not garnered as much attention as some north Indian states and other regions of South Asia. As William Dalrymple has written in *White Mughals: Love and Betrayal in Eighteenth-Century India*, "little serious work has been done on any of the Deccani courts, and this remains especially true of its cultural history." He continues, "for every book on the Deccan sultanates, there are a hundred on the Mughals; for every book on Hyderabad there is a shelf on Lucknow" (xxxviii). For the pamphlet scandal, the problem is even worse, since there has never been a history of that event. I have therefore included literature relating to the pamphlet scandal, primary sources from Hyderabad in the late nineteenth century, and subsequent recent scholarship on Hyderabad of the same period. This list is suggestive but not exhaustive; I have omitted the large number of newspaper, magazine, and journal articles related to Hyderabad.

Several of the prominent participants in the scandal wrote books that directly or indirectly discuss that event. Mehdi Hasan published letters to the editor in different papers across India and in Britain, but his published diary extracts from his trip to London in *Extracts from the Diary of Nawab Mehdi Hasan Khan Fathah Nawaz Jung* provide the most sustained record of his voice. The diary was translated from the original English version into Urdu by Muhammad 'Aziz Mirza, a friend of Mehdi from Lucknow, and published as *Gulgasht-i Firang*. This diary, long forgotten, was subsequently reprinted with an introduction by Omar Khalidi. Khalidi's introduction makes brief mention of the pamphlet scandal. It aims to contextualize Mehdi's journey to the heart of the empire. Mehdi also translated the biography of Salar Jung by Syed Bilgrami, *A Memoir of Salar Jung*, into Urdu as *Muraqqa-i Ibrat*.

After leaving Hyderabad, Server Jung wrote a memoir of his life that includes some allusions to Mehdi and Ellen, although with expected derision, in *My Life: Being the Autobiography of Nawab Server-Ul-Mulk Bahadur.* John Seymour Keay authored several books about Britain's foreign affairs, but none come close to explaining his role in the saga. The same cannot be said for Eardley J. Norton, who published his devastating opening statements in his defense of Mitra in a book, *In the Court of the Superintendent Residency Bazaars, Hyderabad. Nawab Mehdi Hassan V. S.M. Mitra. Mr. Eardley Norton's Opening Speech for the Defence.*

A few works printed at the time of the pamphlet case refer to the event directly or, for instance, to the *lakh* bribe scandal that developed as a part of the pamphlet scandal. A collection of newspaper articles, *Hyderabad in 1890 and 1891,* refers to the *lakh* scandal, and this was followed by *The Lakh Bribery Case, of Hyderabad, Deccan. A Compilation of Articles Published in Several Issues of the Bangalore "Evening Mail."* And, of course, the trial transcript itself was published in north India while the couple was still alive as *The Hyderabad Pamphlet Scandal Case.*

Several histories of Hyderabad State and some of its political participants were written during the time of Mehdi and Ellen's time in Hyderabad. As the first Salar Jung had just died, he was the subject of works such as Syed Bilgrami's *A Memoir of Sir Salar Jung.* Bilgrami played a small role in the pamphlet scandal, writing to Mehdi in defense of Ellen and calling the pamphlet "villainously filthy." Two years later Cheragh Ali's *Hyderabad (Deccan) under Sir Salar Jung* was published. More general histories of Hyderabad State printed at this time include Syed Hossain Bilgrami and C. Wilmott's *Historical and Descriptive Sketch of His Highness the Nizam's Dominions* and A. Claude Campbell's *Glimpses of the Nizam's Dominions.* These works, like so many others, pass over most of Hyderabad's scandals and instead focus on the reforms the city and state were embracing as the nineteenth century came to a close.

Hyderabad city and the Hyderabad State have enjoyed several nostalgic histories. These look back to what the authors view as an almost idyllic time. As such, there is no mention of such unsavory moments as the pamphlet scandal, but these works do provide a valuable service in providing a context for events like the scandal. They also remind us of a time when Hyderabad was less crowded, less polluted, and, at least on the surface, more refined in its everyday interactions. This genre took shape in works such as Harriet Ronken Lynton and Mohini Rajan's *Days of the Beloved,* which looks back at the time of Nizam Mahbub Ali Khan. Other such works include M. A. Nayeem's celebratory *The Splendour of Hyderabad: Last Phase of an Oriental Culture (1591–1948)* and Raza Alikhan's more encyclopedic *Hyderabad 400 Years.*

Some authors have tried to write a comprehensive history of Hyderabad State, such as Narendra Luther's biography of the city as told in *Hyderabad Memoirs of a City.* Others have focused on Hyderabad's economy or place in the larger world, for instance, Y. Vaikuntham's *State, Economy and Social Transformation: Hyderabad State (1724–1948).* Eric Beverley's *Hyderabad, British India, and the World: Muslim Networks and Minor Sovereignty, c. 1850–1950* recasts Hyderabad in a global framework.

More academic texts have taken up the Nizams' relationship with the British Residents and the Raj. These are generally political histories and help to explain the antecedents of the complicated relationships that the Residents faced during the time of Mehdi's tenure in Hyderabad. These relationships had their first sustained examination by Sarojini Regani in *Nizam-British Relations: 1724–1857.* Her work was followed by others, such as Bharati Ray's *Hyderabad and British Paramountcy 1858–1883,* and, later, a more intimate look at the Residents in Omar Khalidi's *The British Residency in Hyderabad: An Outpost of the Raj 1779–1948.* Several communities, groups, or individuals have all received more recent academic attention. Ground-breaking for subsequent generations of scholars of Hyderabad is Karen Leonard's *Social History of an Indian Caste,* which examines the crucial role played by the caste community of *kayasths.* Salar Jung I enjoyed a reappraisal in V. K. Bawa's *Hyderabad under Salar Jung I,* as did the Asaf Jahi family itself, as examined in Rajendra Prasad's *The Asif Jahs of Hyderabad.*

Several doctoral dissertations add valuable insight into the times preceding the pamphlet scandal. The work of Peter Wood, Tara Sethia, and Sunil Chander in their respective theses all merit attention: "Vassal State in the Shadow of Empire: Palmer's Hyderabad, 1799–1867"; "The Railway and Mining Enterprises in Hyderabad State under the British Raj during the 1870s and 1880s"; and "From a Pre-Colonial Order to a Princely State:

Hyderabad in Transition, c. 1748–1865." Three other doctoral theses take the story of Hyderabad through the years of the pamphlet scandal, yet only Parveen's "Contribution of Non-Mulkis for the Development of Administration and Literature in Hyderabad State (1853–1911)" mentions Mehdi's role in the state. Two others address Hyderabad's Muslim identity politics as well as the architectural setting of Hyderabad: see John Roosa's "The Quandary of the Qaum: Indian Nationalism in a Muslim State: Hyderabad 1850–1948" and Alison Mackenzie Shah's "Constructing a Capital on the Edge of Empire: Urban Patronage and Politics in the Nizams' Hyderabad, 1750–1950."

A few critical moments in the story of the pamphlet scandal have been wonderfully illuminated by scholars whose work has helped flesh out some of the major and minor moments in the scandal, within or beyond Hyderabad. During the year that Eardley Norton spent defending S. M. Mitra in the pamphlet case, he compiled a photo album, which has been analyzed by Deborah Hutton in her piece, "Elite Life in Hyderabad and Secunderabad." If not for the globe-trotting of Morton Frewen and his wife Clare, it is unlikely that Ellen would have ever met Queen Victoria, and perhaps the scandal would never have happened. Frewen's life, retold mostly through letters to Clare, can be found in Allen Andrews's *The Splendid Pauper*—splendid indeed.

Mehdi and Ellen began and ended their lives in Lucknow. That city, its surrounding territory, and its history as the princely state of Oudh have been well documented. A few works that provide some context for the time and place from which Mehdi and Ellen emerged include Rosie Llewellyn-Jones's *Engaging Scoundrels: True Tales of Old Lucknow* and *Writings on Lucknow: Shaam-e-Awadh*. A collection of book-length writings on Lucknow can also be found in *The Lucknow Omnibus*. On the middle class of Lucknow, see Sanjay Joshi's *Fractured Modernity: Making of a Middle Class in Colonial North India*. Finally, Barbara Ramusack's *The Indian Princes and Their States* provides context for understanding Lucknow and Hyderabad, both part of princely India.

Sources

PRIVATE PAPERS

Oriental and India Office, British Library, London (OIOC)
Lansdowne Collection MSS. EUR. D/558
Sutherland Collection MSS. EUR. B/397

OFFICIAL RECORDS

Telangana / Andhra Pradesh State Archive and Research Institute, Hyderabad (T/APSA)
Political and Private Secretary's Office files
    Judicial
    Miscellaneous
    Public Charities
    Public Works
"Newspaper Cuttings 1894–1896"
"Newspaper Cuttings 1896–1901"

Chowmahalla Palace Archive (CMP)
Letters

National Archive of India, New Delhi (NAI)
Foreign Department

Oriental and India Office Collection, British Library, London (OIOC)
Crown Representative Records (R/1)
Residency Records (R/2)
Records of the Political and Secret Department of the India Office (L/P&S)

NEWSPAPERS

Advocate of India
Birmingham Daily Post
Bombay Gazette
Deccan Budget
Deccan Mail
Deccan Post

Evening Mail
Hyderabadee
Indian People
Indian Spectator
Leader
Madras Mail
Madras Weekly Mail
Morning Post
New York Times
Pioneer
Times
Times of India

SECONDARY WORKS

Adut, Ari. *On Scandal: Moral Distrubances in Society, Politics, and Art*. Cambridge: Cambridge University Press, 2008.

Ali, Moulvi Syed Mahdi, ed. *Hyderabad Affairs* Vol. 9. London: Talbot Brothers, 1889.

————, ed. *Hyderabad Affairs* Vol. 10. London: Talbot Brothers, 1889.

Alikhan, Raza. *Hyderabad 400 Years*. Hyderabad: Zenith Services, 1991.

"An April-Fool Judgment." *The Indian Jurist* (1893): 212–13.

Andrews, Allen. *The Splendid Pauper*. Philadelphia: J. B. Lippincott Company, 1968.

Bakhle, Janaki. *Two Men and Music. Nationalism in the Making of an Indian Classical Tradition*. Oxford: Oxford University Press, 2005.

Bawa, Vasant Kumar. *Hyderabad under Salar Jung I*. New Delhi: S.Chand & Company Ltd., 1996.

Bayly, C. A. *Empire and Information*. Cambridge: Cambridge University Press, 1996.

The Beauties of Lucknow Consisting of Twenty-Four Selected Photographed Portraits, Cabinet Size, of the Most Celebrated and Popular Living Histrionic Singers, Dancing Girls and Actresses of the Oudh Court and of Lucknow. Calcutta: Calcutta Central Press, 1874.

Beverley, Eric Lewis. *Hyderabad, British India, and the World: Muslim Networks and Minor Sovereignty, c. 1850–1950*. Cambridge: Cambridge University Press, 2015.

Bilgrami, Sayyid Husain. *Muraqqaʻ-I ʻIbrat : Savanih ʻUmri-Yi Navab Salar Jang.* Translated by Mahdi Hasan. [Hyderabad, Deccan]: Matbaʻ-yi Kanzulʻulum, [1880s].

Bilgrami, Syed Hossain. *A Memoir of Sir Salar Jung, G.C.S.I.* Bombay: The Times of India Steam Press, 1883.

Campbell, A. Claude. *Glimpses of the Nizam's Dominions.* Philadelphia: Historical Publishing Co., 1898.

Chernock, Arianne. "Queen Victoria and the "Bloody Mary of Madagascar." *Victorian Studies* 55, no. 3 (2013): 425–49.

Clark, Anna. *Scandal. The Sexual Politics of the British Constitution.* Princeton: Princeton University Press, 2004.

The Code of Criminal Procedure, 1882 as Modified up to December 1888. Calcutta: Superintendent of Government Printing, 1888.

Cohen, Benjamin B. *In the Club. Associational Life in Colonial South Asia.* Studies in Imperialism. Manchester: Manchester University Press, 2015.

———. "The Utility of Scandal: Examples across Disciplines from Europe and India." *History Compass* 14, no. 7 (2016): 304–13.

Cohen, William A. *Sex Scandal. The Private Parts of Victorian Fiction.* Durham: Duke University Press, 1996.

Correspondent, Hyderabad. *Hyderabad in 1890 and 1891.* Bangalore: Caxton Press, 1892.

Dalrymple, William. *The Last Mughal: The Fall of a Dynasty, Delhi, 1857.* New Delhi: Penguin, 2006.

———. *White Mughals: Love and Betrayal in Eighteenth-Century India.* London: HarperCollinsPublishers, 2002.

Fischer-Tine, Harald. *Low and Licentious Europeans: Race, Class and "White Subalternity" in Colonial India.* Hyderabad: Orient Blackswan, 2009.

Fisher, Michael. *Counterflows to Colonialism: Indian Travellers and Settlers in Britain 1600–1857.* Delhi: Permanent Black, 2004.

———. *The Inordinately Strange Life of Dyce Sombre. Victorian Anglo-Indian MP and Chancery "Lunatic."* New York: Columbia University Press, 2010.

Gilmour, David. *The Ruling Caste: Imperial Lives in the Victorian Raj.* New York: Farrar, Straus and Giroux, 2005.

Guthrie, Mrs. *My Year in an Indian Fort.* 2 vols. Vol. 1. London: Hurst and Blackett, 1877.

Hasan, Mehdi. *Extracts from the Diary of Nawab Mehdi Hasan Khan Fathah Nawaz Jung.* London: Talbot Bros., 1890.

Hurst, John F. "Hyderabad and Golconda." *Harpers,* 1888, 440–49.

Hussain, Mirza Bakir. *A Shocking Social Scandal. An Appeal to the Ladies of Hyderabad.* Lucknow, 1892.

Hutton, Deborah. "Elite Life in Hyderabad and Secunderabad." In *Raja Deen Dayal Artist-Photographer in 19th-Century India,* edited by Deepali Dewan and Deborah Hutton, 164–91. New Delhi: Mapin, 2013.

Hyderabad in 1890 and 1891. Bangalore: Caxton Press, 1892.

Joshi, Sanjay. *Fractured Modernity Making of a Middle Class in Colonial North India.* New Delhi: Oxford University Press, 2001.

Khalidi, Omar. "The Amazing Abid of Hyderabad and Devon." *Devon & Cornwall Notes & Queries* 38, no. 6 (1999): 161–68.

———. *The British Residency in Hyderabad: An Outpost of the Raj 1779–1948.* London: British Association for Cemetaries in South Asia, 2005.

———, ed. *An Indian Passage to Europe: The Travels of Fath Nawaz Jang.* New Delhi: Oxford University Press, 2006.

Khan, M. A. *The History of Urdu Press.* New Delhi: Classical Publishing Company, 1995.

Khan, Mahdi Hasan. *Gulgasht I Farang.* Translated by Muhammad 'Aziz Mirza. Agra, 1889.

Khan, Zahid Ali, ed. *Images of Hyderabad.* Hyderabad: Siasat, 1994.

Lawson, Phillip. *The East India Company: A History.* London: Longman, 1993.

Leonard, Karen. "Hyderabad: The Mulki-Non-Mulki Conflict." In *People, Princes and Paramount Power: Society and Politics in the Indian Princely States,* edited by Robin Jeffrey, 65–106. Delhi: Oxford University Press, 1978.

———. "The Hyderabad Political System and Its Participants." *Journal of Asian Studies* 30, no. 3 (1971): 569–82.

———. *Social History of an Indian Caste.* Berkeley: University of California Press, 1978.

Levine, Philippa. *Prostitution, Race and Politics: Policing Venereal Disease in the British Empire.* New York: Routledge, 2003.

Llewellyn-Jones, Rosie. *Engaging Scoundrels: True Tales of Old Lucknow.* New Delhi: Oxford University Press, 2000.

The Lucknow Omnibus. New Delhi: Oxford University Press, 2001.

Luther, Narendra. *Hyderabad: Memoirs of a City.* Hyderabad: Sangam Books Limited, 1995.

Lynch-Blosse, H. R. *Hyderabad Political Notebook.* 1919.

Lynton, Harriet Ronken, and Mohini Rajan. *Days of the Beloved.* Berkeley: University of California, 1974.

Macpherson, J. M. *British Enactments in Force in Native States; Compiled by J. M. Macpherson, of the Inner Temple, Barrister-at-Law, and Secretary to the Government of India, Legislative Department.* Southern India (Hyderabad). Second ed. Calcutta: Superintendent of Government Printing, 1900.

Moodellear, M. Soobaraya. *Hyderabad Almanac and Directory for 1875.* Madras: Foster Press, 1874.

"Mr. Seymour Keay, M.P." *Vanity Fair*, 8 October 1892.

Nayeem, M. A. *The Royal Palaces of the Nizams.* Hyderabad: Hyderabad Publisher, 2009.

———. *The Splendour of Hyderabad: Last Phase of an Oriental Culture (1591–1948 AD).* Bombay: Jaico Publishing House, 1987.

Oldenburg, Veena Talwar, ed. *Writings on Lucknow Shaam-E-Awadh.* New Delhi: Penguin Books, 2007.

The Parliamentary Debates. Vol. 24. London: Eyre and Spottiswoode, 1894.

Parveen, Zareena. "Contribution of Non-Mulkis for the Development of Administration and Literature in Hyderabad State (1853–1911)." Osmania University, 2000.

"Personal Intelligence." *Indian Magazine and Review*, April 1888, 224.

Plowden, Walter F. C. Chicheley. *Records of the Chicheley Plowdens.* London: Heath, Cranton & Ouseley Ltd., 1914.

Prasad, Rajendra. *The Asif Jahs of Hyderabad.* New Delhi: Vikas Publishing House, 1984.

Ramusack, Barbara. *The Indian Princes and Their States.* Cambridge: Cambridge University Press, 2004.

Rau, R. Venkata Subba. *The Hyderabad Pamphlet Scandal Case.* Lucknow: G. P. Varma Press, 1893.

Regani, Sarojini. *Nizam-British Relations: 1724–1857.* Hyderabad: Book-lovers Private Limited, 1963.

Robins, Nick. *The Corporation That Changed the World: How the East India Company Shaped the Modern Multinational.* London: Pluto Press, 2006.

Rock, Joseph. "The New Era at Hyderabad." *The Fortnightly Review* 61 (January–June 1897): 911–22.

Roosa, John. "The Quandary of the Qaum: Indian Nationalism in a Muslim State: Hyderabad 1850–1948." PhD diss., University of Wisconsin, 1998.

Rudolph, Susanne Hoeber, Lloyd I. Rudolph, and Mohan Singh Kanota, eds. *Reversing the Gaze.* Cambridge, MA: Westview Press, 2002.

Ruswa, Mirza Mohammad Hadi. *Umrao Jan Ada.* Translated by Kushwant Singh. 2003 ed. New Delhi: HarperCollins, 1961.

Sarkar, Tanika. "Scandal in High Places: Discourses on the Chaste Hindu Woman in Late Nineteenth Century Bengal." In *Embodiment: Essays on Gender and Identity,* edited by Meenakshi Thapan. Delhi, 1997.

Server-ul-Mulk. *My Life: Being the Autobiography of Nawab Server-Ul-Mulk Bahadur.* Translated by Jiwan Yar Jung. London: Arthur H. Stockwell, 1932.

Sewell, William H. *Logics of History. Social Theory and Social Transformation.* Chicago: University of Chicago Press, 2005.

Shah, Alison Mackenzie. "Constructing a Capital on the Edge of Empire: Urban Patronage and Politics in the Nizams' Hyderabad, 1750–1950." PhD diss., University of Pennsylvania, 2005.

Soneji, Davesh. *Unfinished Gestures. Devadāsīs, Memory, and Modernity in South India.* Chicago: University of Chicago Press, 2012.

Tobin, Beth Fowkes. *Picturing Imperial Power.* Durham: Duke University Press, 1999.

Vaikuntham, Y. *State, Economy and Social Transformation Hyderabad State (1724–1948).* New Delhi: Manohar, 2002.

Wilson, H. H. *A Glossary of Judicial and Revenue Terms.* 2nd ed. Delhi: Munshiram Manoharlal, 1968.

Younger, Coralie. *Wicked Women of the Raj.* New Delhi: HarperCollins, 2003.

Yule, Henry, and A. C. Burnell. *Hobson-Jobson.* 1996 ed. Hertfordshire: Wordsworth Reference, 1886.

ACKNOWLEDGMENTS

I am indebted to an embarrassingly large number of people and institutions. At the University of Utah, Salt Lake City, I want to thank my colleagues and the Department of History for their support. Several times during the research and writing of this book, I taught advanced undergraduate seminars on scandals and events, and I shared the story of Mehdi and Ellen with my students. I thank them for their patience, questions, and enthusiasm for the project. The College of Humanities at the University of Utah provided funding for this project, as well as a chance to speak at the Humanities "Happy Hour" where the project had its first public outing. In 2012–2013, I was a fellow at the Tanner Humanities Center. I am grateful to Bob Goldberg, who was the Tanner Center Director at the time, for his support, as well as to my co-fellows, who all provided feedback on portions of the manuscript. Finally, the University of Utah's Marriott Library interlibrary loan department never failed in helping me track down obscure texts, and I thank them for their assistance.

I presented different sections of this project at various academic conferences across the United States. My gratitude to fellow panelists and audience members at the annual South Asia conferences at the University of Wisconsin–Madison, and at the University of California, Berkeley. I also presented portions of the manuscript at the Western Conference branch of the Association of Asian Studies conference held in Salt Lake City, and at the annual meeting of the

Association of Asian Studies held in Seattle. Again, to my fellow panelists and the audiences, my deep thanks. Charles Nuckolls—a Telugu-speaking colleague here in the Mountain West—invited me to Brigham Young University to give a lengthier presentation on the pamphlet scandal, and I am grateful to Charles and audience members at Brigham Young University for their thoughtful comments. Also, I thank students at Westmont College, where I presented portions of this project.

I wish to thank the staff of the British Library, and in particular, those in the India Office. It was there, on the last day of a frantic research trip, that I found the only copy of the pamphlet at the heart of the scandal, which had been included in a file from a later date. It made this book possible. Many bad things can be rightfully heaped on British rule in India, but I was thankful for its bureaucracy and record keeping on that day.

Leslie Cohen (no relation) and Catherine Howard both read and commented on the manuscript. Their careful readings and comments, both argumentative and technical, immeasurably elevated the quality of the text. At Harvard University Press I was helped by Katherine Brick, Anne McGuire, Mihaela Pacurar, Stephanie Vyce, and Olivia Woods. My thanks to all of them. My editor, Kathleen McDermott, had faith in me and in this story from the beginning. For that faith, and for her wisdom and guidance, I am extremely grateful.

Anonymous readers for the press made invaluable suggestions regarding the manuscript. I thank them all. Some encouraged me to bolster the narrative with heavy academic interventions while others recognized the type of story I wished to tell. My intention has been to tell a story that appeals to many while gesturing to some of the academic possibilities in the endnotes. My hope has always been to let the voices from the past sound clearly in their own words and without distraction.

I want to thank the staff of the National Archive of India, New Delhi, for their support. I am grateful to Purnima Mehta and the American Institute of Indian Studies, also in Delhi. I spent an extremely productive day at the Alkazi Foundation for the Arts in New Delhi and wish to thank the staff there at the time, including Rahaab, Akshay, Meha, Anita, and Mr. Alkazi himself. Also, I offer thanks to the staff at the Uttar Pradesh Archive, Lucknow.

In Hyderabad, special thanks go to Soma Ghosh of the Salar Jung Museum Library. While researching this book, I enjoyed the immense privilege of working in the Chowmahalla Palace Archives. There I was able to track down letters from Ellen and other correspondence that answered some of the pamphlet scandal's mysteries. This would not have been possible without the help of Taqdees Habeeb and the staff who oversee that magical collection. Connected to the Chowmahalla Palace, and incomparable in her own right, is Anu Naik. I am deeply grateful for her help and friendship. Finally, my work at Chowmahalla would not have been possible without H. H. Azmet Jah. No amount of gratitude would suffice to repay his kindness.

The staff and support of the Telangana / Andhra Pradesh State Archive in Hyderabad were absolutely invaluable to the project. Thank you, Chakrapani, Chandrashekar, Ijaz, Khaleel, Moeed, Praveen, Ramesh, Raqeeb, Shankar, and Venkata Ramana. My deepest thanks go to everyone at that institution. I owe very special thanks to Dr. Zareena Parveen, the director, whose very good friendship is now stretching into a second decade.

While visiting Lucknow, I decided (after a late lunch) to go to Fatehpur in search of Mehdi Hasan's grave. Riding through the lush, verdant Uttar Pradesh countryside in a local bus (complete with goat on board) was delightful, and such journeys are among my favorite in India. However, the sun was setting just as I reached Fatehpur. I befriended a cycle rickshaw driver named Nasim, who, after listening to my telling in Urdu of Mehdi Hasan's story, took me to the gate of one of several graveyards. But I had left Lucknow too late, and it was now dark in Fatehpur. Unable to access the graveyards in the dark, yet undaunted, Nasim and I spent the next few hours going around Fatehpur meeting village elders Nasim thought might be able to tell me something about Mehdi Hasan. This was in the early years after America's activities in Iraq and Afghanistan, and I was worried about the reception of an American asking about a long-dead north Indian Muslim. I need not have worried; my reception in Fatehpur was warm and welcoming in every home we visited. Before leaving Fatehpur, I unexpectedly had to visit the police station, but even that detour ended in warmth and hospitality. To Nasim, the village elders, and the police officers I met that evening, I extend my deep thanks.

The only known confirmed photograph of Ellen shows her wearing a particular form of Indian dress as she posed in a photographer's studio scene. To help me unpack that image, I am grateful to Cristin McKnight Sethi for her expertise regarding Indian textiles and knowledge of photographic norms of the time. For his friendship, stretching back to our Earlham College days, many thanks to Sanjit Sethi. I am also grateful to Deborah Hutton; her work on the Eardley Norton album, which he compiled during the pamphlet case, was invaluable in helping me better understand Norton himself.

Over a decade ago, I was in touch with Omar Khalidi. My first book on the *samasthans* (small Hindu feudatories in India's Deccan) of Hyderabad was about to come out, and I had begun investigating the pamphlet scandal to see if it would prove a suitable subject for a book. I wrote to Omar about my work on the pamphlet case, and, in an e-mail response of 21 October 2005, he responded, "How interesting! You are the third person on the planet to know about this matter now." We stayed in touch until his tragic death in 2010. Omar was supportive of my book on the *samasthans* and was equally supportive of my work on the pamphlet scandal. He knew of Mehdi

Hasan from his own work on Hasan's diary of his European trip. Omar's death remains a great loss to scholars of Hyderabad, but I am honored to have known him and grateful for his guidance.

Besides Omar and myself, the third person on the planet to have known about the pamphlet scandal was David Lelyveld. After Omar mentioned David's name, I wrote to him, asking to swap stories about the pamphlet scandal. David not only shared what he knew but graciously sent his own research notes on the topic. Subsequently, he has been a supporter of this project, and I am grateful for his assistance and enthusiasm.

When Omar Khalidi first began investigating Mehdi Hasan for his own introduction to Hasan's diary, he worked with the archivist Syed Shakil Ahmed. Syed retired from the Andhra Pradesh State Archive. When I located him, he not only welcomed me into his home but provided a list of relevant files relating to Hasan. I am overwhelmed thinking of how important that list was, and thus my debt of thanks to Syed is immeasurable.

Karen Leonard has been a pioneer in the study of Hyderabad. As a friend, she graciously read the entire manuscript, and as a scholar, gave me a lengthy list of pointed comments, criticisms, and suggestions that I have tried to follow as best as possible. I am very grateful to her.

Friends and colleagues from my time at the University of Wisconsin–Madison remain much cherished. Thanks to Venkat Dhulipala, Kevin Downey, James Hoover, Scott Levi, and Robert Simpkins. Very special thanks to Chandra Mallampalli, who listened to presentations on this project. He has given me decades of friendship and scholarly camaraderie.

In Hyderabad, friends have offered their company, meals, tea, whiskey, and enthusiasm for this project. For their friendship and tremendous contributions to Hyderabad history, my thanks go to Vasant and Oudesh Bawa, and to Narendra Luther. Siraj Khan has patiently sat with me, sharing stories about Hyderabad of the past and present, and helping me to identify faces staring out of pictures now well over a century old. I am grateful for his friendship and shared enthusiasm. T. Vijay Kumar joined me for a semester at the University of Utah, where he listened to my telling of the pamphlet scandal story and made several invaluable suggestions. I am grateful for his friendship here, there, and beyond. I first met Nandini Rao and her family almost two decades ago, and I am honored to still feel so welcomed at the house on the hill; thank you. K. Vimala Devi and her many family members have been much like my own family—loving and so gracious whenever I prattled on about this or some other project. To the entire Katakaneni family, my deepest thanks.

Since the early 1960s the University of Wisconsin–Madison has maintained and developed a strong program in South Asian studies. My advisor in the Department of History was Robert E. Frykenberg, a scholar of South Asia. In 2000, he decided to retire. One afternoon, he called me to his office to choose some of his books. On top of a stack of books was a bundle of photocopied papers. Knowing I had spent time in Hyderabad, Bob gave me the bundle. When I got to my apartment, I looked at the first few pages. It made no sense; it was a copy of a printed work, but the title page was missing. The story was even less clear. It was neither a history monograph nor a work of fiction. The names were largely unfamiliar, as was the apparent title of the work, "The Hyderabad Pamphlet Case." I had never heard of the case, so I set the bundle aside. Five years later, I reached for the photocopied bundle once more. I read past the opening statement and found myself wading deeper and deeper into the text. Of course, what I was reading was the printed court transcript of the pamphlet case, arguably the most important document in the whole affair. For being a wonderful mentor and a staunch supporter of my telling of the pamphlet scandal story, from the earliest days to his reading of a draft of the manuscript, I owe Bob my deepest thanks.

I owe very special thanks to my in-laws, Errol and Oona Durbach, for their love and support. To my siblings, Edward, Jeffrey, Peter, Tamara, and Susan, their spouses and their families, no words suffice to express my thanks. My parents, Stephen and Roberta, first brought me to India in 1977, and for that and a lifetime of love and encouragement I remain forever indebted to them.

To my children, Miles and Finn, thank you for being the joy in my life and the lights that shine so brightly. My wife, Nadja, has been living with me, as well as with Mehdi and Ellen, for over a decade. She has patiently listened to my every telling of this aspect or that of the pamphlet scandal and read a much-too-long draft. For that—and for *everything*—thank you.

Of course, any mistakes herein are entirely my own.

ILLUSTRATION CREDITS

p. 138.   Eardley John Norton. Lala Deen Dayal, photographer
           (Indian, 1844–1905). Albumen process, albumen print,
           image 4 3/4 × 3 13/16 inches, 1892. Peabody Essex Museum.
           Museum purchase, 2000 PH81.41. © 2011 Peabody Essex
           Museum, Salem, MA. Photography by Walter Silver.

p. 177.   Server Jung. Telangana / Andhra Pradesh State Archives,
           Hyderabad, India.

p. 185.   Breakfast at Bashirbagh palace. Used with permission of the
           Nizam's Private Estate, Hyderabad.

p. 204.   Post-trial victory gathering of the prosecution. Lala Deen
           Dayal, "Residency Bazar Court Chudderghat" from the
           album *Souvenir of Hyderabad 1892–1893*. Albumen print,
           1893, 205 × 275 mm. ACP: 95.0082(71). The Alkazi Collec-
           tion of Photography, New Delhi, India.

p. 210.   Caricature of John Seymour Keay, from *Vanity Fair*, 1892.
           (John) Seymour Keay, "Statesmen No. 602" by Sir Leslie
           Ward. © National Portrait Gallery, London.